TURN THE WORLD UPSIDE DOWN

BLACK LIVES IN THE DIASPORA: PAST / PRESENT / FUTURE

Turn the World Upside Down

EMPIRE AND UNRULY FORMS OF BLACK FOLK CULTURE
IN THE U.S. AND CARIBBEAN

Imani D. Owens

Columbia University Press
New York

Columbia University Press
Publishers Since 1893
New York   Chichester, West Sussex
cup.columbia.edu

Library of Congress Cataloging-in-Publication Data
Names: Owens, Imani D., author.
Title: Turn the world upside down : empire and unruly forms of Black folk culture
in the U.S. and Caribbean / Imani D. Owens.
Description: New York : Columbia University Press, [2023] |
Series: Black lives in the diaspora : past, present, future |
Includes bibliographical references and index.
Identifiers: LCCN 2022049013 (print) | LCCN 2022049014 (ebook) |
ISBN 9780231208888 (hardback ; acid-free paper) |
ISBN 9780231208895 (trade paperback ; acid-free paper) | ISBN 9780231557672 (ebook)
Subjects: LCSH: American literature—African American authors—History and criticism. |
American literature—20th century—History and criticism. |
Caribbean literature—Black authors—History and criticism. |
Caribbean literature—20th century—History and criticism. |
African diaspora in literature. | Black people in literature. | Imperialism in literature. |
Race in literature. | LCGFT: Literary criticism.
Classification: LCC PS153.B53 O94 2023 (print) | LCC PS153.B53 (ebook) |
DDC 810.9/896—dc23/eng/20230207
LC record available at https://lccn.loc.gov/2022049013
LC ebook record available at https://lccn.loc.gov/2022049014

Printed in the United States of America

Cover design: Julia Kushnirsky
Cover image: Anastasia Lembrik / Shutterstock.com

For my parents

In memory of Cheryl A. Wall

CONTENTS

ACKNOWLEDGMENTS

Finishing a book is a long journey, but I did not travel alone. My work would not have been possible without the inspiration of my hometown—Brooklyn—and my adopted home, Harlem. These spaces provided vitality, sustenance, and crucial proximity to the communities that I discuss in this book. My interest in literature and culture further blossomed at Rutgers University under the guidance of pathbreaking scholar—and my favorite professor—the late Cheryl A. Wall. Cheryl advised my undergraduate thesis on Zora Neale Hurston's blues poetics, sharing with me her love of what Hurston called "the will to adorn." She encouraged me to attend graduate school, followed my early career, and remained unwavering in her support of me and my work. This book bears her imprint.

An early version of this project developed at Columbia University in the department of English and Comparative Literature and the Institute for Comparative Literature and Society. I remain grateful for the invaluable direction of Farah Jasmine Griffin, Brent Hayes Edwards, and Robert G. O'Meally. Farah's mentorship has been a sustaining force through each stage of my career. She made sure I always had tea to drink, a place to write, and radical ideas to ponder. She exemplifies the kind of advisor, scholar, and friend I aspire to be. I thank Brent for his generosity, insight, and sharp eye for detail. He read my work with pronounced attention, presented me with copies of out-of-print manuscripts, and encouraged me to push the boundaries of my thinking. Bob took me under his wing from the very start, modeling how to listen as well as how to read. To him I owe my introduction to the Center for Jazz Studies as well as the curatorial group at Jazz at Lincoln Center, which broadened the horizons of what I thought possible as a scholar. I could not have asked for a better team.

I was also fortunate to receive support from the wider academic community at Columbia. I extend thanks to John Gamber and Kaiama Glover, for their generous feedback. I thank the late Marcellus Blount, for sharing his poignant smile as well as the beauty and clarity of his work. Saidiya Hartman provided mind-opening inspiration as well as steadfast support that I will not forget. In the Music Department, George E. Lewis expressed interest in my scholarship and reminded me that "writing is fighting." I feel grateful to Yulanda Grant, program coordinator of the Center for Jazz Studies, for organizing events and receptions that provided sustenance—often literally—for my graduate years. I am lucky to know Shay Harris, a shining star at the Institute for Research in African American Studies, who looked after all the students and provided many laughs over the years. To my fellow Columbia grads, I am so impressed with the scholars and artists you have become. From the very beginning, Victoria Collis, Alvan Ikoku, Patricia Lespinasse, Emily Lordi, and Courtney Thorsson showed me the ropes and helped me to clear each hurdle. I made great memories with Nijah Cunningham, Jean Christophe-Cloutier, Kaveh Landserk, Jang Wook Huh, A. J. Johnson, Jarvis McInnis, the marvelous Matthew D. Morrison, Mariel Rodney, J. T. Roane, Jessica Teague, Huewayne Watson, Autumn Womack, Lindsay Van Tine, Imani Uzuri, and many others. To the other half of the dynamic duo, Courtney Bryan: you're the realest friend anyone could ever ask for. I'm in awe of your talent, persistence, and kindness every day. We made it!

This project hit its stride at the University of Pittsburgh in the Department of English, where I began my assistant professorship. I owe a special thanks to fellow Caribbeanist Shalini Puri, who shared not only her expertise and advice, but also Zumba classes, decadent lunches, and heartfelt talks. Thank you, Shalini. I feel grateful to Nancy Glazener who swapped recipes, invited me on nature walks, and helped lighten the load when I was overwhelmed. I appreciate R. A. Judy for speaking the truth with candor and humor and for always having my back. Bill Scott remained an astute and generous mentor. It was an immense privilege to have known the late

Geri Allen, whose breathtaking genius and generosity continue to inspire me. I am thankful to Dawn Lundy Martin and Lauren Russell at the Center for African American Poetry and Poetics for curating stunning events that made us all dream a little bigger. I thank the Pitt Humanities Center, where I was a faculty fellow, for productive opportunities to share my work. Many thanks to department chairs Don Bialostosky and Gayle Rogers, as well as colleagues across the university: Jonathan Arac, Jerome Branche, Yolanda Covington-Ward, Angie Cruz, Terrance Hayes, Armando García, Karen Gilmer, Michael Heller, Jenny Johnson, Rickey Laurentiis, Neepa Majumdar, Michele Reid-Vazquez, Christel Temple, and many others. The Caribbean Reading Group (CRG), helmed by Shalini Puri and Lara Putnam, was a robust and welcoming intellectual community. I thank Shalini, Lara, and the other members of CRG for sharing their homes as well as their vital feedback on an article that would form the kernel of this book. A shout-out to my dynamic graduate students: Amanda Awankwo, Le'Mil Eiland, Malcolm Friend, Treviene Harris, Gabrielle Rajerison, Lana Sims, Tyrica Terry, Steffan Triplett, and more.

To the unofficial Ace Hotel writing club, Peter Campbell, Jules Gil-Peterson, Paul Johnson, Caitlin Bruce, David Tenorio, and Elizabeth Rodriguez Fielder, this book would not have been possible without our writing sessions, coffee breaks, happy hours, and karaoke. As Peter would say, you all are a-meow-zing. In the brief time that we overlapped at Pitt, Yona Harvey, Lou Maraj, Shaun Myers, Lauren Russell, Khirsten Scott, and I formed a tight crew. Thank you for providing inspiration and joyous community right when I needed it. I am especially grateful for the enduring companionship of my dear friend, poet extraordinaire and fellow afternoon tea enthusiast Lauren Russell. I deeply appreciate the brilliance and compassion of Khalila Chaar-Pérez. I am grateful to Kim at Arriviste Coffee Roasters for providing the caffeine that fueled my writing sessions. I will never forget Nazura Asaseyeduru.

At Rutgers University-New Brunswick I am fortunate to work with a dream-team of colleagues in Black diasporic literature, including Abena Busia, Carter Mathes, Erica R. Edwards, Douglas Jones, Ryan Kernan, Bode Ibironke, Stéphane Robolin, Evie Shockley, and Maurice Wallace. They know how to do the work, but also how to have fun! My colleagues and students in the Department of English have made Rutgers a dynamic intellectual home. I love discussing Hurston with Elin Diamond, who read my manuscript with great care and provided essential feedback. Lunches with Jeff Lawrence, Abigail Zitin, and Kristin Grogan helped me to stay on track. It is not easy settling into a new job during a pandemic, and I am grateful for the support and leadership of Meredith McGill and Rebecca Walkowitz. I am also grateful to Yesenia Barragan, Kim Butler, Brad Evans, Lynn Festa, David Kurnick, Renée Larrier, Deborah Gray White, Mukti Mangharam, Sean Silver, Carolyn Williams, Omaris Zamora, and the many brilliant affiliates of Critical Caribbean Studies. I credit fellow members of the Center for Cultural Analysis seminar, run by Meredith and Colin Jager, for an intellectually stimulating year discussing the Commons. The Institute for the Study of Global Racial Justice (ISGRJ), helmed by Michelle Stephens and enhanced by a vibrant community of fellows, offered crucial support as I completed my book. I am grateful to ISGRJ for sponsoring a manuscript workshop. I owe a great debt to Carter Mathes, who organized the session, and to Deborah A. Thomas and Sonya Posmentier, who understood what I was trying to do and read the manuscript with tremendous care and rigor. Their engagement helped to bring out the best in this work.

I have been fortunate to have the support of various fellowships and residencies. A Ford Foundation Predoctoral Fellowship and a Woodrow Wilson Career-Enhancement Fellowship connected me to a robust cohort of scholars. I was honored to serve as a Riley Scholar-in-Residence in the English Department at Colorado College (CC) via the Consortium for Faculty Diversity. Colleagues at CC provided valuable opportunities to share my work-in-progress and made me feel at home in the Rockies. I would like to extend particular thanks to Claire Oberon Garcia, and to fellow Riley scholars Ryan Bañagale, Heidi Renée Lewis, and my radiant and brilliant friend, Manya Whitaker. A year as a postdoctoral fellow in Princeton's Department of African American Studies broadened the horizons of this book. It was my great fortune to be mentored by the inimitable Daphne Brooks, who remains a source of light, incisive wisdom, and fierce support. Thank you, Daphne. I am grateful to Daphne for convening a manuscript workshop, and to Thadious Davis and Werner Sollors for providing indispensable feedback on the book in its fledgling stages. Many thanks are owed to Wendy Belcher, Wallace Best, Eddie Glaude, Simon Gikandi, Tera Hunter, Naomi Murukawa, Imani Perry, and Michele Tuck-Ponder. I thank the graduate students in the Department of English who invited me to share my work. It was a privilege to share an office suite in Stanhope Hall with the other fellows, Danielle Terrazas Williams and Roderick Ferguson.

A number of archival discoveries, research trips, and fortuitous encounters enabled me to expand the book. My six-month residency at the Schomburg Center for Research in Black Culture was transformative. It was a joy to return to Harlem and the Schomburg, where so much of this project began. I thank Brent Hayes Edwards, who directed our weekly seminar with extraordinary care, and program administrator Sister Aisha H. L. al-Adawiya for ensuring all logistics were in order. I learned so much from the other scholars-in-residence: Hisham Aïdi, Ayesha Hardison, Eric Herschthal, Brian Jones, Tyesha Maddox, Yuko Miki, and Anthony Rodriguez. I will never forget our conversations and those fabulous lunches! I thank the archivists in the Manuscripts, Archives, and Rare Books division, including the enthusiastic and tenacious Alexsandra Mitchell, for assisting me in my explorations. I owe much praise to my research assistant, Naomi Lorrain.

This book would not have been possible without the labor and generosity of the staff at the Beinecke Rare Book and Manuscript Library at Yale University, the Amistad Research Center at Tulane University, the BBC Written Archives Center, and the British Library. In Cuba, I was thankful for the opportunity to present my work at the University of Havana. I deeply appreciate the assistance of the staff at the Fundación Nicolás Guillén, especially Nicolás A. Hernández Guillén and Directora Denia García Ronda, for talking with me at length about Guillén's legacy. Dash Harris of AfroLatinx travel was a vital resource. In Port-au-Prince, Haiti, I was grateful to meet students and faculty at the Institut d'ethnologie, which I visited during a meeting of the Haitian Studies Association. In Panama City, the staff at Museo Afroantillano de Panamá, especially Veronica Forte, went above and beyond to welcome me. It was a pleasure to meet students at the University of Panama, and to hold illuminating conversations with Luis Pulido Ritter and Monica E. Kupfer. For their generous responses to my email inquiries, I thank Demetrius L. Eudell, Antonio López, Aaron Kamugisha, Katherine McKittrick, and Ato Quayson. I appreciated the opportunity to present various versions of these chapters at meetings of the American Studies Association, the American Comparative Literature Association, the Association for the Study of the Worldwide African Diaspora, the Caribbean Studies Association, the Modern Language

Association, the Postcolonial Studies Association, and the West Indian Literature Conference.

I am grateful for permission to reprint portions of chapter 1, which appeared as "'Hard Reading': U.S. Empire and Black Modernist Aesthetics in Eric Walrond's *Tropic Death*" in *MELUS* 41, no. 4 (December 2016) as well as portions of chapter 2, which appeared as "Beyond Authenticity: The U.S. Occupation of Haiti and the Politics of Folk Culture" in the *Journal of Haitian Studies* 21, no. 2 (Fall 2015).

It has been a pleasure to work with the wonderful editorial staff at Columbia University Press. Philip Leventhal believed in my work from an early stage and expertly guided my book through the shifting terrain of publishing during the COVID-19 pandemic. I am also thankful to the editorial board of the Black Lives in the Diaspora series at both Howard University and Columbia University. I compliment the fastidious work of Kat Jorge, Kalie Hyatt, and the entire production team. Many thanks to editorial assistant Monique Briones. I am immensely thankful for the gracious feedback of the anonymous readers who recognized what the book could be and pushed me to refine my thinking in important ways. Freelance editor Vijay Shah, who assisted my work through various stages, was instrumental in helping me to realize my vision for this book.

A magnificent community accompanied me on this journey. To my Zoom writing group, Maleda Beliligne, Crystal Donkor, and Shaun Myers, inspirations all, thank you for keeping me going! To my dear friend Dennis Tyler, thanks for walking alongside me as I neared the finish line. Remember me to Harlem. For their companionship and collegiality, I owe gratitude to Magalí Armillas-Tiseyra, Violet Bryan, Robert Bland, Ashon Crawley, Dasha Chapman, Rafe Dalleo, Danny Dawson, Brittney Edmonds, Harris Feinsod, Julius B. Fleming, Tao Leigh Goffe, Maxine Gordon, Yogita Goyal, Isis Semaj Hall, Ellie Hisama, Tsitsi Jaji, Régine Jean-Charles, Deidre Harris-Kelley, Kelly Josephs, Elleza Kelley, Anthea Kraut, Laurie Lambert, Asia Leeds, Tyesha Maddox, Madison Moore, Uri McMillan, Fawzia Mustafa, Samantha Pinto, Elliot H. Powell, Robert Reid-Pharr, Shanté Paradigm Smalls, Greg Tate, Alex Vazquez, and many others.

To my life-long friends Talesia Felder, Ketty Thertus, Alejandrina Batista, and Esther Spencer, thank you for cheering me on through the long years of coursework, dissertation writing, and book completion—even when it wasn't clear what I was doing! I am especially grateful to college roommate

Dr. Ketty Thertus, who picked me up after every stumble and celebrated every milestone. The Felders in Brooklyn made sure my heart and belly were always full. Thank you for sharing the love. To my goddaughter Bianca: I hope you find something in this book that inspires you!

I owe my most heartfelt thanks to my family, whose love, support, and inspiration are the reason that I persist. My parents, both formidable scholars, showed me what was possible and guided me each step of the way. Mom, thank you for nurturing me through the inevitable highs and lows of this process. Your generous feedback, late-night pep talks, and home-cooked meals have meant everything to me. You are my best reader. Dad, you have inspired me more than you know. Thank you for never wavering in your belief in me and my work. I could not have done it without you. To my brother Shomari, your wit and humor made me smile every step of the way. To my sister-in-law Rebeca, thanks for sharing your light with us. Much love to Cora and Rocco. To my extended Watkins family in Mississippi, my Owens family in California and beyond, and my Willis family all over, I hope to have made you proud. To V., who came into my life at just the right moment, you're the perfect freestyle over a tight beat. Thank you for everything.

TURN THE WORLD UPSIDE DOWN

PROLOGUE

In 1970, the Jamaican cultural theorist Sylvia Wynter wrote a lecture to be given at the UNESCO Regional Conference on Ecology, Archaeology, and Folkdance.[1] Later published in *Jamaica Journal* as "Jonkonnu in Jamaica: Towards the Interpretation of Folk Dance as a Cultural Process," the essay paints a stunning portrait of embodied practices and rituals that were forged by the enslaved on the plantation. Wynter's prose is evocative. In a section entitled "Main Characteristics of Dancing," she makes a striking claim for the transformative potential of Black culture. Dancers, Wynter writes, "through spiritual 'labour' and 'work' deny brute facts of everyday existence through their transcendence in super-reality. They establish in dance 'a putative society' in which they are the elect, the elite. Dance turns world upside-down, liberating participants."[2] Wynter describes not simply a disruption of the social order, but an inversion: to "[turn the] world upside down" is to establish an order in which those on the bottom become the "elect," raising their own subjectivity and personhood into view. In another, quite literal sense, they transformed the very ground on which they stood through the cultivation of crops and rituals that brought them closer to the earth. Black subjects, Wynter suggests, *"rehumanized Nature* and helped to save [their] own humanity against the constant onslaught of the plantation . . . through the creation of a folklore and a folk-culture."[3]

These transformative acts live in tension with the material conditions that enslaved Black people endured, where neither their bodies nor the lands they cultivated and inhabited were considered their own. "The history of folk-culture in Jamaica is the history of this ambivalent relation," Wynter observes. Yet she turns to folk culture not as a romantic antidote to the violence of enslavement and empire, but rather as a site of difficult entanglement with history. Folk culture embodies the "ambivalent relation" between Black subjects and the New World landscape, while also providing an interpretive framework for understanding this tension, precisely through the oppositional gesture of upholding the experiences of "those [people] on the bottom." Adept at making sweeping historical connections, Wynter also slips into the breaks: the "interstices of history." She locates the contradictions and possibilities of culture not solely in grand acts of resistance, but in smaller gestures that constitute a choreography of Black life. Culture "disrupts reality," Wynter suggests, not through romantic escapism but through "labor" and "work," terms that simultaneously invoke the legacy of chattel slavery and the difficult process of collective and individual transformation.[4]

Wynter anticipates Saidiya Hartman's claim that "in the context of social death, everyday practices explored the possibility of transfigured existence and cultivated an imagination of the otherwise and elsewhere, cartographies of the fantastic utterly antagonistic to slavery."[5] In addition to approaching the archives of slavery, Wynter's essay intervened in contemporary cultural politics. She wrote "Jonkonnu" as an emerging cultural critic as well as a dancer, novelist, and playwright deeply attuned to the possibilities of folk culture as a creative praxis. As Wynter later explains, the essay was initially conceived as an effort to contest the "dominant conception" of dance and folk culture that was gaining traction in postindependence Jamaica.[6] As in other spaces across the Caribbean, mass-based folk culture—including folklore, vernacular speech, religion, and embodied performance—became central to postindependence cultural nationalisms, as previously shunned cultural practices were increasingly embraced by the new state as markers of its "authentic" national identity.[7] Folk culture's newfound legitimization also constituted a strategic response to the expanding cultural dominance of the United States in the Caribbean. But Wynter regards the nationalist embrace of folk culture with some caution. In a 1972 review essay, she critiques the ways in which a "sanitized" version of folk culture was deployed

as a prop for political ambitions or as a "weapon for the struggle for hegemony between members of the educated middle classes."[8] Elsewhere, she
warns against the use of folk culture as the basis of a "cheap and easy radicalism" or as a blunt instrument to wield authoritative truths—a warning
more urgent amid her references to the dictatorship of François "Papa Doc"
Duvalier and its violent appropriations of folklore and Vodou in Haiti.[9]
Instead of regarding the uses of folk culture as inherently liberatory, Wynter embraces what the anthropologist Mimi Sheller calls "antiromance," the
imperative to "ask thorny questions about the romantic conventions and
heroes of subaltern history."[10]

What may be the value, Wynter asks, of a critical return to folk culture?
The debates in which Wynter intervened were not new, having raged with
some fury in the 1920s and 1930s, which saw "the precursor movements
to the anticolonial movement that had opened onto my own immediate
political horizon."[11] In various works, she returns to these interwar reevalu-
ations of folk culture. "Jonkonnu," for example, begins with an epigraph
from a text to which she frequently returned: *Ainsi parla l'Oncle* [*So Spoke
the Uncle*], the 1928 ethnography of the Haitian writer, physician, and diplomat Jean Price-Mars:

> We have for a long time cherished the desire to bring to the eyes of the Hai-
> tian people the value of their folklore. . . . By a disconcerting paradox, these
> people who had . . . the most moving history in the world . . . that of the
> transplantation of a human race unto a stranger soil, in the worst possible
> biological conditions, now display a badly concealed embarrassment, even
> shame, to hear speak of their past.[12]

Price-Mars's book was a "cultural breakthrough," according to Wynter,
because it encouraged a generation of Haitian intellectuals to "tear their
eyes from France" and to discover in their own culture "the most moving
history in the world." But writing in 1928, Price-Mars was also responding
to another urgent historical context: the U.S. military occupation of Haiti
(1915–1934), and the rise of U.S. hegemony in the Western Hemisphere. As
Wynter elaborates in her unpublished manuscript *Black Metamorphosis*,
"Price-Mars' book, and the Negritude movement to which it gave rise, was
part of the chain reaction to the United States' neo-colonial occupation of
Haiti. The new colonialism sharpened the consciousness of alienation."[13]

The occupation coincided with the rise of the New Negro Movement and the stirrings of anticolonial revolt in the Caribbean. In Haiti, peasant culture, especially Vodou's alternative social order, offered a subversive challenge to imperial power. Thus, to speak of folk culture in Haiti is to recognize its startling and disruptive contemporaneity.

I begin with Wynter to introduce this book's investment in reinterpreting discourses of folk culture through a Black hemispheric lens. Such a perspective demands attention to what Erica R. Edwards calls "the culture of U.S. empire" and its interplay with the Caribbean's colonial legacies.[14] Wynter's engagement with Price-Mars's Francophone text is an act of cultural and linguistic translation—a process that informs my comparative method, my attention to the ways that the local opens onto the transnational, and my focus on the U.S.-Caribbean region as a point of entanglement for Black expressive culture across five decades. Wynter's body of work encourages us to look for other "secretive histories" of Black folk culture, histories that, as Katherine McKittrick suggests, "are not invested in rehearsing lifelessness, the violated black body, and practices of resistance rooted in authenticity."[15] Such practices are "secretive" not only because they are illegible within the dominant frameworks of the West—or, to use the Haitian anthropologist Michel-Rolph Trouillot's more precise terminology, "the North Atlantic"— but also due to the interpretive labor that they demand, and indeed, the artistic craft necessary to encapsulate them.[16]

As Wynter's descriptions of folk practices reveal, to "turn the world upside down" is also to disrupt form. Her subject matter demands a more dynamic approach to the essay—an imperative to break open the genre. Her prose is often noted for its "allusive density" and "blistering polemical style."[17] But Wynter practices a broader range of formal techniques. "Jonkonnu" uses epigraphs at unexpected intervals, section headings followed by blocks of prose of asymmetrical lengths, numbered lists, and snippets of song. Her text consists of a polyvocal prose that moves in a nonlinear fashion toward an accumulation of meaning. It offers no easy definitions but instead forges an earthbound poetics where both body and language incline toward the Black geographies of the Americas. Like the folk practices it describes, Wynter's writing labors, and demands labor, to be heard.

Turning the world upside down might be understood as an ongoing / recursive gesture, or indeed a choreography of transformation—one that brings together Black writings with various expressive forms to uphold the experiences of "those [people] on the bottom." This book traces a group of interconnected figures who perform the world-overturning act of inverting the gaze (and often the body) toward the cultural practices of "the folk," or as Zora Neale Hurston phrased it, "the Negro farthest down," indicating their subject position as well as their geographical location in the Global South.[18] In the works of Jean Toomer, Eric Walrond, Langston Hughes, Nicolás Guillén, Eusebia Cosme, Hurston, Price-Mars, and Wynter, Black folk culture emerges as an accumulation of unwieldy details that disrupt the normalizing narratives of citizenship, empire, resistance, and radicalization. Critics have often read the turn to Black folk culture as a nostalgic drive to recover an authentic heritage and as a turn away from historicity and radical politics. Following Wynter, this book tells a different story about the uses of folk culture, showing how writers and performers not only crafted alternatives to the tropes of authenticity that circulated in their own artistic movements, but also evaded enclosure by conventional artistic forms. In their portraits of Black labor, movement, speech, folklore, and ritual, these figures reinvent folk culture as a site of upheaval and indeterminacy. Together, they craft new epistemologies of blackness that unfold across a variety of genres and media, including short stories, hybrid forms, ethnography, poetry, performance, and the sonic. Such works demand that we sit with language or performance that is not cohesive or plainly legible, but nevertheless reveals the various ways that Black culture generates meaning. Beginning with the New Negro Movement of the 1920s and concluding with Wynter in the Jamaican 1960s and 1970s, this book names folk culture as a historically contingent process of world-making that powerfully encapsulates the connection between Black aesthetics and politics.

Building on scholarship in African diaspora studies, U.S. empire studies, and Caribbean studies, I show that a multilingual, comparative, transnational method yields a more robust and detailed theory of folk practice as an archive of Black radical innovation than we have previously known. Rather than a unified category that serves to crystalize national identities, folk culture is a conversation across diasporic blackness. It concerns the problem of representation; the interplay between artistic production and ethnography; the function of translation across languages, cultures, and geographies; and the role of poetics, embodiment, and the sonic. For

Toomer and Walrond, folk culture provides a vantage point from which to glimpse the disorienting confluence of death and modernity in the Jim Crow South and the Panama Canal Zone. Turning to U.S.-occupied Haiti, Hurston and Price-Mars experiment with ethnographic form to present folklore and Vodou practices as sites of dynamic suggestion, and yet they come to radically different conclusions about the politics of the U.S. intervention. For Hughes, Guillén, and Cosme, unwieldy performances interrupt established ways of translating and apprehending race in Afro-Cuban poetry and folk culture. Finally, Wynter's early work in London in dance and radio indicates the role of folk culture in the anticolonial project of envisioning "the end of the world, the overturning of the order."[19] At stake in these various experiments is the will to transform reality through folk culture's unruly rehearsals of self-invention.

IMPERIAL ASYMMETRIES

Rather than fixing these various approaches into a universalizing narrative, I trace the imperial asymmetries of folk culture: the ways that Black subjects reimagined folk expression to navigate their uneven relationships to empire in the twentieth century. Drawing from archipelagic American studies, Ifeoma Kiddoe Nwankwo observes that "the history of US-Caribbean relations is a history of asymmetry, especially in terms of geography and power."[20] Asymmetry is also a formal strategy: an element of folk culture that Hurston outlines in her 1934 essay "Characteristic of Negro Expression,"—a work that itself deploys uneven form to raise more provocative questions about blackness than it answers. In exploring cross-imperial asymmetries, my work extends foundational frameworks in diaspora studies such as Paul Gilroy's notion of the Black Atlantic as constituted by "routes" rather than "roots," and Brent Hayes Edwards's signal claim that the "cultures of Black internationalism can only be seen *in translation*."[21] Translation, linguistic and otherwise, remains profoundly central to the discourses of folk culture that underpin the articulations of diaspora and folk culture that I describe in this book. When the Cuban poet Guillén refers to "*negros y el pueblo*" in the barrios of Havana, or Price-Mars describes the "*pèp ayisyen*" that he encounters in the Haitian countryside, it cannot be assumed that they share the same vision of the masses, let alone a commensurate language to describe them.

However, in each of the cases I discuss here, folk culture allows us to glimpse the rise of U.S. hegemony through the lens of what Deborah Thomas names "everyday practice."[22] Accordingly, *Turn the World Upside Down* charts a different set of imperial routes than either Gilroy or Edwards explores. Rather than privileging sites of Black cultural production in urban centers in the North Atlantic, I focus on the Caribbean as a specific "point of entanglement."[23] With its overlapping routes of migration, labor, and travel, the U.S.-Caribbean region is a crossroads from which to glimpse the peculiar technologies of violence that attend the legacy of European colonialism and the rise of U.S. empire. Shaped by the rise of folklore studies and anthropology in the Western Hemisphere, discourses of folk culture emerge at a time when "U.S. [troops] were continually invading one island or another," to use Barbara Christian's blunt phrasing.[24] In December 1898, the United States gained control of Cuba and Puerto Rico and would soon intervene in Panama, Nicaragua, Haiti, the Dominican Republic, and Trinidad. In 1900, Charles Chesnutt remarked: "If certain recent tendencies are an index of the future, it is not safe to fix the boundaries of the future United States anywhere short of the Arctic Ocean on the north and the Isthmus of Panama on the south."[25] Beyond military, economic, and political interventions, U.S. empire labored anxiously to generate and contain cultural knowledge about the dark, tropical, and presumably primitive populations in its newly expanded territories. From scientific fieldwork to sensational travel narratives written by U.S. marines, to zombie films, U.S. empire had much to say about folk culture. In turn, Black cultural producers turned to folk culture to engage, subvert, and ultimately transform imperial ways of knowing.

A robust body of scholarship in Black literary studies, history, performance studies, and critical anthropology informs my understanding of the U.S.-Caribbean region as a problem-space structured by empire. As the work of Stephanie Leigh Batiste, Erica R. Edwards, Nicole Waligora-Davis, Rafael Dalleo, Randi Gill-Sadler, Frank Guridy, Laurie Lambert, Deborah Thomas, Michelle Stephens, Shane Vogel, and others has shown, we gain a better understanding of the politics of artistic production, labor, and social life when we attend to the ways that Black subjects theorize imperial power. In *Caribbean Military Encounters*, Shalini Puri and Lara Putnam assert the need to go beyond indictments of U.S. intervention to address the "actual negotiations of people on the ground," a concern that also animates and complicates the uses of folk culture that I discuss here.[26] Together, this scholarship extends the work of Caribbean theorists such as Wynter and Glissant, whose lives and writings give us a vital framework for charting imperial asymmetries in what Glissant calls "the estuary of the Americas."[27]

Turn the World Upside Down brings these various critical threads into conversation by working across the Caribbean's three major language groups (English, Spanish, and French) to enact a comparative method for Black hemispheric study. I focus on several flash points through which Black subjects articulate the connection between folk culture, imperialism, and Black hemispheric modernity: the African American Great Migration; the construction of the Panama Canal (1904–1914) and its attendant labor migrations; the U.S. military occupation of Haiti (1915–1934) and the subsequent "Golden Age" of Haitian studies; ongoing U.S. intervention in Cuba and the transnational circuits of Afro-Cuban performance; and finally, the emerging contours of the Windrush-era West Indian community in London. Several figures in my study are affiliated with the Harlem Renaissance, and yet their work decenters the cosmopolitan and urban to render a dispersed experimental geography of the periphery. They imagine putatively provincial spaces, such as a cane-field in Georgia or a cemetery in U.S.-occupied Port-au-Prince as transnational sites pivotal to the shaping of history. They depict "the folk" in these sites not to indulge the pastoral or the nostalgic, but rather to show how everyday people contribute to the stirrings of modernity while being excluded from its promises. Such flash points and their ripple effects animate the central questions of my book: How might these events shift our understanding of the historical contexts that underpin the development of Black experimental literature and culture? And further, as Black subjects sought to transmit the terror and the beauty of Black life under empire and Jim Crow, to what expressive forms did they turn?

To place folk culture at the crossroads of U.S.-Caribbean history is not to render the masses more knowable or worthy of assimilation into predetermined models of citizenship or resistance. Rather, what is at stake are epistemologies of blackness that subvert imperial narratives of folk culture's authenticity, premodernity, or obsolescence, leaving us instead with ever-evolving philosophies of self-invention. Furthermore, my interest in asymmetry leads me to displace familiar figures from the contexts in which they are most often discussed. For example, I consider Langston Hughes's participation in a Katherine Dunham production in the post–Harlem Renaissance 1940s, as well as Wynter reciting her early short stories and plays over the air on BBC radio in the 1950s, well before she produced her best-known scholarship. Attending to such moments leads me to archival materials that have been infrequently discussed, if not entirely neglected. My use of such fragments attends to the substance of ephemeral encounters in twentieth-century archives of "the folk."

REINTERPRETING FOLK CULTURE

This book performs a reinterpretation of the familiar, yet "multivalent and slippery" tropes of the folk in Black literary and cultural studies.[28] By engaging discourses of folk culture as sites of both historicity and unruly aesthetics, I read against the grain of criticism that traditionally regards the turn to the folk as an embrace of "romantic culturalism." For example, Gene Andrew Jarrett and Henry Louis Gates Jr. argue that "that ideological turn within the New Negro movement pivoted on [Alain] Locke's hegemonic tropes of the 'folk,'" in which the folk were "romanticized as ahistorical, lower class, and authentically Black." In this constructed vision of the masses, the "folk" do not only problematically embody a Black essence, but also reside in pockets of (often rural) premodernity that are both geographically and temporally removed from their New Negro counterparts in the North. Emphasizing Alain Locke's influence as a cultural ambassador, Jarrett and Gates note a "consequent decline in left-leaning New Negro cultural politics."[29] In a similar vein, in a key intervention following Hurston's recuperation in the academy, Hazel Carby importantly scrutinized vernacular criticism that "uncritically reproduced at the center of its discourse the idea of an authentic, folk heritage."[30] Such critiques have proved instructive for a generation of scholars who have come to interpret the folk not as an "assumed category," but as a "contested vision of collectivity."[31]

To be sure, romantic culturalism held an undeniable allure for Black writers in earnest search of a usable past, as well as white readers and patrons who wanted to grasp the exotic while keeping the masses in their place. Yet it can only go so far to describe the range of experiments in folk culture that emerged in the first decades of the twentieth century. Such a framework can little account for a writer such as Walrond, who between gigs at Marcus Garvey's *Negro World* and Charles Johnson's *Opportunity* wrote scathing critiques of capitalism and U.S. expansion from his Harlem apartment. There is little nostalgia in Walrond's abrasive depiction of Caribbean folk culture in *Tropic Death*, a book of short stories of labor, migration, and death during the U.S. construction of the Panama Canal. And yet Walrond turns to the folk to say something vital about the ways that local culture is imbricated within modernity's global upheavals. Contemplating his sometimes-uneasy fit within the Harlem Renaissance, Walrond classes himself in the "esoteric school" of Black writing, a group that included himself, Toomer, Hughes, Hurston, and others commonly associated with representations of folk life. Walrond uses the word "esoteric" not only to signal insider knowledge—the imperative for the artist to depict "tantalizing Black people he *knows*"—but also to denote a practice of deliberately thwarting expectations for transparency.[32] The formal and thematic difficulty of *Tropic Death*, for which it was both admired and criticized, further serves as a counterpoint to Locke's "hegemonic tropes" of the folk.[33] The esoteric, in Walrond's view, was not only a stance against writerly convention, but also a claim about the unruly form of Black culture itself.

As we will see, alternatives to the construct of an authentic, insular, ahistorical folk (or, for that matter, U.S.-centered notions of Black collectivity) did not just emerge in hindsight but were present in early representations of folk culture themselves. Beyond the esoteric, I turn to other practices that subvert nostalgia, authenticity, and race as stable categories. In Price-Mars's elaboration of how Vodou and folklore humanize the Haitian landscape, Hurston's suggestive trope of "compelling insinuation,"[34] Eusebia Cosme's practiced subversions of Cuban performance culture, and Wynter's descriptions of carnival dancers who "turn the world upside down," I locate epistemologies of blackness that invite (indeed demand) attention to the unruly—that which cannot be readily contained, disciplined, or managed. Through the subversive effects of aesthetics, such experiments venture into more expansive territory than romantic culturalism can encompass. Such efforts are not a disavowal of radical politics, but rather an experimental renegotiation of its terms.

In many ways, the contested nature of folk culture is central to how writers and artists theorize blackness. My analysis of folk culture as a set of indeterminate practices sheds light on scholarly difficulty with defining "the folk." As Anthea Kraut observes, simultaneously a "demographic group, an aesthetic, an ideology, a way of life and a mode of expression," "folk" signifies a term characterized above all by its "remarkable lack of precision."[35] While Carby contends that when Harlem Renaissance writers turned to the folk, "their dilemma was little different from debates over proletarian fiction in the Soviet Union, in Europe, in the Caribbean, and in North America generally: debates that raged over the question of how and by whom should 'the people,' the masses of ordinary people, be portrayed," she also argues that such debates rarely reached consensus.[36] Sonnet Retman deftly reveals that iterations of the folk were "invented, unstable, and shifting, and they served a range of political agendas."[37] While such descriptions stress a critical awareness of the invented and mediated nature of the folk, they also provide a useful vocabulary for the interventions of writers attempting to convey a shapeshifting cultural terrain.

While "the folk" often appears enclosed in quotation marks, "culture" too was an indeterminate concept at the turn of the twentieth century, despite, or perhaps because of, urgent efforts to define it. While the study and documentation of local folklore and customs were not new, the professionalization of folklore studies and anthropology in the Caribbean and the United States shaped discourses of folk culture and authenticity at the turn of the century. As I will elaborate in chapter 2, African American and Caribbean subjects understood anthropology's imbrication with the colonial, as well as with the unfolding U.S. imperial project. In *Inventing the New Negro*, Daphne Lamothe observes how Black folklorists and ethnographers "recognized the epistemological constraints of an academic discipline rooted, as anthropology was, in conditions of colonial conquest and domination."[38] But at the same time, they deploy ethnography as a malleable literary genre through which they could experiment with different methods of observing and defining the quotidian rhythms of Black social life. Rather than simply taking up the "master's tools," they anticipate many of the questions and self-reflexive critiques that engage critical anthropologists today: anthropology's place in what Trouillot coined the "savage slot," the instability of ethnographic authority, and the tensions between the presumed decline of folk culture and its radical aliveness.[39]

I also reevaluate the influence of "salvage ethnography" on discourses of folk culture. Promoted by Franz Boas, salvage ethnography established what Lindsay Reckson terms a "temporality of vanishing," a sense that the cultural forms under study (especially those of Indigenous people and, increasingly, Black Americans) would soon vanish under industrialization.[40] Jean Toomer invokes such a temporality in *Cane*, in which a "son" of the South returns "just in time" to capture Southern folk culture, which was "fading, soon gone." Rehearsing modernist disillusionment with industrialism, Toomer articulated his sense that "the folk spirit is walking in to die on the modern desert," a statement that some critics have taken at face value as a summation of the text. But *Cane's* salvage mission is interrupted by folk culture's unsettling contemporaneity. As the narrator remarks, "I felt strange, as I always do in Georgia, particularly at dusk. I felt that things unseen to men were tangibly immediate. It would not have surprised me had I had a vision."[41] This unwieldy vision bursts the seams of *Cane's* preservationist framework. Shrieks pierce the Southern landscape, disrupting the volume's nostalgic and lyrical poetic voice. Characters speak unintelligibly, their language evading capture. Sugarcane, the volume's purported symbol of wholeness and "deep-rooted" stability, suddenly transports us to the tropics. Death is not in fact an end, but a crossing. The transformative impact of "feeling strange" in Georgia is one of *Cane's* most enduring statements about folk culture. Through its many shifts in form, style, and voice, *Cane* dramatizes the conceptual and aesthetic conundrum of depicting a folk culture in tumultuous transition.

While I explore how writers and performers worked to avoid enclosure by tropes of premodern authenticity, I also acknowledge that tropes of authenticity exerted a profound influence. Hurston touted authenticity when it suited her aims, as with her contrast between "real" Negro spirituals and the Fisk Jubilee Singers' "glee club" adaptations.[42] But in other instances, she emphasized transformation and development, as in her celebration of jook joints as shapeshifting spaces of Black sociality, or in her framing of Black originality as the "modification of ideas." Armed with a different set of motivations, white collectors of folk culture remained all too eager to exploit myths of Black authenticity and primitivism, as Daphne Brooks cogently summarizes: "all of those Black voices down at the bottom of the well, presumably—and mistakenly—'untouched' by the workings of modernity, as that oh-so-familiar myth that stretches back to at least the time of F. Scott and his Jazz Age party people goes, are the repository of our purest traumas and unbridled desires."[43] In his overview of the "cult of authenticity" in folk music studies, Benjamin Filene notes that when the

Lomaxes took the blues guitarist and ex-convict Lead Belly on a whirl-wind tour of New York City, they went to great pains to distinguish his authentic delivery from folk performances that had been tainted by artifici-ality, announcing that "Lead Belly doesn't burlesque."[44] And yet, as Retman also attests, purveyors of Black folk culture (and the writers inspired by them) did, in fact, burlesque.[45] Even when their authors purport to sup-ply access to authentic Black speech, embodiment, folklore, or spirituality, their cultural works ostentatiously stage a failure to offer a cohesive vision of blackness. Such failure, or even refusal, to bring the folk into definitive conceptual focus does not always register as melancholic loss. Rather it opens a dynamic space in which blackness can move.

EXPERIMENTAL VOCABULARIES OF FOLK CULTURE

While declarations of authenticity often serve to elide the recognition of artistic innovation, such innovation is the subject of this book.[46] *Turn the World Upside Down* illuminates a dynamic tension between discourses of folk authenticity and the experiments that are too unruly to be contained by them. I am indebted to a robust body of criticism on Black experimen-tal writing and culture. In many ways, the figures in my study anticipate Glissant's call for formal strategies that favor opacity. "Western thought has led us to believe that a work must always put itself constantly *at our disposal*," Glissant writes, "and I know a number of our folktales, the power of whose impact on their audience has nothing to do with the clarity of their meaning."[47] Glissant's words are sometimes misinterpreted to imply that opaque works and practices are inscrutable or obscure, and there-fore impossible to engage. But when he clamors for "the right to opacity," he is speaking of a poetics that invites interpretive labor. The aim is not to grasp for essences "in a gesture of enclosure if not appropriation." He explains, if "opacities can coexist, weaving fabrics," one must "focus on the texture of the weave."[48] In "Jonkonnu," a drive to engage the opaque com-pels Wynter to tarry with embodied rituals that were illegible to colonial observers. Her aim is not merely to elucidate these practices, but rather to "live with them," as La Marr Jurelle Bruce, echoing Glissant, conveys in his recent work on madness in Black radical art.[49] Following Glissant and Wynter, Samantha Pinto's work on the role of difficulty in diasporic wom-en's writing highlights a Black feminist ethics of interpretation, signaling the "intense engagement that reading opaque, formally experimental texts requires of the modern reader."[50] In my turn to various forms and genres, I extend Pinto's analysis of "non-narrative, or texts in which narrative is decentered, undone, and thwarted" to ask how the refusal of master narratives allows us to tell new stories about Black subjectivity, collectivity, and sovereignty.[51]

This book's engagement with scholarship on global modernism is particularly salient in the reevaluation of the Harlem Renaissance that I offer in chapter 1. As Eric Hayot and Rebecca Walkowitz attest, the point is not simply to locate "more modernism" in previously marginalized geographies, but rather to "ask what happens to the foundational concepts of modernism and to the methods we bring to modernist studies when we approach the field globally."[52] At stake in these efforts is not a drive to make blackness transparent or universal, but rather to take stock of the various ways that Black cultural practices transmit meaning.

Thus, while making larger claims about how artists emphasized the historicity and modernity of Black culture, I also take seriously their interest in aesthetic details—noting the care with which they describe the formal and stylistic qualities of Black culture and the way that these forms inflect their own writing and performance. A turn to detail—stylistic, formal, archival—guides my approach to all the figures in this book, as well as my method of defining folk culture—an elusive term at best. As Alexandra T. Vazquez notes in her study of Cuban music, "details have the ability to jolt the most steadfast of arguments." She recalls being "seduced . . . by the fight against the guiding of Cuban music" and seeking to resist the market's demand to make Cuban music "accessible and available" through description. Such seduction was "cut short" when one of her mentors inquired, "but what do the musicians actually *sound* like?" Vazquez reflects, "To not listen to what the performers are doing would be to enact another kind of violence upon them."[53]

In a similar fashion, I ask: How do these depictions of Black folk culture actually sound (or move, or speak)? Attending to such details does not reduce opaque texts to transparency, but it does honor Glissant's interest in "texture" and relation rather than essence. I examine such details not simply to marshal evidence for scholarly arguments, but to amplify what is "vitally elusive" about these works.[54] An attention to detail guides my interpretive practices, as well as my approach to the archive—whether it is in Toomer's fragmentary prose; Hurston's theory of "compelling insinuation," or the theory of "epigrammatic" Black speech that Wynter first articulates in a radio transcript. While details teach us much about the motivations, collaborative aesthetics, and historical contexts through which Black artists and writers worked, they just as often tend to confound and unsettle, lending ambiguity and nuance to the representations of blackness that they present. Rather than projecting a cohesive vision of how the folk are represented, I consider the ways that writers worked to depict folk culture—and blackness itself—as a site of disruption, experimentation, ambiguity, and flux.

In the first half of this book, I consider folk culture as a disruptive force in interwar Black writing. Chapter 1 locates the folk at the crossroads of the American South and the Caribbean basin. I discuss Toomer's *Cane*, a hybrid collection of poems, short stories, and dramatic sketches set in rural Georgia and its urban borderlands, alongside Walrond's *Tropic Death*, a short story collection about circum-Caribbean labor migration sparked by the construction of the Panama Canal. Often named together as two major stylists of the Harlem Renaissance, Toomer and Walrond have yet to be the subject of an extended comparative reading. As I will show, *Cane* and *Tropic Death* display the radical work of short, experimental forms in depicting Black life amid the disorienting upheavals of Jim Crow and U.S. imperialism. To read them together is to broaden the geographical contours of the Harlem Renaissance and to deepen conversations about Black social death in the American Century. While both texts frame Black modernity as an inexorable and violent transition, they also position their subjects at an illuminating crossroads of transformation, invoking what is dynamically and elusively alive about Black folk culture.

If the completion of the Panama Canal in 1914 represented the "triumph [of the United States] over tropical disorder," the 1915 U.S. invasion of Haiti represented an effort to consolidate power in the Caribbean under the guise of keeping order.[55] Returning to the crossroads of empire and culture, chapter 2 locates the origins of diaspora studies in the robust response to the U.S. occupation of Haiti. I consider Hurston's and Price-Mars's ethnographic writings on Haitian folklore and Vodou as efforts to theorize quotidian practices of sovereignty and self-invention. Both authors name

Haitian folk culture as a praxis of self-determination, as well as formal inspiration for an emergent body of Haitian literature. Yet while Price-Mars vehemently opposes the occupation in his groundbreaking 1928 work *Ainsi parla l'Oncle* [*So Spoke the Uncle*], Hurston's *Tell My Horse* (1938) is often criticized for its jarring praise of U.S. intervention. I understand these problematics as exemplary of the complex negotiations of solidarity that U.S. expansion occasioned for African Americans. Here, I marshal Hurston's theory of compelling insinuation as a framework for reading the contradictions and subtle convergences between *Tell My Horse* and a contemporaneous Haitian intellectual tradition led by Price-Mars. Also termed "dynamic suggestion," compelling insinuation signals the constrained yet provocative agency of Black folk practice, and it also describes a narrative technique that both asserts and destabilizes ethnographic authority. In their own distinct ways, Price-Mars and Hurston imagine folk culture as an alternative mode of occupying space in the face of imperial occupation.

In the book's second half, the literary breaks open into a midcentury performance archive of the folk. Emphasizing an increasingly transmedial approach to folk culture, I draw upon materials such as concert programs, rehearsal notes, scripts for radio programs and plays, and correspondence.[56] Performance poses specific challenges to archival study due to its ephemerality and its resistance to documentation. While I reimagine performances, collaborations, and moments of embodied sociality, I also attend to the ways that performance deliberately evades capture and unsettles frameworks of racial authenticity that are presumed to reside in the body.[57]

In chapter 3, I consider the role of poetics and performance in translating the folk. I turn to the 1946 staging of *Cuban Evening: The Poems and Songs of Nicolás Guillén*, a largely forgotten collaboration between the Katherine Dunham School, the Afro-Cuban *declamadora* Cosme, and the poets Hughes and Guillén. Guillén and Hughes make a familiar pair in scholarship about the challenges of translating race, vernacular forms, and anti-imperial politics. Cosme's performances interrupt this masculinist narrative of transnational collaboration, unsettling folk poetics with the provocative ambiguity of gesture. One of the few women associated with *afrocubanismo* in the 1930s, Cosme became internationally famous for her performances in *declamación*, a theatrical art that involves "not simply recitation, but the physical and aural enactment of written poems."[58]

Cosme's practiced interpretations of Guillén's poems complicate the themes of gender, embodiment, and authenticity already present in his work. Hughes also regarded oral performance as an important part of his translation practice. Drawing his repertoire from a draft of translations of Guillen's poems, Hughes used *Cuban Evening* as an opportunity to experiment with translation effects. Cosme's and Hughes's participation in *Cuban Evening* thus raises key questions about the role of embodiment in acts of cultural interpretation. What difference does it make when the translator is not invisible, but present on stage? In *Cuban Evening*, Cosme and Hughes engage in acts of cultural, linguistic, and formal translation that ultimately disrupt established vocabularies of folk culture through the unwieldiness of the Black performing body.

My final chapter returns to Wynter, recuperating her early career as dancer, playwright, and radio actor in 1950s London. Extending Carole Boyce Davies's framing of Wynter as a "creative/theoretical" who speculates across a variety of forms and media,[59] I turn to an archive of unpublished works, scripts, and correspondence, as well as Wynter's own recollections, to demonstrate the centrality of folk culture to what Wynter calls the praxis of being human.[60] I consider Wynter's participation in the Trinidadian choreographer Boscoe Holder's dance troupe in London before exploring her work for BBC radio: literary commentary, short stories, and a radio play titled *The Barren One*, an adaptation of Federico García Lorca's *Yerma*. In exploring how this work anticipates Wynter's later writings, especially *Black Metamorphosis*, "Jonkonnu in Jamaica," and "Novel and History: Plot and Plantation," I argue for a radical renegotiation of Wynter's interventions into the aesthetics of Black being. Building on Price-Mars's descriptions of how Black subjects humanized the New World landscape through embodied acts of labor, cultivation, and ceremony, Wynter locates the power of folk culture in disruptive practices that momentarily "turn the world upside-down, liberating participants."[61] Even as she works in a medium such as radio that invoked anxieties about immateriality, her creations reveal a persistent and multivalent engagement with the earthbound geographies of folk culture. Looking back at interwar discourses of the folk, and forward toward Jamaica's postcolonial future, Wynter reinterprets culture to imagine new possibilities.

As Davies has remarked, Wynter's early work constitutes the "beginning of an analysis toward 'ontological sovereignty.'"[62] I end the book with a coda that considers the implications of folk culture for Wynter's theories of Black being. As she explains in an interview with David Scott:

> We know about political sovereignty. . . . We do not know about something called ontological sovereignty . . . in order to speak the conception of ontological sovereignty, we would have to move completely outside our present conception of what it is to be human, and therefore outside the ground of the orthodox body of knowledge which institutes and reproduces such a conception.[63]

Meditating on the entangled legacy of European colonialism and the rise of the American Century, Wynter asks what it means for Black subjects to create their own terms for individual and collective existence that are neither containable nor legible within dominant frameworks of national belonging, sovereignty, and the human. According to Wynter, this "alternative form of sovereignty" could only come from the marginalized, "society's expendable damnés" who forge other ways of being outside Western bodies of thought. Wynter's oeuvre suggests many rich opportunities to engage ontological sovereignty through the lens of Black cultural practices.

To take stock of the various genres of the human that Black people have already imagined, Wynter suggests that "we accept folk culture as a point outside the system where the traditional values can give us a focus of criticism against the impossible reality in which we are all enmeshed." While critics have looked to contemporary art practices to imagine new ways of being human (or to move beyond the human entirely), it has been less common to return to early, and presumably familiar, discourses of folk culture as unruly disruptions of our "impossible reality."[64] Yet the articulations of blackness and being that occupy today's critical imagination have a longer history. If such cultural practices offer what Alexander Weheliye terms "alternative modes of life alongside the violence, subjection, exploitation and racialization that define the modern human," the enactment of such alternatives remains a laborious, imperfect, and asymmetrical process that must necessarily be repeated and is always yet to come.[65]

PART I

Writing the Crossroads

Chapter One

GEORGIA DUSK AND PANAMA GOLD

Jean Toomer, Eric Walrond,
and the "Death" of Folk Culture

Legend has it that the blues icon Robert Johnson sold his soul to the devil at the crossroads of two highways in the Deep South, at the stroke of midnight, in exchange for his prodigious skills on the guitar. This tale—which Johnson perpetuated himself—persists even though the lyrics of his famous song "Cross Road Blues" (1936) make no mention of such a transaction, but rather chronicle the terror that Johnson may have felt as a Black man hitchhiking through the Mississippi Delta in the era of Jim Crow. But the lyrics are no less a part of the legend. They position Black artistic mastery in the context of the racial violence that marks Black modernity. Of course, this tale is larger than Johnson, as the crossroads has long been imagined in Black diasporic culture as a space where one might acquire folk mastery or spiritual insight through a mysterious encounter with the supernatural. In some versions of the legend, this mysterious force at the crossroads is not the devil, but "a big Black man"; in other versions, the figure becomes Papa Legba, a West African and New World gatekeeper of the crossroads, an intermediary between the living and the dead.[1]

The crossroads also marks the intersection of U.S. and Caribbean culture, history, and geography. As the poet Yusef Komunyakaa suggests, Johnson's tale simultaneously encompasses the local and conjures other landscapes just south of the South. He writes, "I glimpsed that legendary figure standing somewhere in the Mississippi Delta night, clutching his guitar, ready to make a Faustian deal with the Devil. But, of course, it wasn't long before the Delta night became a countryside road somewhere in Haiti."[2] In Black diasporic culture, crossroads function as a scene of spatial and temporal intersection and transition, a site of creativity, and frequently as a space of encounter with death. Moreover, the crossroads is also a figure of comparison, invoking what Natalie Melas calls "a ground for comparison that is in common but not unified."[3] As M. Jacqui Alexander elaborates in *Pedagogies of Crossing*, the crossroads are "the space of convergence and endless possibility; the place where we put down and discard the unnecessary in order to pick up that which is necessary. It is that imaginary from which we dream the craft of a new compass. A set of conflictual convergences."[4]

This chapter draws upon the trope of the crossroads as a liminal, transformative space with specific resonance in the context of the Americas. I turn to *Cane*, Jean Toomer's 1923 hybrid-genre portrait of the U.S. South, and *Tropic Death*, Eric Walrond's 1926 short story collection depicting migration between the Panama Canal Zone and the surrounding Caribbean. Both texts frame death and crossing as markers of Black hemispheric modernity. Toomer wrote that "the folk spirit is walking in to die on the modern desert," words that are commonly read as a nostalgic lament for a Southern folk culture "fading, soon gone."[5] And yet to read *Cane* alongside *Tropic Death*'s portrait of deadly canal labor is to think Black death more expansively, to further illuminate what that "modern desert" might signify in the interconnected geographies of the South and the Caribbean. While the United States oversaw the construction of the Panama Canal (1904–1914), the bulk of the hard labor—the dredging, digging, clearing of brush, and handling of explosives—was completed by laborers recruited from surrounding Caribbean islands (figure 1.1). While *Cane* is haunted by the legacy of plantation slavery and the modern specter of lynching, *Tropic Death* reveals the deadly entanglements of colonialism, Jim Crow, and U.S. imperialism evident in Panama Canal construction and various other industrial projects throughout the Caribbean. In distinct ways, *Cane*'s and *Tropic Death*'s stylistic experiments seek to illuminate contemporary forms of violence that were insidious, pervasive, and often confounding.

FIGURE 1.1 Unfinished locks, Panama Canal, ca. 1913. *Source:* Library of Congress, Prints and Photographs Division, LC-USZ62-9604.

While both texts anticipate contemporary conversations about Black social death, they also explore the idea that "death can be proliferative."[6] At the crossroads, the moment of "fading" is an opportunity for unique insight, as the narrator of *Cane* implies: "I felt strange, as I always do in Georgia, particularly at dusk. I felt that things unseen to men were tangibly immediate. It would not have surprised me had I had a vision."[7] *Cane*'s "vision" unfolds across thirty-one poems, short stories, and sketches as a set of formal practices: strategies by which Toomer both reveals and obscures the contours of Black folk culture. Similarly, *Tropic Death*'s structure, a short story cycle, enables its geographical leaps as well as its inexorable, machine-like rendering of death across space and time. Walrond's language—here fragmentary, there dense and intricate—registers the U.S. empire's failure to contain tropical disorder. Through a series of surprising juxtapositions, Walrond depicts the vitality—and vital elusiveness—of Black folk life. By noting their investment in what Kevin Quashie calls "Black aliveness," I do not mean to suggest that either text concludes triumphantly.[8] Rather, each text insists on the interplay between Black life and death. By engaging Black folk culture at a moment of transition in U.S.-Caribbean history, both texts propose that death is not an end, but a crossing. In so doing, they continue an Afro-diasporic tradition of communion with death. Speaking of death and burial practices in Jamaica, Vincent Brown observes that for Black subjects, "the end was the beginning, that death arrived not only to finish the living, but to cultivate important features of social life."[9] Although these texts transmit the painful and disorienting legacy of slavery and modern imperial violence, they also convey, in distinct ways, the unruly process of Black living.

In discussing Toomer and Walrond together, I further extend our now-expansive framework for considering the geographical parameters of the Harlem Renaissance, exemplified by Brent Hayes Edwards's turn to the cultures of Black internationalism in Paris. Here, I trace the contours of a Black hemispheric poetics invested in complex renderings of death, labor, and modernity at the crossroads of the Americas. In the process, I revise existing critical vocabularies for formal and thematic innovation in Black writing. Although Toomer and Walrond were frequently named together by their contemporaries and later critics as two of the Harlem Renaissance's most promising experimental writers, they have not yet been the subject of an extended comparative reading.[10] Situating Walrond's work in the context of American modernism, Michelle Ann Stephens observes that "in a manner remarkably similar to that of Jean Toomer in his descriptions of the Southern United States in *Cane* . . . Walrond literalised the metaphor of the modern 'wasteland' on Caribbean shores."[11] Stephens's reference to T. S. Eliot's modernist long poem *The Waste Land* is appropriate in more than one sense. The three authors shared the same publisher, Boni and Liveright, which in the 1920s eagerly acquired works that displayed disillusionment with modernity.[12] However, even though *Cane* and *Tropic Death* share the bleak, disorienting tone of other modernist texts, they may instead belong to what Seth Moglen calls "another modernism . . . that emerged alongside the familiar canonical works—and, like them, developed experimental formal strategies in order to map a process of social transformation so vast that it could be perceived only in fragments." Unlike the diffuse, general anxiety present in these better-known texts, "their works insist on the historical specificity of the destructive social forces at work in a modernizing America—and, in varied ways, they are committed to resistance."[13]

Moglen offers a useful frame for the intersection between *Cane*'s and *Tropic Death*'s experimentalism and historicity. Both expand the repertoire of historical themes in modernist writing and also reframe discourses of race, region, and folk culture that circulate in the Harlem Renaissance and throughout the Black Americas, suggesting new ways of reading "small places" and the folk that inhabit them.[14] Both works are set in the first two decades of the twentieth century, with its major waves of migration and shifts in the social landscape of Black communities. And each book reveals how narratives of modernity's progress are burdened by the weight of a brutal history. Furthermore, both *Cane* and *Tropic Death* framed a period of furious literary activity in which short forms—including stories, essays, poems, and plays—increasingly served as a site of experimentation, as well as a testing ground for young writers eager to make their mark on a rapidly changing literary sphere.

But as we will see, more than transposing the modernist impulses of white writers, both texts also belong to a Black diasporic tradition of formal innovation, and even difficulty—what Walrond labels the esoteric. He first used the term "esoteric school" in his 1925 essay "The Negro Literati," where he outlined a generational debate about the form and politics of Black writing. Whereas the older generation had been "obsessed by the inferiority complex," the work of "Jean Toomer, Countee P. Cullen, Zora Neale Hurston, Rudolph Fisher, Gwendolyn Bennett, Langston Hughes and Esther Popel in its 'flyest' moments is notoriously devoid of this irritating taint." Walrond singles out *Cane* for special praise: "Of the group Toomer is by far the strongest. *Cane* . . . didn't take particularly, and for a reason that would hold true to the major work of this esoteric school. In the first place, these swashbuckling neophytes are not going in for Charity or Uplift work. They don't give two hurrahs in hell for the sort of writing that attempts to put the Negro on a lofty pedestal." Instead, Walrond insisted that the writer should paint pictures of "tantalizing Black people—he knows."[15] Walrond anticipates Langston Hughes's 1926 manifesto "The Negro Artist and the Racial Mountain," which criticized the "Nordicized Negro intelligentsia" and instead praised the "low-down folks, the so-called common element, and they are the majority—may the Lord be praised!"[16] Like Walrond, Hughes suggests that Black folk culture constitutes a "great field of unused material." Both writers aimed to set an agenda that was at once ideological and aesthetic, urging a move away from the conventional in both subject matter and form.

However, Walrond's adjective "esoteric" deserves specific attention, as it registers the aesthetic and conceptual challenges that these texts posed to the Harlem Renaissance, as well as mainstream Black culture. Walrond had in fact used the phrase earlier, in a personal letter to Alain Locke following the successful publication of several of his stories in 1924: "I've been doing a lot of stuff since I last saw you, but much of it, I imagine, is a bit too esoteric for provincial consumption."[17] While Walrond delivers this line with a bit of snark, he also evinces real frustration with numerous enjoinders from critics to make his work more legible. On one hand, Walrond uses the phrase "esoteric school" as an umbrella term for those younger writers who, as Shane Vogel puts it, were "against uplift," departing from one conventional frame in which Black literary production had been apprehended.[18] On the other hand, if their critical reception is any clue, their work was also esoteric in a more straightforward sense: it defied legibility, leaving contemporary readers with a mix of admiration and bafflement.

Indeed, despite *Cane*'s now-hallowed place in the canon of the Harlem Renaissance, and *Tropic Death*'s robust recuperation, both texts perplexed contemporary readers. As Arna Bontemps reflected in 1966, "there are many odd and provocative things about *Cane*, and not the least is its form. Reviewers who read it in 1923 were generally stumped. Poetry and prose were whipped together in a kind of frappé. Realism was mixed with what they called mysticism, and the end result seemed to many of them confusing."[19] The esteemed W. E. B. Du Bois remarked that Toomer's "art carries much that is difficult or even impossible to understand," adding that "I am myself unduly irritated by this sort of thing."[20] Putting it more bluntly, a reviewer for the *New York Herald Tribune* complained that "at moments his outbursts of emotion approach the inarticulately maudlin," ruling out the possibility that *Cane*'s "inarticulate" outbursts might indeed be part of its artistic strategy.[21] Reviews of *Tropic Death* displayed a similar response, and Walrond faced the added pressure of presenting a Caribbean cultural landscape considered foreign to many of his American readers. Mary White Ovington, a white founder of the National Association for the Advancement of Colored People (NAACP) lamented that "Mr. Walrond's style . . . is at times trying. . . . He has the modern method of making sentences out of words. . . . He does not seem to realize that his milieu is unusual and that if he wishes us really to see the pictures that flood his mind he must take a little more pains in presenting them to us."[22] Beyond its "modern method,"

Tropic Death's unwieldy transnationalism constituted another aspect of its difficulty for its readers. Echoing his assessment of *Cane* three years prior, Du Bois called *Tropic Death* a "distinct contribution to Negro American literature," but he worried that "the book's impressionism, together with its dialect, make it often hard reading and difficult to understand in parts."[23] Even the modernist writer Waldo Frank, a staunch defender of his friend Toomer's experimental prose, regarded Walrond's prose as a distraction from his subject matter: "The reader finds . . . himself thinking of Mr. Walrond's language: finds himself seeing (and often being moved by) Mr. Walrond's words; rather than by the pictures and the dramas they are supposed to flesh."[24]

Rather than dismiss these reviews as mere misreadings or evidence of an impatience with formal difficulty that has since been overcome, I would like to retain a sense of what was "esoteric" about these texts: their refusal of transparency in depictions of "Negro folk life." I am informed here by Samantha Pinto's understanding of difficulty as requiring a kind of "challenging literacy" that reframes the way that we read difference in diasporic texts.[25] Revising the conventions of local color tales, which often depicted the South and Caribbean as ahistorical, provincial spaces frozen in premodern time, both texts grapple with disorienting historical upheaval: the transition from the plantation economy to industrialism, the subsequent waves of migration to industrial centers, and the changing shape of racial violence and systematic oppression in the first decades of the twentieth century. Each text crafts a poetics of Black life and death that compels readers to question what they know about the South and the Caribbean. Although both writers were featured in Locke's seminal 1925 anthology *The New Negro*, they also revise Locke's view of Black migration as a "deliberate flight not only from countryside to city, but from medieval America to modern," which signifies a geographical *and* temporal divide between folk in the Global South and their counterparts in Northern cities.[26] In contrast, the folk in *Cane* and *Tropic Death* are not merely "relics worthy of preservation," but laborers, migrants, performers, and producers of knowledge who contribute to the stirrings of modernity even as they are denied its promises.[27] Subverting notions of geographical and temporal fixity, authenticity, and ultimately decipherability, both Toomer and Walrond search for a form and language with which to represent "the modernity of the geographically 'non modern.'"[28]

My aim in this chapter is not only to bring disparate texts into relation, but also to highlight the comparativist elements already present in
these works. Walrond enacts such a juxtaposition with the words, "It wasn't
Sepia, Georgia, but a backwoods village in Barbados."[29] This evocative
phrase announces the setting of *Tropic Death*'s first story, "Drought." Such
language not only insists on the particularities of place—the story's setting
in a rural Barbados ravaged by drought and industrial labor—but it also
alludes to the Georgia landscape of *Cane*.[30] Walrond had favorably reviewed
Cane in several of his writings of the period, and his 1926 essay "From
Cotton, Cane, and Rice Fields" demonstrates his attunement to one of the
book's major themes—the stirrings of the African American Great Migration. In leaving behind the trace of *Cane*'s Southern elsewhere, Walrond
suggests not equivalences but resonances between the African American
and Caribbean literary geographies. Such connections appear in the form
of evocative imagery: snatches of folk song, "dark, brilliant, black faces of
West Indian peasants"; "canes spread over with their dark rich foliage into
the dust-laden road," and other markers of rural life that echo Toomer's
portrait of the U.S. South.[31] Such allusive language also illuminates traces
of the Caribbean in *Cane* itself: the economies of sugar suggested by *Cane*'s
central symbol, (sugar)cane, and the West Indian geographies of poems
such as "Conversion," "Georgia Dusk," and "Portrait in Georgia."

Cane was inspired by Toomer's own journey to the South in the fall
of 1921, when he served as the acting principal at the Sparta Agricultural
and Industrial Institute in Georgia. His grandfather, the prominent P. B. S.
Pinchback, had been born in Macon, Georgia. Born in 1894 and raised in
Washington, DC, Toomer was eager for the opportunity to return to the
"heart of the South."[32] In Sparta, Toomer encountered a landscape quite different from his middle-class upbringing in Washington, DC. Here, he was
captivated by Negro spirituals, which he found "sad and rich and joyous and
beautiful." At the same time, the specter of racial violence loomed, as evident in "Portrait in Georgia," which was first published in *Modern Review*
alongside "Face" and "Conversion" as "Georgia Portraits."

> Hair—braided chestnut,
> coiled like a lyncher's rope,
> Eyes—fagots,

Lips—old scars, or the first red blisters,
Breath—the last sweet scent of cane,
And her slim body,
white as the ash
of black flesh after flame.[33]

Perhaps more than any other work in his oeuvre, this poem demonstrates Toomer's claim that "mystery cannot help but accompany the deep, clear-cut image."[34]

Toomer's juxtaposition of "clear-cut" images suggests mysterious and yet fundamental entanglements: in this case between the preservation of Southern white womanhood, the lynched Black body, and a Southern landscape indelibly marked by that violence.[35] But while the poem's imagery is entrenched in the specificities of racial violence in the South, the "last sweet scent of cane" also transports us elsewhere. What would it mean to read the poem with attentiveness to the resonance of sugarcane in the literature of the Black Americas? As Toomer writes in the story "Carma," "time and space have no meaning in a cane field."[36] Read alongside *Tropic Death*, then, the scent of cane evokes not only the "lingering odor of death that clings to the sensuous southern landscape" as Vera Kutzinski observes, but also the cane field's enduring legacy as a symbol of labor, violence, and resistance in Black transnational literature.[37] Together, these texts reveal the dynamic modernity of local spaces, attuning us to a crossroads poetics of Black life and death under empire and Jim Crow.

A BLACK VAUDEVILLE OUT OF THE SOUTH

In his essay "A Century of Negro Portraiture in American Literature," Sterling Brown frames Toomer's and Walrond's writing in terms of an oblique and evocative poetics. Arriving at the section on the Harlem Renaissance, Brown declares that the "poets of the period spoke more deeply than the novelists," privileging works that eschew the master narrative of the novel.[38] Though he first lists poets such as Claude McKay, Countee Cullen, and Langston Hughes, Brown's idea of poetics is capacious enough to encompass the "evocative" and "impressionistic" prose of two of the movement's "striking books":

Two striking books of this movement were Jean Toomer's *Cane* (1923) and
Eric Walrond's *Tropic Death* (1926). . . . Toomer is a poet in the few lyrics in
Cane, and even more so in his evocative prose. No imaginative work since
The Souls of Black Folk had so deeply explored Negro life in the deep South,
in border cities, in the North, among the folk, the urban masses, the bour-
geoisie, the intellectuals; and none had revealed it so beautifully. Walrond's
Tropic Death is a brilliantly impressionistic, obliquely, subtly communicated
series of portraits of the author's native West Indies.[39]

Here Brown encapsulates the central role of formal and stylistic innovations in Toomer's and Walrond's portrayals of race and region. Both writers
depict black life in their respective regional settings—a task Brown himself
undertook in his poetry collection *Southern Road* (1932). In Brown's view,
each text's panoramic vision of black life is inextricable from its formal
dynamics—a premise also evident in the parallel Brown draws between
Cane and Du Bois's *The Souls of Black Folk*. The organization of both books
into a collection of shorter works allows for both sweeping breadth and distilled vision. Their form enables their movement between "life in the deep
South, in border cities, among the folk, the urban masses," or in Walrond's
case, succession through a "series of portraits" of the West Indies.[40] To
emphasize the importance of short forms is not to detract from the significance of book-length contributions. On the contrary, short forms served as
an experimental testing ground on which writers re-imagined the novel, or
in Toomer's case—crafted inventive alternatives to it.

Although the Harlem Renaissance has often been framed in terms of
its great novels, the movement's growth and development were catalyzed
through short forms: the short story, the poem, the play, the essay, the
vignette. Short stories were the most published genre in *Crisis and Opportunity*, including 135 published by Black women.[41] In a practical sense, short
forms enabled circulation and exposure, as the work was able to move in
various literary journals, anthologies, and little magazines. Such circulation
meant that writers' work could be framed in various and often opposing
ways, as well as for distinct audiences. Toomer published in the NAACP's
uplift-focused *Crisis*, as well as the socialist *Messenger*. In 1923, Walrond
published five stories on Caribbean themes that served as a "dress rehearsal
for *Tropic Death*."[42] Novelists such as Hurston and Richard Bruce Nugent
also wrote short stories and plays, eager to try their hand in a publishing

industry experiencing unprecedented growth during the interwar years. And while some writers opted for traditional plots, realist prose, or classical verse, others used short forms to test the boundaries of representation.[43]

Yet few were prepared for the arrival of *Cane*. The form of *Cane* has long been contested, and the stakes of classification are often high. Writing at the time of *Cane*'s republication by Harper and Rowe in 1969, Darwin Turner asserts that the book "is not a novel, not even the experimental novel for which [Robert] Bone pleaded to justify including it in his study of novels by Negroes. It is, instead, a collection of character sketches, short poems, and a play, which forms one of the distinguished achievements in the writings of Americans."[44] Here, Turner refers to Bone's influential 1966 study, the *Negro Novel in America*. By including *Cane*, Bone aimed to classify not only *Cane*'s genre, but also the book's weight and significance.[45] However, Toomer's reflections on the process of writing *Cane* reveal that he did not conceive of the book as a novel, but as a "free woven narrative" assembled from a variety of genres, as Waldo Frank suggests in a 1922 letter to Toomer.[46] "I feel my form is slowly crystallizing," Toomer responded, referring simultaneously to the creation of *Cane* and to his own artistic development.[47] In the 1910s and early 1920s, Toomer read the short story cycles of Sherwood Anderson, as well as the imagist poets. By the time *Cane* was published in 1923, several of its poems and stories had already appeared in such magazines as *Broom*, *Crisis*, *Double Dealer*, *Liberator*, *Little Review*, *Modern Review*, *Prairie*, and *S 4 N*. To understand *Cane* as a collection rather than a novel is to attend to the process of the text's formation.

Although *Cane* emerged in separate pieces, Toomer felt the need to publish a book, for reasons both professional and aesthetic. As he explained to Frank, "the concentrated force of a volume will do a great deal more than isolated pieces possibly could."[48] During this period, Toomer's correspondence shows him searching for a new form in which to transmit the Black experience. If one did not exist, it would have to be invented. Assembled from published works and new material, *Cane* was a whole animated by its eclectic parts, to which Toomer referred not as chapters but rather "pieces" and "vignettes." *Cane*'s tripartite structure traces the route of the Great Migration: Part I explores Black life amid the dusk and lyrical folksongs of rural Georgia. Part II "swings upward" into the fast-paced yet stifling lives of migrants in Washington, DC, and Chicago. Part III, "Kabnis," is a dramatic sketch that catalogues a tortured poet's return to the rural South.[49]

Juxtaposing poems, short stories, vignettes, and drama, Toomer "adopts an aesthetics of assemblage," suggesting that no one form could capture the multiplicity of Black life.[50]

In the dust jacket sketch on the original edition of *Cane* (figure 1.2), Toomer provocatively declares, "*Cane* is Black vaudeville. Black super-vaudeville out of the South." He further elaborates, "Its acts are poems, sketches, short stories, and one long drama. There can be no cumulative and consistent movement, and of course no central plot to such a book. It is sheer vaudeville. But if it be accepted as a unit of spiritual experience, then one can find in *Cane* a beginning, a progression, a complication, and an end."[51] Such phrasing has been attributed to the influence of an overzealous marketing team eager to promote primitivist, sensationalized images of the Black South, and indeed, the correspondence between Toomer and his publisher demonstrates the pressures that he faced in this regard.[52] However, as Barbara Foley notes, the term "Black vaudeville" appears in various handwritten drafts of the sketch among Toomer's papers, and it is furthermore consistent with Toomer's "insistence upon the book's avant-garde features—its lack of a central plot or 'cumulative or consistent movement'—[which were] integral to his claim that it is impossible to designate a single experience as the Negro experience."[53] Furthermore, while critics often link Toomer's experimentalism to his engagement with a white literary avant-garde, here he frames *Cane* in terms of contemporary Black

FIGURE 1.2 *Cane* by Jean Toomer, dust jacket of the first edition. *Source:* James Weldon Johnson Collection in the Yale Collection of American Literature, Beinecke Rare Book and Manuscripts Library, Yale University, New Haven, CT.

performance traditions. As Jayna Brown explains, emerging in the context of Black performers' exclusion from white vaudeville circuits, the "fluid structure and mutability of the variety stage acts rejected the monologic narratives of the dramatic play."[54] In his reference to Black vaudeville, a contemporary performance tradition, Toomer casts folk culture in terms of transformation and development rather than obsolescence.

Vaudeville serves as only one of the many metaphors that critics have used to describe the form of *Cane*. T. Austin Graham calls *Cane* a "field recording, an attempt on Toomer's part to catch a disappearing musical culture in words and to preserve it in literary form."[55] While such a metaphor registers the preservationist impulse that informs *Cane*'s narration, it tends to emphasize Toomer's documentation of folk materials rather than their performative transformation. While folklorists such as Alan Lomax turned to field recordings as a mode of realistic access to supposedly authentic folk culture, they also found that "surface noise obfuscated certain frequencies and reminded the listener that his or her experience was mediated."[56] It may be said that obfuscation *is* in fact one of *Cane*'s formal strategies, with its unwieldy mix of forms and asymmetrical structure serving to amplify rather than reduce surface noise in its representation of Black culture.

But to imagine *Cane* as Black vaudeville is to question the premise that the book aims to record folk culture to begin with. Indeed, the vaudeville stage's "medley of apparently unrelated elements" constituted another type of modern technology, one that dramatized the mediated nature of the spectator's encounter with Black culture by incorporating disruption into the form of the performance.[57] While most discussions of *Cane*'s aesthetics have emphasized a free-flowing musicality inspired by the "sorrow songs," I take interest in what Toomer called "terse lyricism" as a kind of vaudevillean aesthetic. As he writes in a letter to the poet Lola Ridge, "I think my own contribution will curiously blend the rhythm of the peasantry with the rhythm of machines. A syncopation, a slow jazz, a sharp intense motion, subtilized, fused to a terse lyricism."[58] "Terse lyricism" not only implies the emotional longing of the lyric, but also emphasizes that which is concise, abrupt, and elliptical. While critics typically attribute such qualities to *Cane*'s northern sections, they are central to *Cane*'s southern poetics, as well as its themes.

In the introduction to the 1975 edition of *Cane*, Turner contends, "[P]oetically ambiguous, *Cane* may appear to be a jungle through which original trails can be hacked by readers seeking their own myths and symbols."[59] By imagining *Cane* as a "jungle through which original trails can be hacked," Turner perhaps inadvertently points to a politics of encounter and interpretation framed in explicitly imperial terms. Natalie J. Ring argues that in the early twentieth century, a "transnational circuit of rhetoric and reform encouraged American cultural imperialists to construct the U.S. South as a tropical space in need of colonial uplift, much like the tropical possessions acquired as a result of American imperialism."[60] Indeed, with its tropical landscape and foliage, the dust jacket of *Cane*'s first edition conjures an exotic landscape to be interpretively "hacked."[61] But it is this very dynamic that *Cane* itself dramatizes and ultimately subverts. If *Cane*'s readers were drawn to the text in search of easily digestible depictions of folk culture, they instead encountered the disorienting challenges of *Cane*'s hybrid, itinerant structure, its "performative lyricism," its eruptions of song and other utterances, and ultimately the unruliness of the folk.[62]

POUR THAT PARTING SOUL IN SONG

As Mark Whalan has observed, *Cane* did much to suggest "a critical terrain that would figure largely in the decade; the interest in 'the folk,' the politics of the observer—namely who had the authority to observe, and how one's situation affected what could be seen; and the political value of formal experimentalism."[63] The book approaches these issues through its signal trope of the "spectatorial artist," a phrase coined by Toomer's contemporary, Gorham Munson, to describe the poetic persona who moves like a shadow throughout the pages of the book, observing what he sees and hears in the Georgia landscape. His quest is captured best in "Song of the Son," the poem that sets the elegiac tone for the first section of *Cane*:

> Pour O pour that parting soul in song
> O pour it in the sawdust glow of night
> Into the velvet pine-smoke air to-night
> And let the valley carry it along.
> And let the valley carry it along.[64]

In "Song of the Son," the journey south is figured as a poet's quest to the birthplace of a Black folk culture born out of the slave experience, but now seeming to fade in the face of modern industrialization and Black migration to Northern cities. Using apostrophe, a poetic phrase addressed to a recipient who is not literally present, the poet addresses his song directly to an apparently fading folk culture and a mystical Southern landscape nearly obscured from view. The poet intones, "O land and soil, red soil and sweet gum tree / so scant of grass so profligate of pines / Now just before an epoch's sun declines / Thy son, in time, I have returned to thee, / Thy son, I have in time returned to thee." On the one hand, the inverted phrasing of the previous two lines suggests somewhat paradoxically that the poet has returned just in time: "Though late, O soil, it is not too late yet / To catch thy plaintive soul leaving soon gone." On the other hand, these lines imagine the poet's return to the Southern landscape as a journey back in time to a space not only geographically, but also temporally removed from modern urban life.[65]

Central to the poet's song is the desire to "catch" folk culture, in the hope that it might serve as "an everlasting song, a singing tree"—the raw material for new, modern art. Toomer was certainly not the first to insert an artist-observer into his text. Such a traveling figure is also seen in the work of Du Bois, James Weldon Johnson, and later in Hurston. These writers were influenced in no small part by the burgeoning field of anthropology and its emphasis on travel and fieldwork. As Daphne Lamothe contends, the rise of anthropology offers a frame for understanding "the geographical locations identified by, and socially mediated gazes used by, Black intellectuals in the early decades of the twentieth century."[66] This new ethnographic work remained in dialogue with (and often sought to revise) a long tradition of imperial travel writing that had been preoccupied with representations of "primitive" and presumably premodern life in the New World. Like much writing of the New Negro era, *Cane* engages imperial ideologies and methods. Although *Cane*'s spectatorial artist is a "native son," his art seems never completely disentangled from the problematics of observation and enclosure.

While Lamothe reads these anthropological adaptations as attempts to "name and create a cohesive, collective, modern Black identity," I argue that Toomer's text ultimately dramatizes the problematics and painful limitations of observation.[67] The desire of "Song of the Son" to recover a coherent narrative of the past (transmitted through easy, flowing lyricism) is soon challenged by more fragmented voices—voices that challenge its mission as a recovery project. Over the course of the book, the poet persona encounters a cultural terrain that is far more expansive and elusive than he had imagined. By the time we arrive at "Kabnis," the dramatic sketch that comprises *Cane*'s final section, the poet's voice is stripped of the lyricism and hope that characterized the first part of the text: "Dear Jesus, do not chain me to myself and set these hills and valleys, heaving with folk-songs, so close to me that I cannot reach them," Kabnis laments.[68]

Such lines are often interpreted as evidence of Kabnis's and, by extension, Toomer's own geographical and class distance from the Southern folk whom he aims to represent. And not without reason: as Toomer put it bluntly in a letter to Waldo Frank, "Kabnis is *Me*."[69] Noting the breakdown of the lyrical poetic voice in the final section of *Cane*, Karen Jackson Ford observes, "*Cane*'s song of an end regards the very end of song, the inability of the modern black poet to transform the last echoes of the spirituals into a new poetry."[70] *Cane* certainly seeks to dramatize this failure, particularly through the figure of Kabnis, a frustrated poet for whom expression seems to emerge only in incoherent stammering. Ultimately, Ford suggests, such fragmentation tells us just as much about the narrator's distance from his subjects as it does about the presumed disintegration of folk culture itself.

While I agree with Ford's suggestion that Kabnis ultimately fails to fulfill the quest of "Song of the Son," I depart from her conclusion that this failure signals the "end of song." On the contrary, *Cane*'s disintegrations mark its greatest moments of poetic possibility. The breakdown of lyric, so lamented by the spectator, becomes a formal practice of folk culture itself. In many respects, "Song of the Son" finds a response in the prose piece that follows it: "Fern," a story about a mysterious woman of the same name. "If you walked up the Dixie Pike most any time of day," the narrator explains, "you'd be most like to see her resting listless-like on the railing of her porch." The narrator feels drawn to Fern, especially her eyes, which are mysterious and magnetic and contain "hardly a trace of wistfulness." Fern seems so rooted in her surroundings that it is difficult to imagine her anywhere else. The narrator considers the possibility of bringing her up North, but quickly dismisses it: "Besides picture if you can, this cream-colored solitary girl sitting at a tenement window looking down on the indifferent throngs of Harlem. Better that she listen to folk-songs at dusk in Georgia, you would say, and so would I."[71]

Indeed, even as the Great Migration provides the context for *Cane*, women often seem rooted in their surroundings, while the narrator is shown whizzing by in trains or carriages, or even walking the dirt roads on foot. The fact that Fern lives in a lonely shack by the railroad, where she can see the searchlight of the evening train, is significant—in another kind of narrative, she would be a blues woman. Nevertheless, in the final pages of "Fern," we encounter perhaps one of the strangest and most trans- formative moments in the entire text. The narrator remarks, "I felt strange, as I always do in Georgia, particularly at dusk. I felt that things unseen to men were tangibly immediate. It would not have surprised me had I had a vision. People have them in Georgia more often than you would suppose." As dusk settles with a "purple haze" around the cane, Fern springs up and begins to sing:

> She sprang up. Rushed some distance from me. Fell to her knees, and began swaying, swaying. Her body was tortured with something it could not let out. Like boiling sap it flooded arms and fingers till she shook them as if they burned her. It found her throat, and spattered inarticulately in plaintive, convulsive sounds, mingled with calls to Christ Jesus. And then she sang, brokenly. A Jewish cantor singing with a broken voice. . . . Dusk hid her; I could hear only her song.[72]

Fern is lost in the dusk, and the narrator (and by extension, the reader) cannot see her: "Dusk hid her, I could hear only her song." Fern's song of suffering and prayer is all that remains, but it too is marked by brokenness. Her body, as the narrator imagines it, is both beautiful and "tortured." Sap, which Toomer elsewhere calls a fount of authenticity and deep-rooted sus- tenance, does not nourish; instead, it boils and burns. Expression emerges not lyrically, but in intermittent snatches. Fern's broken voice does not stand alone. Rather, such moments echo throughout the text in the broken voices and inarticulate mumblings of its characters, in "convulsive sounds," and, most notably, in fleeting, fragmented images.

This apparent breakdown of self-expression is commonly read as an omen of folk culture's inevitable demise, or relatedly, as Toomer's silenc- ing of his female characters. As Susan L. Blake remarks, the men of *Cane* "are the active characters, artist figures with the will to limit control, define experience. The women, silent, passive, elusive—represent the experience that the men are trying to grasp. They embody the beauty, suffer the pain, and above all accept the domination of the natural chaos."[73] However, although the narrator's gaze and hearing would aim to capture Fern, her voice is not merely passive. It rather exemplifies what Nathaniel Mackey has called a "telling inarticulacy," a quality of Black artistic expression characterized by obliqueness, incompleteness, and abstraction. While the fragmented voice has been considered a hallmark of modernist expression, telling inarticulacy consists more specifically of "an introspective gesture that arises from and reflects critically upon an experience of isolation or exclusion." Evidencing a "given frustration with and questioning of given articulacies, permissible ways of making sense," the persistence of such a gesture in *Cane* complicates Toomer's purported trope of obsolescence.[74] If folk expression is indeed fading, it does not recede from view like the soft edges of a vignette. Rather, its breakdown seems to embody, in its very form, a critique of its own embattled history of exclusion.

Significantly, *Cane* locates this modernist innovation in the voice of a woman whose failure to be a muse opens the door to other dynamic possibilities. Returning to the concept that *Cane*'s many pieces constitute vaudeville acts, one might posit that the women in *Cane* perform what Daphne Brooks calls "spectacular opacity," through expressive acts that emphasize improvisation, fragmentation, inarticulacy, and other nonrepresentational modes of meaning-making.[75] Brooks augments Édouard Glissant's concept of poetic opacity by emphasizing the key role of embodiment in expression and indeed, knowledge production. By preserving the ambiguity of these performances, *Cane* complicates masculinist discourses of artistic mastery, as well as the imperial epistemologies of Black culture that underpin its own trope of the spectatorial artist.

In many ways, this vision of Fern parallels Toomer's description of the agonizing experience of writing *Cane*: "*Cane* was a lyric essence forced out with great effort despite my knotted state. People have remarked its simple easy-flowing lyricism, its rich natural poetry, and they may assume that it came to bloom as easily as a flower. In truth, it was born in an agony of internal tightness, conflict, and chaos . . . the book as a whole was distilled from the most terrible strain that I have ever known."[76] The concept of lyricism distilled from "terrible strain" provides a framework for understanding one of *Cane*'s central tensions: the paradox of artistic composition. "Rich, natural poetry," Toomer suggests, does not bloom as organically as a flower, but rather emerges from forced effort and internal agony.[77] Through the lens of "terrible strain," we might read differently Toomer's own narrative about the time that he spent among the Southern folk as a teacher in Sparta, Georgia. In a now-famous reflection, Toomer writes:

> The setting was crude in a way, but strangely rich and beautiful. I began feeling its effect despite my state, or perhaps, just because of it. There was a valley, the valley of "Cane," with smoke-wreaths during the day and mist at night. A family of back-country Negroes had only recently moved into a shack not too far away. They sang. And this was the first time I'd ever heard the folk-songs and spirituals. They were very rich and sad and joyous and beautiful. But I learned that the Negroes of the town objected to them. They called them "shouting." They had victrolas and player-pianos. So, I realized with deep regret, that the spirituals, meeting ridicule, would be certain to die out. With Negroes also the trend was towards the small town and then towards the city—and industry and commerce and machines. The folk-spirit was walking in to die on the modern desert. That spirit was so beautiful. Its death was so tragic. . . . And this was the feeling I put into *Cane*. *Cane* was a swan-song. It was a song of an end.[78]

This account is frequently read at face value, as a definitive confirmation of Toomer's romantic culturalism. In many ways, the passage *is* laden with what Mackey terms the "elegiac weariness and weight" that characterize *Cane* as a volume. In emphasizing the perspective of an urban artist coming into contact with folk culture for the first time, Toomer draws a classic binary between premodern and modern Black artistic forms. On one hand, there are folk songs and spirituals, which are "rich and sad and joyous and beautiful," and yet maligned; on the other hand, there is jazz, whose dissemination is mediated by modern technologies such as the Victrola. Such a binary might seem to suggest a tendency to see Black artistic forms in terms of discontinuity rather than evolution, a narrative that would have been disrupted by a consideration of blues music as a Black vernacular form that encompassed the experiences of both the town and the "back-country," of both the "folk spirit" and "industry commerce and machines."

However, while establishing a tragic sense of discontinuity is imperative to Toomer's autobiographical self-fashioning as a preservationist, it does not hold in *Cane* itself. Consider Toomer's contrast between his own appreciation of the songs and the objections of the "Negroes of the town." Unlike Toomer, the townspeople—who do not live up North but just a ways down the road—do not find the spirituals lyrical or nostalgic. Instead, they register as disruption: "they called them shouting." At first glance, their rejection resembles a familiar rehearsal of respectability politics: attempting to distance themselves from "low" forms of Black expression, the townspeople misread (or in this case, mishear) the spirituals and are unable to appreciate their value. Their dismissal makes Toomer's preservation all the more heroic and necessary.

But what would it mean to read the label of "shouting" not merely as a mischaracterization, but rather as an aesthetic insight? How might shouting, a constitutive part of Black folk expression, offer a useful counterpoint to the more common notion of spirituals as lyrical and pleasing to the ear? Such "shouting" might unsettle the equilibrium of genteel parlors, drown out the music of the Victrola, and compete in real time with the modern technologies presumed to replace them. Unlike the singing fruit, "caroling softly souls of slavery" idealized in "Song of the Son," shouting amplifies the embodied presence of the folk and their unsettling proximity to the artist who wishes to record them, but also prefers to hold them at a distance. At the same time, shouting defies the documentary impulse, its high-frequency sound lending itself less easily to transcription or capture by recording technologies. Along with other unruly modes of Black performance, shouting unsettles the pastoral soundscape, serving as a startling reminder of the urgent contemporaneity of the folk.

Such disruption occurs most unsettlingly in *Cane*'s closing act, "Kabnis." Kabnis becomes increasingly disturbed by the shouting of a woman in a nearby church. A tortured poet who laments his inability to transform the beauty of the Southern landscape into true poetry, Kabnis does not find all forms of folk expression equally inviting: "Singing from the church becomes audible. Above it, rising and falling in a plaintive moan, a woman's voice swells to shouting. Kabnis hears it. His face gives way to an expression of mingled fear, contempt, and pity."[79] The shouting is distinct from song. The voice "swells"; it rises above the melodious singing to reach a startling, affective climax. While critics often view Kabnis's reaction through the lens of his misapprehension of Black spiritual traditions, I find it useful to linger on the notion of the shout as a disturbance. The shout disturbs Kabnis precisely because it stirs something in him that he would rather not explore.

"Her voice, high pitched and hysterical, is almost perfectly attuned to the nervous key of Kabnis."[80] Such is the devastating paradox of his encounter with the Black voice: even though Kabnis would disavow the shout, the shout is "perfectly attuned" to his tumultuous interiority.

While this "nervous key" is perfectly consonant with Kabnis's interiority, it contrasts sharply with the idealized portrait of folk life that he imagines earlier in the piece: "a cabin silhouetted on a knoll about a mile away. Peace. Negroes within it are content. They farm. They sing. They love. They sleep."[81] Shouting, permeated by the trace of embodiment that Roland Barthes calls the "grain of the voice," does not lend itself easily to such idealization or disembodiment from the material realities of Black life.[82] Kabnis is reminded that just beyond the cabin where he sits looms the modern violence of lynching. Through the shout, one encounters not the free-floating folk spirit, but the body in all its vulnerability. Ultimately, Kabnis is a modern artist tortured not by unbridgeable distance, but rather by visceral connection and proximity.

A form of sonic and embodied knowledge, shouting transmits the modern violence of the Georgia landscape, and more specifically, frames the piece's narrative of the lynching of Mame Lamkins. In a voice "uniformly low and soothing" (a chilling counterpoint to the shouts), Kabnis's companion Layman recounts the murder of Mame Lamkins and her unborn child. Layman's retelling is sparse and matter-of-fact, yet nevertheless it affects a mounting terror with each successive image:

> She was in th family-way, Mame Lamkins was. They killed her in th street, and some white man seein th risin in her stomach as she lay there soppy in her blood like any cow, took an ripped her belly open, an th kid fell out. It was living; but a nigger baby aint supposed t live. So he jabbed his knife in it an stuck it t a tree. And then they all went way.[83]

This passage is a fictionalized account of the lynching of Mary Turner, who was killed by a white mob in Lowndes County, Georgia, along with her unborn child on May 19, 1918, after speaking out against her husband's lynching the previous day. The story of Mary Turner's lynching became well known and was referenced in the NAACP's antilynching campaigns. In 2010, a historical marker was placed near the site, calling it "one of the deadliest waves of vigilantism in Georgia history."[84] If Turner's story stresses the vulnerability of Black women's bodies to gendered modes of racial violence, it is also a testament to the resonance of Black women's voices. While Toomer's version alters the details—Mame Lamkins is killed not for her defiant speech, but because "she tried t hide her husband when they was after him"—the story is nevertheless framed by the Black woman's voice. At the end of Layman's retelling, as if on cue, "a shriek pierces the room."[85]

This moment in "Kabnis" does more than document or memorialize violence and death in the Jim Crow South. It seeks to outline what one cannot know through conventional historiography or field research. The sonic does not merely heighten or more deftly "express" the terror of this story; rather, it offers an alternative—another way of knowing that is "perfectly attuned" to the traces of violence in the present. Its urgency ruptures a framework of nostalgia in which the Black subject is frozen in time. I am influenced here by Fred Moten's attempt to grapple with the scream of Frederick Douglass's Aunt Hester, "which [Douglass] recalls and reconfigures throughout his body of autobiographical work in successive iterations of the brutal sexual violence to which it violently and aninaugurally responds." As Moten explains, "I began to consider that the scream's content is not simply unrepresentable but instantiates, rather, an alternative to representation. Such consideration does no such thing as empty the scream of content. It makes no such gesture. Rather, it seeks after what the scream contains (and pours out), and after the way that content is passed on—too terribly and too beautifully—in black art."[86] Following Saidiya Hartman's foundational efforts to trace the "diffusion of terror" in quotidian, even seemingly mundane scenes, Moten attends to those moments in Black art and performance in which the content and context of violence are "diffused but not diluted." Such an approach enables an analysis of sound and Black folk production as never divorced from, but rather produced by, the material realities of Black life and death. As Ashon Crawley writes, the scream "carries the trace and weight of its source of emanation."[87]

It might be said that what Kabnis experiences in the Georgia landscape, and what he hears in the shout, amount to just such a diffusion. In many respects, his discomfort is an invitation to ask just what the shout "contains and (and pours out)": to search for its epistemological value, its ongoing purchase as a form of Black self-knowledge. It is important to note that Aunt Hester's scream (which Moten discusses) and the vocalizations in "Kabnis" exist along distinct sonic registers. This difference is partly a matter of form. Over the course of the piece, Kabnis hears not just one shout, but a cacophony of shouts, shrieks, and screams that might variously invoke terror, pain, spiritual ecstasy, and defiance. The shout might be an appeal, an acknowledgment, or a hailing. Or most perplexingly, it might consist of all of these. While the shout may originate in a Black religious context, its spiritual possibilities, like the sound itself, exceed the confines of the church.

CONVERSION

The "shout" of Kabnis does not mark an isolated moment in the text. It returns us to the diasporic landscape of "Conversion," a poem that appears in *Cane*'s first section. Toomer alludes to the poem in Kabnis's complaint about "a gin soul that gets drunk on a preacher's words. An Screams. An shouts." Juxtaposing these two pieces, we might view folk culture not through the lens of fading, but conversion:

> African Guardian of Souls,
> Drunk with rum,
> Feasting on a strange cassava,
> Yielding to new words and a weak palabra
> Of a white-faced sardonic god—
> Grins, cries
> Amen,
> Shouts hosanna.[88]

"Conversion" was originally published in *Modern Review* as part of a series entitled "Portraits in Georgia." Yet the poem suggests a landscape that moves beyond the South. As Karen Jackson Ford notes, "Rum and cassava place this conversion in the West Indies," the original site of enslavement and supposed cultural conversion in the New World.[89] While "Conversion" looks backward to a violent colonial past, it also suggests linkages to contemporaneous economic and cultural processes in the Caribbean. Rum recalls sugarcane, the book's central metaphor. Sugarcane appears mysteriously, voluptuously, on the book's title page: "Oracular / Redolent of fermenting syrup, / Purple of the dusk, / Deep-rooted cane." Critics have read Toomer's preoccupation with sugarcane more as evidence of his desire for a symbol of sensuous authenticity and rootedness than as an indication of the crop's actual economic significance, since, as Barbara Foley has noted, sugarcane occupied a "relatively marginal place in the farming economy" of 1920s Georgia.[90] Conversely however, the Caribbean's sugarcane industry was expanding, and its production was increasingly in the hands of the United States. Interpreted more broadly, "Conversion" traverses time and space, linking the colonial past to modern agricultural imperialism.

To link "Conversion" to contemporary processes in the Caribbean is to complicate readings of the poem that cite it as the loss of authentic African beliefs.[91] To be sure, one might read this conversion as indoctrination: authentic African spirituality replaced with white religion; native language interchanged with "weak palabra," signifying empty speech and the linguistic echoes of Spanish colonization. And yet, with its focus on culture-as-process, *Cane* also contributes to anthropological conversations on folk culture that increasingly turned to the Caribbean. A quest for African survival in the New World fueled the anthropological experiments of Melville Herskovits, Lomax, and, of course, Hurston. These researchers often viewed their work in the Caribbean and their work in the South as related enterprises. They constantly bumped up against the question of authenticity, finding it at best a sticky concept in the cultural crucible of the Americas. To what extent are African traditions lost or retained through the process of enslavement? Conversely, how is Christianity itself transformed?

Cane suggests that poetry might approach these ethnographic questions by conveying, and perhaps preserving, the ambiguities of Black culture. Throughout *Cane*, Black spirituality bears these African and Caribbean traces. From this perspective, when the African guardian of souls "shouts hosanna," it is not clear precisely who, or what, has been converted. This poem enacts a process akin to spirit possession, in which the Black subject's "conversion" is marked precisely by their departure from fixed meaning or "permissible ways of making sense."[92]

The placement of "Conversion" in the volume—right before "Portrait in Georgia," Toomer's metonymic poem about lynching—serves to link the Caribbean and the American South to both past and contemporary scenes of violence and cultural transformation. As Farah Jasmine Griffin observes, "Portrait in Georgia" and "Blood Burning Moon" are *Cane*'s most explicit statements about racial violence. Appearing as they do right before *Cane*'s upward swing into the North, these pieces "establish violence on the Black body as a trope to signify the violence of the South as the major catalyst for migration."[93] It may seem that the text itself migrates to the North, aiming to escape less sophisticated (and therefore quintessentially not modern) forms of racial violence. The lynching in "Blood Burning Moon" takes place in an abandoned factory, presumably a symbol of the Southern town's failed entry into the industrial age. Yet as a contemporary tool of violence supported by modern technologies, lynching is constitutive of Southern modernity rather than fundamentally at odds with it. The placement of "Blood Burning Moon" right next to "Seventh Street," with its whizzing streetcars, would seem to indicate a connection between, rather than a rupturing of, modern innovation and mechanisms of violence such as lynching. Such connections complicate Toomer's fading model of folk culture's transition into modernity because they suggest that its demise is manufactured by social forces rather than an inevitable consequence of time. It is through *Cane*'s poetics of disruption, its unintelligible bursts of song, religious shouting, and the mysterious traces of "canebreak loves and mangrove feastings" that burst through the lyrical seams of the text that we might locate the South as a contemporary landscape in flux, if we would only dare to listen.

WRITING THE CROSSROADS OF THE AMERICAS

While *Cane*'s renegotiation of Southern folk culture, in Margo Natalie Crawford's words, "would be too heavy and disorienting for some to hold onto," *Tropic Death* further leans into the perplexing potential of unruly folk.[94] Positioned at a U.S.-Caribbean crossroads, both Toomer and Walrond chart alternative routes of migration, labor, and imaginative exchange to broaden the geographies of Black diasporic modernity. Whereas *Cane* limns the elusive yet profoundly immediate traces of racial violence, *Tropic Death* foregrounds wholesale social disintegration and death. Unlike *Cane*, *Tropic Death* lacks a spectatorial voice. And yet its narration, though omniscient, often withholds context. On *Tropic Death*'s form, Du Bois succinctly remarked: "Here is a book of ten stories of death, which, with impressionistic pen and little plot, show forth with singular vividness the life of Black laborers of the West Indies. There is superstition, unusual dialect, singular economic glimpse; but above all, there is truth and human sympathy."[95] Du Bois's review highlighted *Tropic Death*'s twofold contribution. First, the text performs a significant geographical shift by locating its portrait of Black migration and labor in neither Harlem nor the U.S. South, but rather in the Caribbean basin. Second, the text's artistic innovations—its "impressionistic pen and little plot"—establish Walrond's reputation as one of the key stylists of Harlem's emerging avant-garde.

Despite this auspicious debut, *Tropic Death* fell from view in subsequent decades, much as Walrond himself did. He left New York on a Guggenheim fellowship, with the intention of writing a history of Panama Canal construction entitled *The Big Ditch*. That project never materialized, and Walrond relocated to Europe, where he continued to publish, perhaps most strikingly in the *Roundway Review*, the monthly publication of the psychiatric hospital where he was admitted as a voluntary patient.[96] Elsewhere, I have commented on *Tropic Death*'s critical neglect and subsequent recuperation by Louis J. Parascandola, James C. Davis, Arnold Rampersad, and Carl A. Wade.[97] Davis's recent biography makes a crucial contribution in this vein. As Davis observes, in light of "a transnational understanding of the Harlem Renaissance and a diaspora approach to Caribbean writing— Walrond's significance takes on a different cast."[98]

Here, I want to make a case for reading *Tropic Death* alongside *Cane* as two contributions to a Black hemispheric literature—a literature of difference and convergence at the crossroads of the Americas. While the internationalist thrust of diaspora studies offers a useful context for reading *Tropic Death*, the book's distinct orientation is the Western Hemisphere. It explores the experiences of a Caribbean migrant workforce that official narratives of canal construction often rendered invisible. At the center of the text looms the construction of the Panama Canal, initiated by France in the 1880s and completed by the United States. The canal's construction precipitated one of the largest mass migrations the region had ever witnessed as workers from across the Caribbean flocked to the isthmus in search of the higher pay promised, but not always delivered, in the Canal Zone. Through a dynamic regional lens, *Tropic Death* traces the contours of this labor migration as it moves between Panama, Barbados, Honduras, and Jamaica.

The interconnected geographies of *Tropic Death* invoke Walrond's own liminality: Is he a writer of Harlem, British Guiana, or Panama? Indeed, he himself was a product of isthmian migration. After living in British Guiana and Barbados, Walrond and his family moved to Colón in 1911. In Colón, he attended secondary school and became fluent in Spanish, trained as a stenographer, and became a clerk in the Health Department of the Canal Commission in Cristóbal. He also made his start as a journalist, working as a reporter and sportswriter for the Panama newspaper *Star and Herald* before migrating to New York in 1918. In a personal note that accompanied his story "The Godless City," Walrond wrote: "I am spiritually a native of Panama. I owe the sincerest allegiance to it."[99] Yet as the Panamanian critic and novelist Luis Pulido Ritter notes, given Walrond's interest in showing "the fissures, the paradoxes, the contradictions, the breaks," his work does not belong to literatures of Panamanian nationalism that rehearse the romantic and homogenizing ideology of "mulatto-mestizo ethnicity, the Spanish language and the Catholic religion."[100] In many ways, Walrond's "restless itinerary" mirrors the migratory patterns of the folk whom he depicts in *Tropic Death*.[101] The Panama Canal is both central to the U.S. imperial project and a liminal space between the Atlantic and Pacific, between Central American inland and the surrounding Caribbean basin, between old empires and new. Such in-betweenness illuminates my reading of *Tropic Death*'s crossroads poetics, in which liminality (and its attendant ambiguity and disorientation) emerges as a key framework for reading the folk in the first decades of the twentieth century.

In its preoccupation with U.S. imperialism as a catalyst of Black migration and death, *Tropic Death* revises the dominant narrative of canal construction as exemplary of prosperity and progress. Instead, the book delivers a relentless catalog of untimely demise, disease, and ecological disaster. The book's bleak atmosphere put a special shock to readers who approached the text expecting the tropical and quaintly exotic. As Mary White Ovington remarks with unfeigned surprise: "To those of us who know the West Indies as a pleasant winter resort . . . Eric Walrond's picture is like a stomping blow. . . . One asks oneself can it be true? Is life so terrible in this exquisitely beautiful and seemingly happy land? . . . One wonders whether many people will have the courage to finish a book which by its very title promises death as a constant companion."[102] True to Ovington's observation, the aesthetic unity of *Tropic Death* does not cohere around distinct, linear plots, but rather around the recurrence of death. Whereas *Cane*'s composition rests on its interplay of various forms, *Tropic Death* takes shape through repetition. A grisly death awaits one or more of the characters at the end of each of the ten stories. A hungry girl dies after stuffing herself with marl rock. A rebellious worker is stalked and killed by a white American marine who oversees the Jim Crow work site at the Canal Zone. A woman is trampled on a ship (that erstwhile symbol of masculine mobility) as she travels between Honduras and Jamaica. Ubiquitous and inexorable, this litany structures the text. The causes are multiple—starvation, murder, accident, natural or supernatural disaster—but the outcome is the same. In each case, death arrives rapidly and without pathos. The process of dying is not made explicit until the reader is startled by the sudden appearance of a corpse.

Framing the canal project in terms of danger and death was no imaginative stretch for Walrond, who worked as a journalist in Colón before migrating to New York in 1918. In that interocean city, he catalogued not only beatings and brawls, but also a staggering number of deaths. Indeed, work on the canal was a treacherous enterprise. Irma Watkins-Owens notes that "during the decade of canal construction, thousands of Black men died or sustained permanent physical injury through premature or delayed explosions of dynamite, asphyxiation in pits, falls from high places, train wrecks, landslides, and cascading rocks in the canal cut."[103] In a letter to the Isthmian Historical Society in the 1960s, one canal worker from Nassau, Bahamas, Albert Peters, vividly recalls the ubiquity of death:

> Every evening around 4:30 one could see #5 engine with a box car and the rough brown coffins staked one upon the other bound for Mt. Hope which was called Monkey Hill in those days. The death rate was high. The most deaths were from pneumonia and malaria, some from accidents. There were [sic] no Yellow fever at that time that I knew of. If you had a friend that you always see and missed him for a week or two, don't wonder, he's either in the hospital or at Monkey Hill resting in peace.

As a reward for contributing his story, the Isthmian Historical Society paid Peters fifty dollars, the equivalent of 100 days of labor.[104]

Beyond documented threats to life, limb, and livelihood, U.S. imperialism in *Tropic Death* is an insidious force whose workings are not fully understood. Critics have noted *Tropic Death*'s use of the Gothic mode: its atmosphere of gloom and terror, its preoccupation with sensational, supernatural occurrences, its violence. Robert Bone, who classified *Tropic Death* as an antipastoral countering *Cane*'s pastoral, saw Walrond's employment of the "lethal dangers of the tropics" as an attempt to discredit technologi-cal optimism: "His snakes and sharks and vampire bats, his droughts and fires and tropical diseases, serve as grim reminders of mankind's tenuous position in the universe."[105]

Yet along with *Cane*, *Tropic Death* joins a hemispheric literary tradi-tion of linking grim phenomena to "terrors of American history."[106] The book prefigures Maryse Condé's description of Panama Canal migration in her 2009 essay "What Is a Caribbean Writer?" in which she describes the canal's construction as an epic tragedy on the stage of modern Caribbean life. The workers who built the canal would "pay with their lives for this technical feat, this marvel that split the world in two, and would die buried in the mud of Gatun. Marcus Garvey . . . saw for himself the immense mis-ery of his fellow countrymen and thought up the idea of a massive return to the lost continent, Mother Africa."[107] The image of the canal as a mass grave belies the narrative of modernity's triumphant march. In Condé's account, the material and symbolic consequences of the event reach far beyond the region, with specific implications for Black leadership and cultural produc-tion. To be a Caribbean writer, Condé suggests, is to encounter death as a historical condition of Black hemispheric modernity.

Tropic Death encapsulates Condé's call for attention to the entangle-ments of migration and death in Caribbean writing. Such a task raised questions about both form and content. In addition to exposing the disori-enting violence of imperialism, Walrond gestures toward another poten-tially generative kind of upheaval: the instability of Black identities and the messy exchange of culture, nation, and language that defines Black hemispheric experience. Canal migration and resettlement epitomize such disorder. Such a collision of elements imbues the isthmus with a mysteri-ous, pulsating energy: "As it grew dark the hewers at the Ditch, exhausted, half-asleep, naked but for wormy singlets, would hum queer creole tunes, play on guitar or piccolo, and jig to the rhythm of the *coombia*. It was a *brujerial* chant, for *obeah*, a heritage of the French colonial, honeycombed the life of the Negro laboring camps."[108] The hybridity of the Canal Zone remains salient above all in its cultural practices, a "queer creole" mix that infused the labor camps with a vibrant, transformative power in the face of impossible conditions.

Walrond's representation of the diversity of the circum-Caribbean exem-plifies what Louis Chude-Sokei calls *Tropic Death*'s "linguistic excesses."[109]

In "The Yellow One," on a sea voyage between Honduras and Jamaica, a simple request for hot water takes various forms:

> "How de bleedy hell dem heckspeck a man fi' trabble tree days an' tree whole nights beout giv' him any hot watah fi' mek even a can o' tea is somet'ing de hagent at Kingston gwine hav' fi pint out to me w'en de boat dey lan'—"
>
> "Hey, mistah hawfissah, yo' got any hot watah?"
>
> "Hot watah, mistah?"
>
> "Me will giv' yo' a half pint o' red rum if yo' giv' me a quatty wut' o' hot watah."
>
> "Come, no, man, go get de watah, no?"
>
> "Ripe apples mek me t'row up!?"
>
> "Green tamarin' mek me tummack sick!"
>
> "Sahft banana mek me fainty!"
>
> "Fish sweetie giv' me de dysentery."

The cultural flux of the Caribbean is also present in the narrator's conjectures about the various things that one might do with a cup of the "precious liquid": "Into it one might pour a gill of goat's milk—a Cuban *señora*, a decker of several voyages, had fortified herself with a bucket of it—or melt a sprig of peppermint or a lump of clove or a root of ginger. So many tropical things one could do with a cup of hot water," Walrond writes.[110]

In a departure from popular local color tales of the era, Walrond's use of regional dialects does not serve to ground the stories in predictable local contexts. Often, various dialects meet and clash within a single story, and dialect is not a reliable marker of location. Reviews of the text not only revealed frustration with the ubiquity of vernacular speech, but also noted Walrond's failure to "translate" the dialect into standard English.[111] Insofar as *Tropic Death* fails to put itself at the disposal of its readers, this failure might be understood as an intentional part of the text's experimental project. Anticipating Glissant's focus on the "right to opacity," *Tropic Death* deliberately tests the limits of translatability, experimenting with what may or may not translate across regional boundaries in terms of language, culture, and historical vision.[112] This notion of failure operates internally among characters from different shores who frequently misapprehend each other. But such failures also herald the text's commitment to incommensurability and difference.

On one hand, the circum-Caribbean migration depicted by Walrond fits with narratives of modern agency and mobility. It exemplifies the pattern of "movement, transformation and relocation" that Paul Gilroy describes as being part of the condition of Black modernity.[113] However, *Tropic Death* broadens Gilroy's focus on sites in the north Atlantic by illustrating a range of Black migrant experiences at a crucial moment in history for both the Caribbean and the United States. The text expands our knowledge of Black migration narratives by introducing routes of migration that defy a north-south trajectory. Circum-Caribbean migration, *Tropic Death* demonstrates, is as much a part of the modern Black experience as the northbound flight from "cotton, cane, and rice fields" that looms so large in the African American artistic imagination.[114] Remittances from Panama and other industrial sites often paved the way for later travel to the United States. However, prior experiences in Panama and elsewhere are a reminder that Caribbean residents were already transnational citizens by the time they arrived in Harlem, a fact that, as Lara Putnam contends, "should shift our sense of the origins of the Black internationalist thinking and organizing that made interwar Harlem 'new.'"[115]

On the other hand, *Tropic Death* discards an easy correspondence between migration and agency. The book's rejection of triumphant models of transnationality or diasporic homecoming has perhaps posed another obstacle to its recuperation. To begin with, *Tropic Death* challenges triumphant Caribbean narratives of isthmian migration. As Rhonda Frederick notes, the scenes of grueling labor, violence, and poverty in many of *Tropic Death*'s stories constitute a drastic departure from popular narratives that portrayed the "migrant-as-dandy, known for his jewelry, assumed accent, cosmopolitan air, and North American–styled clothes."[116] In *Tropic Death*, the possibilities of migration are inextricable from its risks, often ironically so. For example, in one story, "Panama Gold," a worker returns to Jamaica, his experience on the canal marked by his gold chains, his colognes, and a missing leg. It is toward such realities that *Tropic Death* directs our gaze, emphasizing a uniquely modern experience of cultural exchange and flux far from the streets of Harlem.

SUBJECTION

A reading of several of *Tropic Death*'s stories elucidates what Langston Hughes called the text's "sun-bright hardness," alluding to its stylistic, historical, and affective challenges.[117] Such qualities converge in "Subjection," which inhabits the physical center of the book, halfway through the ten stories. The story is also *Tropic Death*'s conceptual center, where the brutal enforcement of the color line, the exploitation of the environment, and the manipulation of official narratives are shown to constitute the business of industrial imperialism. In "Subjection," a migrant worker named Ballet challenges an American marine engaged in the brutal beating of another worker. Young and defiant, Ballet is the only man who manages to "whip up the courage of voice" in support of his peer.[118] He pays for this transgression with his life, and evidence of his murder is promptly erased from the record. In addition to exposing Ballet's murder, Walrond takes pains to illustrate the devastating predominance of the color line, from Jim Crow wages and housing to surveillance and the systematic erasure of diverse migrant identities. "Subjection" thus illuminates the ways in which, as Kaysha Corinealdi states, "US officials set about making the Canal Zone an extension of the United States."[119]

The story begins with the image of land being pulverized by Black workers: "Toro Point resounded to the noisy rhythm of picks swung by gnarled black hands. Sunbaked rock stones flew to dust, to powder." Their work song "seasoned the rhythm" of the picks, adding their own voices to the industrial soundscape. However, the song is suddenly interrupted, or perhaps completed, by the harsh voice of a white American marine: "The blows rained. The men sang—blacks, Island blacks—Turks Island, St. Vincent, the Bahamas—Diamond gal cook fowl botty giv' de man / 'I'll show you goddam niggers how to talk back to a white man—.'" The marine's voice is met with ominous silence, curtailing the sonic exchange of the story's opening lines. Moments later, a conflict arises at the work site, unfolding only as a mysterious sequence of images:

> A ram-shackle body, dark in the ungentle spots exposing it, jogged, reeled and fell at the tip of a white bludgeon. Forced a dent in the crisp caked earth. An isolated ear lay limp and juicy, like some exhausted leaf or flower, half joined to the tree whence it sprang. Only the sticky milk flooding it was crimson, crimsoning the dust and earth.[120]

Here, we encounter not the beating itself, but its shadow. The assailant is invisible. His presence is indicated only by the phrase "white bludgeon" after the moment of impact has already occurred. Instead, the images highlight the way both body and earth respond in the immediate aftermath of the violence. On one hand, the land is indelibly marked by the violence done to the body: as it lands, the nameless, faceless, "ramshackle-body" forces a dent in "crisp caked earth." On the other hand, the imagery goes even further to join body and nature: the half-severed ear is like an "exhausted leaf or flower"; the body is a "tree" and the blood is a "sticky milk" that literally crimsons the dust and earth. By the end of this sequence, body and earth are indistinguishable. But as Whalan writes of the Georgia soil in *Cane*, this is not an organic connection. The land is "crisp" and barren. Like those who work on it, it has been exhausted by the violence that has occurred there.[121] With a force of imagery that anticipates Billie Holiday's 1939 "Strange Fruit," the assault depicts both body and land as sites of disorienting violence.[122]

The passage is often cited as evidence of Walrond's "impressionistic" style. Such a description, however vague, provides a clue to the effect of his stylistic choices. If Walrond succeeds in giving an impression of a scene rather than representing it with photographic realism, his point is precisely to capture those connections that the camera cannot see. As Jesse Matz observes, fragments can often invoke, through their very abstraction, a fuller and more nuanced version of reality: "If 'fiction is an impression' it *mediates* opposite perceptual moments. It does not choose surfaces and fragments over depths and wholes but makes surfaces show depths, make fragments suggest wholes, and devotes itself to the undoing of such distinctions."[123] A juxtaposition of such fragments suggests relationships that would not be perceptible otherwise. Walrond's imagery certainly "makes fragments suggest wholes," revealing startling historical entanglements of race, violence, and geography.

The moments where Walrond's prose erupts into impressionism, therefore, are not merely ornamental; they deepen the content of his anti-imperialist critique and, in some cases, mobilize the plot of his stories. In "Subjection," for example, the assault serves as a catalyst, a signal event that precipitates the rest of the story's action. As the marine carries out this brutal beating, Ballet looks on in anger: "Irrefutably, by its ugly lift, Ballet's mouth was in on the rising rebellion which thrust a flame of smoke into the young Negro's eyes."[124] At the work site, silence has become the code of survival, and the other workers are well aware that defiant speech is a

form of resistance for which one pays with one's life. Yet Ballet nevertheless manages to "whip up the courage of voice": "Yo' gwine kill dat boy," he
says, as the "older heads" of the gang look on in incredulous disapproval.
"Yo' coward yo'—a big able man lik' yo' beatin' a lil' boy lik' dat. Why yo'
don' hit me? Betcha yo' don' put down yo' gun and fight me lik' yo' got any
guts." The marine, a nameless, khaki-clad white American, turns on him:

> "You mind yer own goddam business, Smarty, and go back to work," said
> the marine. He guided an unshaking yellow-spotted finger under the black's
> warm, dilating nostrils. "Or else—"
> He grew suddenly deathly pale. It was a pallor which comes to men on
> the verge of murder. Mouth, the boy at issue, one of those docile, half-white
> San Andres coons, was a facile affair. Singly, red-bloodedly one handled it.
> But here, with this ugly, thick-lipped, broad-chested upstart, there was need
> for handling of an errorless sort.[125]

The marine labels the men in the homogeneous language of U.S. racism.
The victim of the beating, "Mouth," probably named so due to his penchant
for "talking back," is called a "half-white coon." Ballet is labeled a "thick-
lipped upstart," or simply, as the marine adds later, a "black bastard." The
marine's categorizations are an attempt to "handle" the men: to impose a
familiar racial order by acquainting the West Indian and Central and South
American workers with the rigid workings of the color line. Yet the men
are by no means a homogenous group. Among them are migrants from
San Andres, Colombia, Turks Island, St. Vincent, and the Bahamas. There
are "Bajan creoles," "black taciturn French colonials," "tempestuous Jamaicans"; there are Panama men from "Bottle Alley," Boca Grande, and Silver
City.[126] Walrond's rendering of the incredible diversity of the Canal Zone
cuts a vivid contrast against the marine's homogenizing epithets.

If Ballet's rebellion represents the possibility of resistance, the consequences of his action are clearly foreshadowed: the marine "grew suddenly
deathly pale. It was a pallor which comes to men on the verge of murder."
From this moment on, violence seems inexorable. As the sole provider for
an impoverished household, Ballet is compelled to return to work the next
day. He speeds through Colón on his way to the work site, assailed by the
sun's oppressive heat. He flies past "dinky bathhouses . . . grog shops, chink

stores and brothels,"[127] and scores of Black men trekking to work. As one group clears a patch of jungle with cutlasses, they sing a work-song that simultaneously foretells Ballet's fate and heralds the relentless march of modernity: "Comin' Ah tell yo'! One mo' mawin,' buoy."[128]

His arrival hastens his confrontation with the marine, who cries, "Stand up and take yer medicine, yer goddam skunk." Ballet flees, taking shelter behind the spokes of a wagon wheel in a toolshed on the edge of the jungle. His situation now hopeless, he is quickly tracked down. With chilling matter-of-factness, the narrator recounts the youth's final moments:

> Behind the wheel, bars dividing the two, Ballet saw the dread khaki—the dirt-caked leggings.
>
> His vision abruptly darkened.
>
> Vap, vap, vap—
>
> Three sure, dead shots.
>
> In the Canal Record, the Q.M. at Toro Point took occasion to extol the virtues of the Department which kept the number of casualties in the recent native labor uprising down to one.[129]

This passage's dry realism stands in stark contrast to the fragmented prose of the pivotal beating scene at the beginning of "Subjection." Serving as bookends, these two scenes depict a violent atmosphere that ranges between the uncanny and the quotidian. Indeed, the story's unceremonious ending suggests that the erasure of Black life was routine. The truth of Ballet's death goes undocumented in the Canal Commission's official publication, or rather, it is incorrectly documented as a "native labor uprising." In addition to denying his murder, the *Canal Record* subsumes Ballet's identity and history under the category of "native," a term that is misleading at best in the context of the Canal Zone's largely migrant labor population. Yet the term reveals the canal authorities' attempts to keep a non-U.S. Black population "under de heel o' de backra."[130] Before the marine kills Ballet, for example, he exclaims, 'I'll teach you niggers *down here* how to talk back to a white man."[131] Moreover, as Frederick observes, the manipulation of the record enables the "fiction of U.S. benevolence at the Canal Zone to continue."[132] This erasure constitutes the final and perhaps most devastating act of violence in "Subjection."

MARL DUST AND GUAVA BUDS

The disturbing clarity of Walrond's anti-imperial critique in the Panama setting of "Subjection" helps us to understand the complicated machinery of death at work in the volume's other stories. Importantly, although the Panama Canal stands at the literal and conceptual center of the text, it also serves as a flash point whose effects ripple outward. Several of *Tropic Death*'s stories establish a link between that large-scale project and the many smaller industrial projects taking place far from the shores of Panama. Walrond achieves this connection partly through imagery: a ubiquitous white "marl" dust, unleashed by the drilling at various work sites, quietly pervades many of the book's ten stories. Baked and dried by the oppressive heat of the sun, the suffocating industrial waste takes on a life of its own: "Marl . . . dust," "thick adhesive marl," "hot creeping marl."[133]

The marl's sinister presence is illustrated viscerally in *Tropic Death*'s opening story, "Drought," in which industrial drilling and natural disaster produce a ravaged landscape in rural Barbados. The story follows a protagonist, Coggins Rum, who works at the site. On his daily trek home from the quarry, Coggins gasps at the "consequences of the sun's wretched fury": "The sun had robbed the land of its juice, squeezed it dry. Star apples, sugar apples, husks, transparent on the dry sleepy trees. . . . Undug, stemless— peanuts, carrots—seeking balm, relief, the caress of a passing wind, shot dead unlustered eyes up through the sun-etched cracks in the hard, brittle soil." The people are equally robbed of their vitality. In the face of this "dizzying spectacle," they sink to their knees and pray for rain. With the crops dead, and with Coggins's meager wages barely sustaining them, Coggins's wife, Sissie, is "running a house on a dry-rot herring bone, a pint of stale, yellowless corn meal, a few spuds. . . ."[134]

But the focus soon shifts to Coggins's daughter, Beryl, standing on the marl road: "Six years old; possessing a one-piece frock, no hat, no shoes. . . . Victim of the sun—a bright spot under its singeing mask—Beryl hesitated at Coggins' approach. Her little brown hands flew behind her back." In light of the all-around scarcity, the girl has adopted the habit of eating the only thing that the landscape provides in abundance—marl rocks. Coggins frequently admonishes her behavior, to their mutual distress: "A gulping sensation came to Coggins when he saw Beryl crying. When Beryl cried, he felt like crying, too . . . [b]ut he sternly heaped invective upon her. 'Marl'll make yo' sick . . . tie up yo' guts, too. Tie up yo' guts like green guavas. Don't eat it, yo' hear, don't eat no mo' marl.'" These warnings quickly grow ominous, painfully highlighting the family's inability to provide any alternative. In the face of poverty, the physical environment has turned deadly.[135]

This foreshadowing nevertheless fails to prepare us for the story's startling climax. Approaching the family's empty rainwater keg, Coggins encounters Beryl's motionless body: "Beryl, little naked brown legs apart, was flat upon the hard, bare earth. The dog, perhaps, or the echo of some fugitive wind had blown up her little crocus bag dress. It lay like a cocoanut flap-jack on her stomach."[136] The tone here is one of clinical understatement; the flat description belies the horror of the girl's demise. Here, the lifelessness of land and body merge with disturbing clarity. Soon, the narrative abruptly shifts to the girl's autopsy, a scene revealed only in fragments:

> "Marl . . . marl . . . dust. . . ." It came to Coggins in swirls. Autopsy. Noise comes in swirls. Pounding, pounding—dry Indian corn pounding. Ginger. Ginger being pounded in a mortar with a bright, new pestle. Pound, pound. And. Sawing. Butcher shop. Cow foot is sawed that way. Stew—or tough hard steak. Then the drilling—drilling—drilling to a stone cutter's ears!
> "Too bad, Coggins," the doctor said, "too bad, to lose yo' dawtah."[137]

The precise moment of death eludes us. Afterward, the reality of the girl's demise slips in and out of consciousness in "swirls" of sound and image. Yet it is precisely in this moment of fragmentation that the link between the family's impoverishment, the exploitative labor, and the disintegration of the landscape becomes remarkably vivid. Ironically, the "[n]oise" of the autopsy mimics the preparation of the food items that the girl's family lacks: "dry Indian corn," "[g]inger," "[c]ow foot," and "[s]tew." The incessant pounding and sawing, which elevate at the final moment to drilling, are reminiscent of the backbreaking industrial labor that fails to provide sustenance for the workers and their families. Here, as elsewhere in the text, Walrond's use of fragments brings into focus a harsh and disorienting reality. The story's unsentimental examination of the cause of death constitutes its own kind of autopsy. The text moves beyond realistic documentation to uncover a visceral relationship—a malevolent one—among the people, the land, and the work that is done there. *Tropic Death* enacts a poetics of labor that stresses the fraught relationship between Black bodies and the modernity that they help to facilitate, even as they are deprived of its promises.

At the same time, the itinerant structure of *Tropic Death* allows drastic contrasts in its representation of the Caribbean landscape. In the next story, "Panama Gold," nature becomes a source of sustenance and creativity for the main character, Ella:

> The wind tossed the lanky guava tree. Scudding popcorn—white, yellow, crimson pink guava buds blew upon the ground. Forwards and backwards the wind tossed the guava tree. It shook buds and blossoms on the ground—moist, unforked, ground—on Ella Heath's lap, in her black plenteous hair. Guava buds fell in Ella's bucket, and she liked it. They gave flavor to the water. All of nature gave flavor to Ella, wrought a magic color in Ella's life. Green, wavy moss—rhubarb moss . . . brought color to the water, gave body flavor to it. Gave the water a tang.
>
> Cast up on a bare half acre of land, Ella came to know the use of green, virgin things. Ore; green ore—spread over the land. . . . A wild, mad, hectic green—the green of young sugar canes. . . . Corn, okras, gunga peas, eddoes, tannias, tomatoes—in such a world Ella moved.[138]

Not to be confused with the idealized pastoral, such a scene instead conveys a deep knowledge, ingenuity, and sensual enjoyment of the Caribbean landscape that is rarely granted to women "folk" characters. Such a moment serves as a crucial interlude, a quiet yet powerful reprieve from the book's various stagings of death.

THE GODLESS CITY

Walrond's experimental vision, however bleak, offers a different way of reading literary representations of the folk. His focus on dying and impoverished *bodies*—his concern with the material circumstances of folk life—situates his folk firmly in the present. Their tragic deaths mark their contemporaneity: their paradoxical, yet distinct experience of modernity. Stopping short of the jubilant celebration of Black folk culture and identity often performed by their peers, both Toomer and Walrond paint a portrait of modernity in which death and transformation are fundamentally intertwined.

I conclude with a reading of Eric Walrond's 1924 short story, "The God-less City," which offers a counterpoint to *Tropic Death*'s catalog of death by revealing the mysterious power of folk culture in the looming shadow of an ongoing U.S. military presence. It begins with the ominous image of a U.S. Navy ship keeping watch at the entrance to the Panama Canal: "In the night the U.S.S. Manodnock [sic] glowed like a bronze pebble on the tropic sea; slowly, slowly—like a cop on the beat—kept vigil; guarded the gateway to the canal."[139] While *Tropic Death*'s stories place the reader in the thick of canal construction, "The Godless City" is set in Colón (then named Aspinwall) after its completion in 1915. Dwelling in the aftermath of that event, the story is a portrait of a transnational community surging with life against imperial containment.

Following France's failed attempt to build the canal in the 1880s, the United States had framed its own completion of the project in 1914 as a "triumph over tropical disorder," as well as a triumph of new empire over old.[140] But "The Godless City" subverts this narrative: the story's Carib-bean and Central American subjects do not experience the American century as a moment of radical rupture with European empire, but rather as a moment of disorienting reverberation. As night descends upon the "lust-ridden inter-ocean city," Aspinwall's French colonials—"believers in the magic of Obeah"—share tales that transform the history of the canal's construction through the prism of local folklore:

> One of the most cherished tales of this decaying decade in the history of Boca Grande related to the French engineers who failed to build the Canal. Some had it that a young dusky beauty from Martinique had been the consort of one of the French officers. . . . This girl kept a *Maubé* shop on Bottle Alley. *Maubé* is a French colonial pop similar to the "ginger beer" of the Negroes of Guianas. After years of chemical experimenting, the girl concocted an 'abor-tive' mixture which she threw into the emerald waters of Limon Bay. As she did it, she took an oath that the French would never build the Canal! Others of doubtful origin ended the same way, but substituted De Lesseps' name for the anonymous engineer's.[141]

Ferdinand de Lesseps, the developer of the Suez Canal, had attempted to repeat the task on the Panamanian isthmus. It was a doomed project, hin-dered by the enormous scale, complexity, and danger of the task, as well as the epidemic of malaria and yellow fever that claimed at least 22,000 lives. More than simply the tale of a lover's revenge, the local memory of the event frames folk ritual and "experimenting" as a particularly potent form of resistance to the imperial project, forged no less from conditions of intimacy.

However powerful this folk intervention, it is not an act of transcendence over empire—after all, this tale of France's engineering failure is recalled in the shadow of a U.S. naval ship. And yet, while the "abortive mixture" did not prevent U.S. dominance in the region, it did signal another promise: the continuation of the very "tropical disorder" that the United States claimed to vanquish. Indeed, disorder reigns in Walrond's eclectic portrait of folk culture and its interventions—supernatural and otherwise—into the historical record. Moving past the formidable image of the ship, he depicts the pulsating, intricate, and sensuous energy of the city: "Down Cash Street there meandered a river of creole cafés. In them, as the night cast her wings over the lust-ridden inter-ocean city, the crust of the Black Art idolators were in the habit of gathering," he writes. "They were chiefly Negroes from St. Lucia and Martinique, who cut roses and dug graves and planted anemones up at the cemetery at Monkey Hill . . . they took with them various pieces of primitive musical instruments—flutes, *gobies*, banjoes, goatdrums, steel, harmoniums. Far into the tropical night they would sip liquors and dance—quadrilles and lancers and calidonias."[142] This vignette describes, on one hand, the labor that brings these workers into intimate proximity with the rituals of death and mourning—the digging of graves and the planting of flowers at the cemetery. On the other hand, the nightly social rituals of music and dance encapsulate in the life-sustaining practices of folk culture that span various diasporic and colonial crossings.

As if to demonstrate this power, by the end of the story, Aspinwall / Colón lies in ashes. The city did in fact experience three devastating fires—in 1885, 1915, and 1940. While the white inhabitants frame the conflagration as a moral cleansing of the unsavory Black and brown inhabitants of this "godless city," the story's denouement suggests another interpretation. Barely escaping the blaze, Captain Wingate of the U.S.S. *Manodnock* returns to his ship to encounter a strange scene: "Ezekiel, the Negro cabin boy, was there, cleaning up the ashes—as cool and as prophetic as if nothing had happened."[143]

If "The Godless City" depicts folk practices as experimental, prophetic— "oracular," as Toomer phrased it—and exacting in retribution, his later volume, *Tropic Death,* focuses on their vulnerability and the material conditions of their death and survival. In both depictions of folk culture, Walrond exchanges premodern authenticity for unsettling contemporaneity. The depiction of a contemporary folk unsettles the very project of U.S. imperialism, which depends on the fiction of their premodernity. But the fiction of premodern folk not only circulated through U.S. imperial rhetoric, but also was a discourse of interwar Black literary production—one that was adopted, adapted, subverted, and often, like a strange potion cast into the sea, disrupted by its writers. Like the other figures in this study, Walrond unsettles the idea that the folk in the Global South live not only geographically apart, but also in a separate temporality from their New Negro counterparts in the North.[144] Rather than merely serving as the source of a usable past, folk culture is the lens through which the present and future are reimagined.

Toomer's and Walrond's focus on the vexed relationship between death, labor, folk practice, and imperialism raises questions about what it means to be in the tumultuous wake of slavery, but not yet in the wake of empire. Such a question was especially urgent in the ethnographic experiments of the 1930s, which extended the New Negro Movement's drive to "make it new" by turning to everyday practices of cultural transformation. Chapter 2 extends this chapter's mediation on the crossroads as a site of death and transformation by turning to Toomer's and Walrond's contemporaries, Hurston and Jean Price-Mars. In their ethnographic writings about Haitian Vodou and folklore in the era of U.S. occupation, they theorize the crossroads as a site of subversion and ambiguity that productively stretches the limits of ethnographic fieldwork and writing. In the process, they excavate new understandings of Black humanity, self-invention, and sovereignty.

Chapter Two

COMPELLING INSINUATION AND THE USES OF ETHNOGRAPHY

Zora Neale Hurston, Jean Price-Mars, and the U.S. Occupation of Haiti

The 1930s have been rightfully called "a golden age for Haiti studies."[1] Zora Neale Hurston made two trips to Haiti on a Guggenheim fellowship between 1936 and 1937, resulting in the publication of *Their Eyes Were Watching God* and her ethnography and travel narrative, *Tell My Horse*. She was among several students of the pioneering anthropologist Franz Boas to visit Haiti during these years. In 1934, Melville and Fanny Herskovits lived in the Mirebelais Valley, where they conducted fieldwork for the influential 1937 book *Life in a Haitian Valley*. With a letter of introduction from Melville Herskovits, the ethnomusicologist Alan Lomax (who had earlier accompanied Hurston to record music rituals in Eatonville, Florida) arrived in Haiti in December 1936 near the middle of Hurston's first visit. Armed with state-of-the-art sound recording equipment loaned to him by the Library of Congress, Lomax recorded 1,500 tunes within five months.[2] Also in 1936, Katherine Dunham, then a graduate student in anthropology at the University of Chicago, landed in Port-au-Prince. As she later recounts in *Island Possessed* (1969), she had many lively conversations about "politics, vaudun, and methods of research in ethnology" with Haitian intellectuals, including the ethnographer Jean Price-Mars and his wife, Cécile.[3]

In this flood of activity, one might locate the early stirrings of Black hemispheric studies. Haiti's emergence as a key site of anthropological inquiry in the 1930s was no coincidence. While the Black republic had long held a revered place in the imagination of Black people who neither conducted fieldwork nor visited the island, the nineteen-year U.S. military occupation put Haiti on the map for the general U.S. public. As Mary Renda notes, "Haiti became not only a point of protest, but also, with new vigor, an object of cultural fascination—indeed, an object of desire, a valuable commodity."[4] A rapidly growing imperial literary culture stoked such fascination. Sensational travel narratives written by U.S. marines and other white travelers, such as William Seabrook's *The Magic Island* (1929) and John Houston Craige's *Cannibal Cousins* (1934), gained wide readership and played a significant role in justifying the civilizing mission of the United States in Haiti. The texts contained lurid accounts of Vodou rites, offensive illustrations, and other content that emphasized the primitivism of Haitian culture. Although such works "stimulated the dramatic turn" to Haiti in U.S. anthropology, American anthropologists also distanced themselves from these sensationalist accounts by situating their authority in a new scientific and literary genre—the ethnography—that drew upon participant observation to craft cultural descriptions of the folk. When the American anthropologists turned to Haiti, they were not the first to enter the field. Galvanized by U.S. intervention, Haitian scholars drew upon their own intellectual history of "racial vindication," as well as a formidable legacy of peasant insurgency, to frame folk culture not merely as a recovery of roots, but as a contemporary form of resistance to U.S. hegemony. Coterminous with the New Negro Movement, such work raises questions about the politics of observation and the stakes of Black hemispheric solidarity. If the revolution of 1804 made Haiti central to formulations of Black self-determination and resistance, the renewed threat to Haiti's sovereignty sharpened debates about what it meant to be Black in the Americas—to navigate the narrow space between U.S. empire and Jim Crow.

This chapter discusses two major Black ethnographies of the interwar period, Jean Price-Mars's *Ainsi parla l'Oncle* (*So Spoke the Uncle*) (1928) and Hurston's *Tell My Horse* (1938). Each a pioneering figure in their own right, Price-Mars and Hurston are often discussed separately: Price-Mars, a father of Négritude and champion of Haitian self-determination; and Hurston, a revered innovator of folk expression in the United States who nevertheless seemed to falter when she approached the Caribbean folk as a cultural outsider. I aim here to give a more robust sense of the intellectual and creative field of which Hurston and Price-Mars were part, as well as the challenges they faced as they engaged in the difficult work of "constructing a culture to study."[5] To read these works together is an exercise in imperial asymmetry, a practice of dwelling *au carrefour* (at the crossroads), where "conflictual convergences" of culture, belief, and politics rise into view.[6] Together, their work illuminates the shifting ground of ethnographic authority in an age of U.S. intervention: the vexed question of who gets to observe, define, and theorize Black folk culture, and to what end. Both texts belong to the "anthropology of Caribbean peasantries," which, as Deborah Thomas observes, have been linked to the question of sovereignty: "how it is to be framed, addressed, and expressed."[7] Beyond considering the immediate threat of the occupation and its aftermath, both authors anticipate Sylvia Wynter's question of *ontological sovereignty* as they search for a language and method to pronounce Haitian folk culture's philosophies of Black invention and self-possession.[8]

Founder of the Institut d'ethnologie in Haiti, an ethnographer, a medical doctor, and a diplomat, Price-Mars was influenced by a nineteenth-century tradition of antiracist Haitian scholarship (figure 2.1). Price-Mars's

FIGURE 2.1 In the Faculté d'Ethnologie in Port-au-Prince, a large portrait of Jean Price-Mars hangs in one of the classrooms. *Source:* Taken by the author.

expertise allowed him to serve as an intellectual guide to U.S. researchers during their visits to the island, easing their way into a social milieu
that was (rightfully) suspicious of their motives. But he differed from some
of his American colleagues in his unwavering, vehement opposition to
U.S. intervention. In *Ainsi parla l'Oncle* (*So Spoke the Uncle*), Price-Mars
turned to the stock of Haitian "oral traditions, legends, tales, songs, rid-
dles, customs, observances, ceremonies, and beliefs" as the foundation of
an anti-imperial politics and a revitalized national literature.[9] The book
had an explosive impact on Haiti. Price-Mars critiqued what he saw as the
elite's delusional cultural allegiance to France and was among the first to
affirm Vodou as a legitimate religion with the "social virtue of bringing us
together in community"—long prefiguring its official recognition in 2003.[10]
In Kreyòl, he found "a language of great subtlety" that could serve as the
basis for a national literature.[11] Overall, the rehumanizing force of Haitian
folk culture was a vital defense against the designs of "nations impatient for
territorial expansion, ambitious for hegemony, to erase the society from the
map of the world."[12]

Yet Price-Mars's work also reveals his positionality as an ethnographer
and member of the very *lelit* (elite) he had critiqued—and a cultural outsider to the folk rituals that he was attempting to witness. On one expedi-
tion to the peasant countryside in 1920, he recalls a startling encounter:

> I interrupted a legally forbidden ceremony and my clothes were a principal
> reason for my mistake that caused the participants of the ceremony to scatter.
> In effect, clothed in a horseback-riding outfit, wearing a khaki helmet, legs
> encased in a yellow flannel, a gun in a bandolier, I resembled an officer in
> the rural police force. Thus my initial attempt to dissuade the runaways, my
> engaging pleas, failed to inspire their confidence and I was unable to ascer-
> tain the principal elements of the celebration and what it was celebrating.[13]

As Michael Largey explains, the encounter is typical of what many elites
would have experienced when coming face-to-face with Vodou in the
countryside: "an unsettling, frightening, and vaguely dangerous encounter
with people who fear reprisals."[14] More specifically, it is also a reminder
of the "legal regime against Vodou," which the occupation had strength-
ened and enforced. As Kate Ramsey observes, laws against *les sortilèges*
(spells) were not merely the result of longstanding intolerance of folk forms
among the Haitian elite. Rather, occupation officials regarded Vodou as a

catalyst of native insurgency.[15] Price-Mars's encounter was thus more than an uncomfortable instance of mistaken identity—it was also symbolic of the thorny power dynamics that mediated his study of the folk.

As Wynter later observes, "Price-Mars' book, and the Negritude movement to which it gave rise, was part of the chain reaction to the United States' neo-colonial occupation of Haiti."[16] No less a part of this "chain reaction" was Hurston's 1938 ethnography and travel narrative, *Tell My Horse*, now infamous for its praise of U.S. military intervention and its problematic misreading of Haitian politics. In one particularly jarring passage, Hurston reimagines the invasion of U.S. marines as a parable of salvation: "The smoke from the funnels of the U.S.S. Washington was a Black plume with a white hope."[17] Her support of the occupation was not an anomaly among African Americans. As Brandon Byrd notes, even though many of Hurston's contemporaries eventually condemned the occupation, more than a few initially "struggled to reconcile their imagined connection to Haiti with their claims to national citizenship." Adopting the rhetoric of racial uplift, some vowed to "save Haiti from itself."[18]

However, beyond the complex negotiations of solidarity that U.S. expansion occasioned for African Americans, *Tell My Horse* reflects Hurston's struggle to find her footing not only as a foreigner, but also as a woman in a male-dominated political milieu. Doing ethnography in the aftermath of the occupation posed distinct challenges for her. Shortly before Hurston's arrival, the government of President Sténio Vincent doubled down on the repression of Vodou rituals with a 1935 law banning "*les pratiques superstitieuses*" (superstitious practices), even as Vodou-inspired folkloric forms were ushered onto the national stage as symbols of Haitian identity.[19] Echoing Price-Mars, Hurston rejects the logic of occupation-era repression by describing spirit possession and folklore as transformative modes of political resistance against authority, both local and foreign. On the other hand, as Leigh Ann Duck has argued, Hurston's political commentary reflects her wariness toward the ascendance of "*noiristes* or Griots [who] linked the study of folklore not only to racial essentialism, but also to an explicitly authoritarian political agenda."[20] Such ideology later fueled the dictatorship of François "Papa Doc" Duvalier, who rose to power in 1957 through his folkloric styling and strategic appropriation of Price-Mars's pioneering work.

As Wynter later observes, there were two variants to the challenge of "neo-colonial occupation" by the United States: "One thrust, that of

Price-Mars, laid the emphasis on the calling into question the distortions of Western ethnographic accounts of Vodoun. The other, that of Francois Duvalier (and his Noiristes), was to manipulate Vodoun, together with its secret society system as a powerful semi-official tool with which to displace the hegemony of the largely mulatto-upper class elite, replacing it with its own socially mobile lower middle black, but no less educationally Westernized, elite."[21] In some ways, Hurston's critique of cultural nationalism anticipates this turn. By listening to the resonances between Price-Mars's and Hurston's work, this chapter raises questions about the uses of folk culture: its dual potential as a tool of liberation and as fuel for a regime of authenticity.

Price-Mars and Hurston anticipate anthropology's later self-reflexive debates about ethnographic authority and the politics of knowledge production. In his classic 1983 essay "On Ethnographic Authority," James Clifford details the myriad rhetorical and formal techniques by which "unruly experience [is] transformed into an authoritative written account" in twentieth-century ethnography.[22] Conversely, in this chapter, I ask: How do Black ethnographic practices attend to unruly experience? By attempting to register the vitality of Black folk practices that were increasingly under assault during the occupation and its aftermath, Price-Mars and Hurston do not just seek to preserve their historical significance. Rather, they aim to puzzle over what Colin Dayan calls folk culture's "project of thought," citing "the intensity of interpretation and dramatization it allowed." As Dayan elaborates, with its attention to details and fragments and its elaborate embodied rituals of possession and service, Vodou embodies the "process of thought working itself through terror."[23] Dayan echoes Wynter's claim that Vodou presents a mode of "reflective thought" and a different "understanding of man's humanity," which, with its ethics of collective cooperation, was directly opposed to the cultural logic of the occupation.[24] Following Dayan and Wynter, I argue that in the face of imperial possession, Haitian folk culture enacts ontological sovereignty as an ongoing process of invention that draws upon collective ritual, polyvocality, and embodied knowledge. Faced with the challenge of recording *pèp ayisyen* (Haitian lower classes), who are not just objects of study but agents of knowledge, both Hurston and Price-Mars show folk authenticity and ethnographic authority to be unstable at best. By emphasizing the perplexing mutability of folklore and Vodou, dramatizing their distance from their subjects, or presenting intractable informants who talk back or defiantly return the ethnographic gaze, each text shows how folk culture both unsettles and enriches ethnography.

AN ETHNOGRAPHY OF COMPELLING INSINUATION

If, as I argued in chapter 1, Jean Toomer and Eric Walrond subvert nostalgic myths of a premodern folk, Price-Mars and Hurston grapple with folk culture's potential to disrupt imperial regimes of knowledge. Faced with sonic, embodied, and spiritual practices that defied description, they develop strategies of ethnographic experimentation that resonate with the cultural practices they describe. In my reading of the interplay between folk and ethnographic knowledge, I draw upon Hurston's theory of "compelling insinuation," a mode of Black folk performance characterized by "calculated and captivating restraint." Relying on understatement to produce meaning, compelling insinuation suggests a politics of ethnographic writing—one that emphasizes dynamically suggestive modes of resistance, alternative modes of *occupying* space in the face of imperial intervention. In "Characteristics of Negro Expression," Hurston writes:

> Negro dancing is dynamic suggestion. No matter how violent it may appear to the beholder, every posture gives the impression that the dancer will do much more. For example, the performer flexes one knee sharply, assumes a ferocious face mask, thrusts the upper part of the body forward with clenched fists, elbows taut as in hard running or grasping a thrusting blade. That is all. But the spectator himself adds the picture of ferocious assault, hears the drums and finds himself keeping time with the music and tensing himself for the struggle. It is compelling insinuation. That is the very reason the spectator is held so rapt. He is participating in the performance himself—carrying out the suggestions of the performer.[25]

As an aesthetic, a performative strategy, and a mode of critique, compelling insinuation encapsulates the dynamic interplay between performer and audience. Compelling insinuation is one of several "characteristics" that might frame a reading of Hurston's ethnography. In her discussion of *Tell My Horse*, Samantha Pinto provocatively deploys "asymmetry" as "a method of reading [Hurston's] innovative critiques of existing orders of modernity," as well as a marker of the book's own uneven form: the book features a short section on Hurston's travels in Jamaica before devoting most of its chapters to Haiti.[26] Here, I turn to compelling insinuation to indicate formal gestures that are subtle, evocative, or anticipatory.

I use the term in two ways. First, compelling insinuation is a ritual practice of folk culture. It is evident in Price-Mars's descriptions of how enslaved Africans "humanized" the New World landscape through suggestive, embodied acts of labor and ritual that do not always read straightforwardly as resistance. It exists in Hurston's portrait of the subversive potential of spirit possession, particularly the provocative *banda* dances practiced by the Gede spirits, or *lwa*. Although Hurston coined the term before traveling to Haiti, her prior investment in evocative movement and speech may have explained her preoccupation with the Haitian Gede spirits. Gede (also spelled "Guede" or "Ghede"), boisterous guardian of the crossroads between life and death, pronounces the words "*parlay cheval ou*" ("tell my horse") and proceeds to do and say "the things that the peasants would like to do and say," usually in the form of devastating critiques of power.[27] Dancing the *banda*, Hurston explains, Gede "cavorts about, making coarse gestures, executing steps like the prancing of a horse, drinking and talking."[28] Both ethnographers explore the implications of what the dance scholar Celia Weiss Bambara terms "materiality of the body and the transformation of movement" for the writing of ethnography and the challenges of participant observation.[29] The transformative potential of these embodied and narrative acts rests precisely in what Daphne Brooks calls their "performative threat": their ability to suggest "ferocious assault" through quotidian acts of insinuation that reclaim the body from the violence of occupation.[30]

Second, compelling insinuation is a narrative strategy that unsettles ethnographic practice by dramatizing the challenges of cultural description. If, as Emily Maguire observes, early twentieth-century ethnography worked to assert scientific authority by "establishing the ethnographer as the sole interpreter of the culture that he or she had studied, and thus as the primary narrative voice of the text itself," the ethnography was nevertheless "a literary text, connected to the literary conventions of the other genres (such as travel writing) from which it had sprung."[31] It illuminates the provocative tension between Price-Mars's and Hurston's efforts, on one hand, to assert ethnographic authority according to the emerging norms of the genre, and on the other hand, to use ethnography as a porous site of experimentation in which a number of dissonant voices, styles, and genres subtly permeate the text. While both authors make bold and emphatic claims about the uses of folk culture, they also employ understatement, irony, and suggestion to allow folk culture to talk back. In both texts, the voices of local folk informants alternately amplify, correct, and subvert the narratives set forth by their authors. Musical scores and photographs interrupt (and sometimes contradict) ethnographic description, and in the case of *Tell My Horse*, the text's circuitous and asymmetrical organization destabilizes scientific order. In other words, compelling insinuation functions as both a characteristic of folk culture and as an ethnographic practice that performs new ways of describing Black agency. Price-Mars's and Hurston's works not only allow but invite such interpolation. Their approach to observing and writing about the folk suggests that what was true for the folk artist might also be true for the ethnographer: "nothing is too old or too new, domestic or foreign, high or low, for his use."[32]

PRICE-MARS AND THE SCENE OF OCCUPATION

As Michel-Rolph Trouillot observes, given the incursion of U.S. hegemony and the enduring legacy of European colonialism, it is no coincidence that "in the 1920s and 1930s, many Caribbean-born writers, such as Price-Mars in Haiti and Pedreira in Puerto Rico, saw the study of culture as inevitably tied to history."[33] Born in 1876 in Grande-Rivière-du-Nord, a province in northern Haiti, Price-Mars dates his decision to study anthropology to a pivotal moment in 1899 when as a medical student in Paris, he became acquainted with the racist theories of the French sociologist Gustave Le Bon. While browsing books in a shopping arcade near the Théâtre de l'Odéon, Price-Mars encountered Le Bon's 1894 *Lois psychologiques de l'évolution des peuples* (*Psychological Laws of the Evolution of Peoples*). He recalls, "It was with a religious fervor that I approached the reading of this work of Le Bon. Alas, I would be disillusioned. The writer who, at that very moment, was enjoying a grand vogue and who directed the Library of Scientific Philosophy where so many works of high value were published, had constructed a theory on the immutability of character. . . . And Mr. Le Bon, by virtue of this theory, divided the races into four categories: The primitive races, the inferior races, the middle races and the superior races." Much to young Price-Mars's dismay, Le Bon invoked the example of Haiti (Saint

Domingue) to provide incontrovertible proof of Black inferiority: "When the mix of whites and of Blacks, he wrote, is inherited by chance, as in Saint Domingue, from a superior civilization, that civilization rapidly descends into a miserable decadence." As Price-Mars plainly recalls, "Reading that book decided my vocation."[34]

What Price-Mars was discovering was the role of anthropology in the construction of what Trouillot called the "Savage slot." As Trouillot contends, "[A]nthropologists never give the people they study the right to be as knowledgeable or, more precisely, to have the same kind of knowledge about their own societies as ethnographers."[35] Instead, anthropology occupies the "Savage slot." Trouillot elaborates, "It is a stricture of the Savage slot that the native never faces the observer. In the rhetoric of the Savage slot, the Savage is never an interlocutor, but evidence in an argument between two Western interlocutors about the possible futures of humankind."[36] Price-Mars vowed to draw upon anthropology to systematically refute arguments about the inferiority of Blacks and their unfitness for self-governance—claims that had profoundly threatened the Black republic's self-determination. In doing so, Price-Mars joined what Gérarde Magloire and Kevin Yelvington call a "Haitian intellectual tradition of racial vindication," exemplified by the work of the anthropologist and diplomat Anténor Firmin, whose 1885 book *De l'égalité des races humaines* (*On the Equality of Human Races*) refuted the racist theories of Arthur de Gobineau and others.[37] Price-Mars was named after the Haitian diplomat and poet Hannibal Price, who in 1900 authored the influential *De la réhabilitation de la race noire par la République d'Haïti* (*On the Rehabilitation of the Black Race by the Republic of Haiti*). Together, the work of Firmin, Price, and Price-Mars demonstrates the ongoing relationship between antiracist scholarship and political involvement in Haiti. As Jhon Picard Byron explains, "Even from the moment of anthropology's first stammerings, Haitians presented themselves as anthropologists."[38]

Price-Mars, however, departed from Firmin and Price in important ways. As J. Michael Dash points out, Price-Mars's predecessors were "not so much interested in Haiti's originality but in demonstrating that Haiti was as civilized as Europe."[39] But by the twentieth century, there was need for a response to the United States and its increasing subjugation of its neighbors in the hemisphere. If the completion of the Panama Canal announced the start of the American Century, military intervention sharpened the localized impact of U.S. hegemony. The United States occupied Haiti in July 1915 following the events of July 28, in which President Vilbrun Guillaume Sam was assassinated after his massacre of some 167 political prisoners. Although framed as a necessary intervention to restore order to a country plagued by instability, the United States had long held a strategic interest in Haiti. As Magdaline Shannon explains, the establishment of control was swift: "within a month [the United States] had established martial law, assumed military and civil control of Haiti, restricted the Haitian press, and seized control of five services: customs, finance, the constabulary, public works, and public health."[40] Marines also revived the *corvée*, an obsolete law that required citizens to labor on the public roads under conditions comparable to slavery. In 1918, a new constitution granted property rights to foreigners for the first time. The occupation also waged an assault on Haitian folk culture: U.S. marines ransacked Vodou *ounforts* (temples) and confiscated cultural objects that they feared could inspire peasant insurgency. With military precision and rhetorical force, the United States restructured citizenship in Haiti.

In his report for the National Association for the Advancement of Colored People (NAACP) in 1920, James Weldon Johnson observed that the assassination of President Sam did not cause the intervention but merely furnished the long-awaited opportunity: "When the United States found itself in a position to take what it had not even dared to ask, it used brute force and took it."[41] As Johnson recalls, his exposé of the U.S. occupation—a series of essays published in *The Nation* in August 1920 under the title "Self-Determining Haiti"—resulted from extensive conversations "with almost every important Haitian, many of them men of wide political knowledge and experience, who realized the difficulty of the situation, but were determined to take every feasible step for the restoration of Haitian independence."[42] One of these interlocutors was Price-Mars. In an April 1920 letter, he writes, "My dear M. Johnson: When I left you last Thursday night, I forgot to inquire about M. Seligmann whether he was come back or not from his trip. Anyhow, enclosed you will find a word for him in order that he may join us tomorrow if he is in Port-au-Prince. Yours truly, Price-Mars."[43] Price-Mars was referring to Herbert Seligmann, who had sailed with Johnson to Haiti in February 1920. In July 1920, Seligmann would also publish an exposé of the occupation in *The Nation* entitled "The Conquest of Haiti." In April 1920, Price-Mars left several calling cards inviting

Seligmann to join him for lunch "in the company of Mr. Johnson and several other friends" in Petionville, an affluent enclave outside the city center, on Sunday, April 18, 1920. ("*Voulez-vous accepter à dejeuner avec moi en compagnie de M. Johnson et de quelques autres amis à Petionville, dimanche prochain 18, à midi?*")[44] Such correspondence offers a small glimpse into the activities of an elite circle of intellectuals who gathered to debate the politics of the occupation.

Given Price-Mars's stature as an ethnographer, physician, and diplomat, both Johnson and Seligmann likely were consulting with him on the essays they were currently writing. Price-Mars, in turn, likely sought to exert some influence over representations of the occupation published in the U.S. press. By the time of their meeting, Price-Mars had already served as the secretary of the Haitian legation to the United States. In 1919, he published *La vocation de l'Élite*, in which he recalled his alarm at the "state of disarray in which I found the elite of this country since American intervention into the affairs of Haiti."[45] Of course, Price-Mars was a prominent member of the very elite that he critiqued. Yet his work afforded him an unusual intimacy with a peasant class he dubbed "*ceux d'en bas*" (those down below), anticipating Hurston's spatially inflected phrase "the Negro farthest down."[46] In Price-Mars's case, contact with the folk actually required spatial ascension. A practicing physician, he often traveled to the mountains on horseback to treat patients. These visits to *paysans montagnards* (mountain peasants) became part of his fieldwork, enabling him to hear folktales and eventually gain entrée to over one hundred Vodou ceremonies.[47] But the field of Price-Mars's research was no provincial site removed from the contemporary scene of the occupation. On the contrary, these peasant communities were a literal and symbolic site of peasant insurgency. From the early stages of the occupation, the *cacos* had taken up armed resistance. In 1919, Charlemagne Péralte led a revolt at Port-au-Prince, vowing to "drive the invaders into the sea and free Haiti."[48] The revolt was violently suppressed and its leaders executed. U.S. authorities implicated Vodou and other cultural practices in militant resistance, and this association served to justify frequent raids of temples and confiscation of sacred objects. Official documents of the occupation attributed barbaric acts to *cacos* and rendered the terms "peasant" and *caco* interchangeable. Thus, in the language of U.S. imperialism, to be a peasant was to be an insurgent.[49]

Caco resistance was only one part of a robust response to the occupation. Across class lines, Haitians engaged in various modes of anti-imperial activism, including student protests and urban strikes. No less consequential, as Grace Sanders-Johnson notes, was the local activism of Haitian market women.[50] In 1925, a group of writers founded the nationalist group La Nouvelle Ronde, whose core members went on to establish the short-lived but influential journal *La Revue Indigène*.[51] The journal's inaugural issue featured an essay by Price-Mars entitled "La famille paysanne: Moeurs locales et survivances africaines" ("The Peasant Family: Local Customs and African Survivals"), which later became the final chapter of *So Spoke the Uncle*. But however salient the activities of the elite were, Price-Mars pressed for more action by making a strategic contrast between the two classes. Whereas the masses had taken the initiative, Price-Mars lamented, the elite had simply thrown up their hands in defeat. Whereas the masses hoped to cast off colonial chains, the elite participated in a system that perpetuated disenfranchisement, even while living off of peasant labor in a "state equivalent to parasitism."[52] Furthermore, whereas the masses had embraced Haitian cultural forms as a bulwark against U.S. imperialism, the elite clung to French ideals, suffering from an identity crisis that Price-Mars (in a somewhat ironic reference to Gustave Flaubert's 1856 novel *Madame Bovary*) dubbed "collective bovaryism," (*bovarysme collectif*) which was "the faculty of a society seeing itself other than it is."[53]

Given Price-Mars's concern with cooperation between the lower and upper classes, as well as his preoccupation with the "*vocation*" of the elite (most forcefully translated to mean a calling or destiny), his admiration for his distinguished contemporary Booker T. Washington should be unsurprising. Eager to compare the condition of African Americans with those of Haitians, Price-Mars visited Tuskegee in 1904 during a trip through the U.S. South. During the trip, he remembers being affronted with "all the indignities of color prejudice. One time, over the course of my voyage through the Black belt, I was almost penned inside a compartment of livestock, I was often turned away at the door of restaurants, refused in hotels, and insulted in streetcars" (*J'ai affronté toutes les ignominies du préjugé de couleur. Une fois, au cours de mon voyage dans le black belt, j'ai été presque parqué dans un compartiment de bestiaux, j'ai été souvent mis à la porte des restaurants, refusé dans les hôtels, insulté dans les cars*).[54] But although Price-Mars named Washington "the most powerful American orator of our days," he did not merely pattern his own politics after Washington's. To begin with, Washington and Price-Mars differed on one crucial point: Haitian self-determination. In an essay for the *New York Age* shortly before the end of his life, Washington called the U.S. occupation an "absolutely necessary" measure, noting that the Haitian people are "easily led and guided."[55] Price-Mars revises Washington's project of racial uplift—perhaps best epitomized by a bronze statue at Tuskegee depicting Washington lifting the veil of ignorance from the eyes of a kneeling slave. In contrast, Price-Mars's campaign of *"relèvement moral"* (moral recovery) sought to reform the elite rather than the masses.

In 1932, Price-Mars engaged Washington's ideas in a three-part essay entitled "A propos de la Renaissance nègre aux États-Unis" ("On the Negro Renaissance in the United States"). But Price-Mars's *"Renaissance nègre"* encompasses not only the Harlem Renaissance, but also earlier advancements of African Americans since emancipation. In a gesture that would no doubt have been surprising to the progressive figures of 1920s Harlem, Price-Mars revisits the most infamous part of Washington's 1895 Atlanta Exposition speech—the parable of the ships.[56] In the original speech, known sardonically as "The Atlanta Compromise," Washington urges Blacks to cast down their buckets into the "common occupations of life" and into efforts to advance the mutual progress of the races. Of course, this mantra of self-sufficiency also implied a deferral of the very substance of citizenship: social equality and political power.

In Price-Mars's hands, however, Washington's parable is radically transformed from a call for compromise to an anti-imperialist statement.[57] Echoing Washington's imperative to "cast down your buckets where you are," Price-Mars encourages Haitians to *"plongez vos baquets."* Unlike Washington, Price-Mars rejects the dichotomy between technical training and intellectual and artistic endeavors. His version of the parable calls for immersion not only in the "common occupations of life," but also in the riches of Haiti's expressive culture. "To all our intellectuals," he exclaims, "to all those who live in and of this country, and who are unaware of the potential richness in human values, to all those who are unaware that they might find art and beauty in the intangible bronze that is our community, I say in symbolic fashion, 'plunge your buckets!' "[58] If Price-Mars casts Haiti as a ship in distress, his repetition of the phrase *"plongez vos baquets"* becomes a call for immersion in Haiti's rich internal resources—its folklore, its rituals, and the integrity and ingenuity of the people. Bringing his allusion to Washington's speech full circle, Price-Mars shows that the distressed vessel had never needed intervention to begin with: "the ship in distress had been navigating the mouth of the Amazon and had not even perceived it."[59]

In effect, Price-Mars performs what might be called a strategic misreading of an African American text. Whereas Washington had stressed compromise—the forfeiture of social equality and political power—Price-Mars shifts the parable to a call for citizenship and self-determination. And whereas Washington had mused, "I hope this country will be equally patient and more than patient in dealing with Haiti—a weaker and more unfortunate country!," Price-Mars envisions transnational relations as a *"code de la solidarité entre gens de mer"* (code of solidarity between people at sea). Crucially, Price-Mars's use of "solidarity" does not imply uplift or paternalism. While maintaining a posture of mutual cooperation, the two ships are nevertheless independent vessels.[60]

Price-Mars's revision of Washington's speech is an example of compelling insinuation. In place of rebutting Washington's ideas outright, Price-Mars modifies Washington's imagery. In the process, he highlights the ways in which, as Kevin Gaines argues, "the rhetoric of racial uplift often resembled the imperialist notion of the civilizing mission."[61] Price-Mars's engagement with Washington mines the tensions between a politics of uplift, which sought to rehabilitate Haiti, and a politics of cultural immersion, which sought strategies for resistance in the riches of Haitian culture. Led by Price-Mars, Haitian artists and intellectuals would "plunge their buckets" into Haitian cultural riches, deploying ethnographic work as a means of nationalist resistance. His use of anthropology—a discipline "integral to colonial apparatuses of power/knowledge" gave him further opportunity to mine these tensions as he sought to interrogate the field from within.[62]

SO SPOKE THE UNCLE:
ETHNOGRAPHY AND POLITICS OF THE VOICE

An influential member of the elite by the 1920s, Price-Mars secured his status as an innovator of the study of Haitian folk culture with the publication of *So Spoke the Uncle* in 1928. A collection of essays culled from his many public lectures, *Uncle* valorizes the African origins of Haitian culture and calls for a national literature based in the contributions of the masses. Price-Mars's preface begins with a frank statement on the book's purpose: "We have nourished for a long time the ambition of restoring the value of Haitian folk-lore in the eyes of the people. This entire book is an endeavor to integrate the popular Haitian thought into the discipline of traditional ethnography."[63] Price-Mars does not present the book as an effort to valorize Haiti in the eyes of Europe and the United States, but rather as an attempt to elevate its value in the eyes of its own people. He frames his object of study as *"pensée popular haïtienne"* (popular Haitian thought), suggesting that Haitian folklore is an intellectual project that might contribute to, if not revise, traditional ethnography. Price-Mars thus advances a challenge to conventional assumptions about who produces knowledge and who serves to benefit from its practice.

Above all, Price-Mars's attention to Haiti's "moving history" destabilizes the myth of an ahistorical, homogenous folk that had persisted in anthropological discourse:[64]

> These people who have had, if not the finest, at least the most binding, the most moving history of the world—that of the transplantation of a human race to foreign soil under the worst biological conditions—these people feel an embarrassment barely concealed, indeed shame, in hearing of their distant past. It is those who during four centuries were the architects of black slavery because they had force and science at their service that magnified the enterprise by spreading the idea that Negroes were the scum of the society, without history, without morality, without religion, who had to be infused by any manner whatsoever with new moral values, to be humanized anew.[65]

Price-Mars reconstructs Haiti's history as a New World epic: through the Middle Passage crossing, to the crossroads of the Americas. He deconstructs Western myths of Black inferiority, which had disastrously "magnified the enterprise" of slavery and colonialism. Setting aside these fictions, he redefines what it means to be "humanized anew," and vows to reveal "our presence on the point of the American archipelago which we have 'humanized,' the breach that we have made in the process of historic events in order to secure our place among men."[66] In other words, it was not Blacks who required humanization by the civilizing hand of Europe, but rather they who had humanized the colonial landscape through embodied acts of labor, ritual, and resistance. As Wynter later argues, Price-Mars shows how these cultural inventions "convert the Nature of Haiti into the cultural ecology of the black man."[67]

Wynter's engagement with Price-Mars, on which I elaborate further in chapter 4, amplifies the stakes of his project. Although both authors uphold the importance of African retentions, they emphasize not their unaltered preservation, but their transformation in what Wynter calls "a great syncretic process [that] re-established itself as the cultural subsoil of the peasant relation to the new land; which reinvented religion, folksongs, folklore, folk beliefs, peopled innumerable 'duppy plants' with the spirits of ancestors, with old and new gods. It was this stream which fed the roots of culture."[68] Price-Mars anticipates Wynter's focus on the provision ground—lands granted to the enslaved for cultivation—as a site of this process of rehumanization. Thus, when Price-Mars links the "agrarian sacrifice *du manger yam*" (of eating yam) to contemporary practices of sacrifice in Vodou, it is to emphasize a particular philosophy of man's relationship to the earth: "that the earth and the seasons and their rhythm belong to a mystical scale of things to which man owes reverence."[69] He suggests that Haitian subjects and their ancestors had long sustained a different relationship to the landscape than the occupation allowed—with its system of forced labor, seizing of land as property, and a regime of cultural repression.

Price-Mars thus approaches ethnography as a historical project. His engrossment in the writing of what Trouillot called "culture-history" is evident in the form and organization of the text. After two brief chapters on folklore and popular beliefs, the book takes a seemingly circuitous route through the study of African societies before returning to a discussion of Vodou. In his review of the 1986 translation of *Ainsi parla l'Oncle*, Trouillot calls attention to the "didactic necessity" of this detour, "which may now seem awkward to the modern reader": without the reevaluation of African societies and cultures, "the Haitian reevalution is impossible."[70] Trouillot adopts a similar approach in his own book *Peasants and Capital*, in which "history generates the first unit; political economy helps make sense of the second. The reader enters the village-level ethnography only two-thirds of the way through the book."[71] The purpose of such a "*promenade ethnographique*" (ethnographic promenade), as Price-Mars phrases it, is to connect the village to the world and to frame culture as a historical process rather than as static artifact.[72]

But the book's intervention into the construction of historical knowledge is first announced by its title. The phrase "so spoke the uncle" is commonly used by storytellers to invoke the folkloric hero Uncle Bouqui, "a force borne of patience, resignation, and of intelligence, just like the expression which we are able to detect in the mass of our mountain folk." Price-Mars elaborates: "Bouqui is typical of the '*nègre bossale*' newly brought from Africa to Saint Domingue whose clumsiness and stupidity were the object of frequent bullying and merciless joking by Ti Malice, personification of the '*nègre créole*' generally considered as more adroit and even a little sly." But there is another side to the humble uncle. The word "Bouqui," Price-Mars speculates, may in fact be derived from "Bouriqui," the name of an ethnic group from the Grain Coast whose members were rumored to be "unmanageable" and who became distinguishable by their "eccentricities and the unassimilable nature of their temperament so unlike other Negroes promptly mixed into the indistinct mass of slaves."[73] Such a description suggests that underneath Bouqui's apparent "resignation" and docility was unruliness, and even a posture of defiance to the colonial regime. Price-Mars suggests that Bouqui's closeness to his African origins had served as an advantage rather than as a detriment to his survival in the New World. Furthermore, his unmanageability was perfectly suited to the needs of the present, for was it not the "*paysans montagnards*" (mountain folk) who had been the first to resist the occupation? With the use of "so spoke the uncle," Price-Mars becomes a spokesman as well, speaking through this folk figure and all he represents. As a performative utterance, the phrase announces the book's intention not merely to recall the uncle's words, but to speak *as* the uncle and thereby embody his wisdom, authenticity, and sincerity. The book's title, therefore, provides a clue to the tensions at work in Price-Mars's desire to privilege folk utterance while maintaining his own authority in the text.

The question of voice thus rises to the fore. Where does one locate the voice of the ethnographer in this project? Where does one locate the voices of the folk, commonly dubbed the *pèp ayisyen*? As Yarimar Bonilla observes, the questions "Whose voice can be deployed as evidence of culture? Whose as ideology? And whose as theory?" are key to Caribbeanist anthropology.[74] They also help us to evaluate the "epistemological status" of folk discourse in literary studies. Thus, while noting Price-Mars's authoritative voicing of the uncle and his attempts to establish historical continuity between Haiti and Africa, I am also interested in the text's polyvocality, as well as its attention to historical gaps and loopholes. His use of the storytelling phrase "so spoke the uncle" leads him to a discussion of language: "It is thanks to Creole that our oral traditions exist, are perpetuated and transformed . . . tales and legends have found in the Creole language an entirely unexpected manner of expression, subtle and penetratingly acute."[75] Price-Mars stresses the "ingenuousness" of Kreyòl, rather than French, as being key to a collective identity, since it is "the only instrument that we and the masses can use for expressing our mutual thoughts." But it is also a "resonant instrument," a musical idiom with the power to ground meaning as well as destabilize it. It obtains its subtlety, Price-Mars insists, through the "unsuspected depth of the ambiguities that it insinuates by its innuendoes, by the inflection of the voice itself, and especially by the mimetic face of the speaker." Thus, while the title "so spoke the uncle" pronounces the importance of speech acts to the production of knowledge, Price-Mars emphasizes not only their content, but also their sonic and embodied form. In Kreyòl's "priceless sonority and delicacy of touch," he locates a particularly resonant form of compelling insinuation.[76]

Price-Mars's writing traces the very texture of aurality. As Alejandra Bronfman observes, his attention to sound also highlights "the ways the presence of a plurality of voices—and their emanation from raced and gendered bodies—stretched the possibilities of politics."[77] It is fitting, then, that before the end of the first chapter, Price-Mars turns to song. A chorus of other voices intervene in his ethnographic narrative:

Ah! melancholic chants of the slave, submissive and bruised under the whip of the commander, calling out to immanent justice; passionate chants, countless wailings, wild chorus of half-starved rebels shouting their defiance of death in the onslaught at Vertières in the sublime stanza:

Grenadiers à l'assaut
Ça qui mouri zaffaire à yo!
Nan point manman na point papa!
Grenadiers à l'assaut!
Ça qui mouri zaffaire à yo![78]

In the last stanza, Price-Mars transcribes a battle cry from Vertières, the last battle of the Haitian Revolution on November 18, 1803. (Grenadiers, to the attack! Whoever dies, so be it! We have no mother or father!)

It is in this "wild chorus" that Haiti finds its voice:

> I really think that one could justly define the Haitian: a people who sing and who suffer, who grieve and who laugh, who dance and are resigned. . . . He sings in the furor of combat, under the hail of machine-gun fire, or in the fray of bayonets. He sings of the muscular effort and the rest after the task, of the ineradicable optimism and humble intuition that neither injustice nor suffering are eternal and that, moreover, nothing is hopeless since "bon Dieu bon."[79]

In referencing the "furor of combat," Price-Mars invokes Haiti's epic battle for independence as well as its struggle under the occupation. Songs are filled with commentary on local politics, offering a rich repertoire for resistance in the present: "satirical couplets lashing the puppets of the moment and unmasking the hypocrisy of leading politicians." But beyond this "fierce choir" of overtly militant utterance, there are songs that operate on another frequency: "O melancholic songs of the wounded," "absorbing lullabies," "Liturgical nocturnes," "hymns of love and faith."[80] Furthermore, he highlights the role of women: "You know that the woman has a preponderant role in the gatherings where people tell and sing tales. If she is not always the leader of the chorus, she is at least a pre-eminent figure whom the populace calls the queen of song, queen forever so to speak, given the considerable importance that the chant in all its forms holds in the life of our people."[81] In all of these examples, Price-Mars is drawn to the way, in Haitian Kreyòl, that the "image often bursts forth in the simple repetition of analogous sounds which, in creating onomatopoeia, accentuate the musicality of the idiom."[82]

But in his turn to the voice, Price-Mars also encounters the ephemerality of the medium: it is material that "persistently disappears with unaccommodating frequency because it is essentially an oral tradition." Through apostrophe ("O melancholic chants!"), Price-Mars calls to the music itself as if to an absent lover: "can I gather you reverently, gather your brilliant frondescence into an immortal gesture whereby the race would recapture an intimate sense of its genius and the conviction of its indestructible vitality?" Such an endeavor proves elusive. "Wishful thinking, alas! Idle ambition!," Price-Mars laments.[83] Perhaps more than the other materials, Price-Mars's discussion of folk songs reveals the limitations of cultural recovery. As he attempts to reproduce the songs, he admits that many of the "airs have not survived." However, he adds, if the Negro American tradition stands as any comparable example, the body of songs must have been rich.[84] While Price-Mars dramatizes the elusiveness of these materials, he implies folk culture's modernity rather than its obsolescence. In other words, to understand culture as historically contingent is also to acknowledge that it is subject to change, loss, and ultimately transformation. Price-Mars undertook the task of transforming these materials, participating in the very folk aesthetic of juxtaposition that is the subject of his study.[85]

It is with this philosophy that Price-Mars endeavored to set some of the old lyrics to new music with the help of the Haitian composer Ludovic Lamothe. The choice of Lamothe, a classically trained composer who was inspired by folk forms and contributed to a new genre of "Vodou music / *musik savant ayisyen*," was significant.[86] Price-Mars reproduces the resulting musical scores on the page in a similar fashion to the sorrow songs in W. E. B. Du Bois's *The Souls of Black Folk*. The juxtaposition of these scores with Price-Mars's text suggests a dynamic interplay between his scholarship and folk materials that possessed a vibrant life of their own. Many of the songs also express loss "under the sign of love and in a minor key."[87] Price-Mars thus imagines the archive of folk culture as both an abundant resource and as something provocatively incomplete. But rather than replacing what has been lost, Price-Mars performs what Brent Hayes Edwards, referencing blues poetry, calls an "apostrophe of form," in which the text not only discursively hails an object of affection who is absent but also "calls out to an absent music, its missing chord changes, and the two apostrophes are set in an uneasy, jagged coexistence."[88] In leaving a suggestion of what is absent, Price-Mars's text performs compelling insinuation, constructing a model for collective meaning-making. In this more dynamic view, folk culture is an unwieldy, living force with implications for Haiti's modernity and its active role in contemporary anti-imperial struggles.

THE DWELLING PLACE OF THE SPIRIT

The book's most provocative model for polyvocal and embodied forms of expression emerges in its descriptions of the Vodou ceremony. In ritual possession, Price-Mars locates an excess of meaning that bursts the seams of any single master narrative—even, crucially, his own. Revising the work of Haitian author J. C. Dorsainvil who classed possession as a "religious, racial psychoneurosis,"[89] Price-Mars instead motions toward what M. Jacqui Alexander calls a pedagogy of the Sacred, a praxis of "collectivized self-possession" based on Vodou's philosophies of healing, embodied knowledge, and self-invention.[90] For the Black masses—the *pèp ayisyen*—possession represents a form of individual agency enabled by communal ritual. Its dynamic choreographies serve to transform the individual, granting each one a voice that remains elusive in everyday life. Price-Mars suggests that Vodou's synthesis of multiple traditions, its adaptation to the needs of its practitioners, and its reliance on the interplay between individual and group could serve as an important model of national unity and struggle. Far from being a shameful chapter of Haiti's past, such rituals were "the mirror which reflects most accurately the restless countenance of the nation."[91]

But in describing what it meant to serve the divine *lwa*—commonly termed *les invisibles*—Price-Mars faced difficult questions of representation. What does it mean to observe Vodou's complex choreographies, while preserving the unseen "mystères of the faith"? In short, how does one write about the invisible? Such a seeming contradiction, Jenny Sharpe argues, lies at the crux of a worldview that daily transgresses the boundaries between the material and spiritual worlds. While the visual artists that Sharpe discusses craft a "vodou archive," replete with the iconography of the crossroads, Price-Mars summons the paradoxes of performance.[92] He portrays the Vodou ceremony as a finely choreographed ritual: a form of compelling insinuation that transmits meaning through suggestion and collective response. In a chapter entitled "The Religious Sentiment of the Haitian Masses," Price-Mars describes the "special atmosphere" required to facilitate possession:

> The subject, in this case—most often, but not always—requires a special atmosphere, that of the worship ceremony which unfolds only in a setting

where the mystères of the faith hover. . . . The high priest inaugurates the ritual of worship with the consecration of the premises. He offers libations to the gods, scatters wheaten flour on the ground, pours spirituous liquors as he pronounces the liturgical words. The deep and muffled voice of the drums prolongs the vibration of the chants and incantations. The *Hougan* invested by his insignia intones the liturgical *melopée* [recitative chant] that the whole audience takes up in chorus.

Agile dancers, as if spirits, leap about the arena and increase the rhythm of pace to the cadence of nostalgic sounds and those evoking orgiastic frenzies. Abruptly the possessed one bursts out from the crowd where his attention was intensely concentrated on the movement of the ceremony and mixes with the dancers, or else dancing by himself, he is more and more intoxicated by the sounds and movements and dances, dances madly. But then he stops, dazed. He staggers, shrieks, sinks to the ground, prostrate or shaken by violent contortions. He rises again by himself or with the help of an assistant. His face assumes a tortured expression. Often the drums become silent at this moment. The audience is pensive and the possessed in an altered voice tremulous with the tumult of his mind improvises an air in honor of the god by which he is possessed and who identifies himself through the lips of the subject. And the possessed transmits a new momentum to the dance with an enhanced power that is irrepressible, inexpressible.[93]

Price-Mars begins this remarkable description not with an image of the possessed devotee, but rather by first passing through a series of elements that advance the ceremony, gradually preparing the way for the entry of the *lwa*. This process is a carefully orchestrated "ritual of worship," with specific roles for all participants. The priest (*oungan*) begins the ritual by consecrating the space—with libations, blessings, and other gestures—a repertoire which up to this point resembles a Catholic liturgy. The musicians also play a key role. The "voice" of the drum extends the chants of the *oungan*, adding resonance to his words. At this point, the audience is invited to take up the chant. The ceremony now moves from a single chant to a chorus of voices. Sound constitutes only one layer of this collective performance; the other is movement. Dancers "leap about the arena and increase the rhythm" of the music and the incantations. Meanwhile, the person to be possessed has his "attention intensely concentrated on the movement of the ceremony." The ceremony moves toward its climax. It is only then that the *lwa* is able to *monter la tête* (mount the head) of the chosen devotee. The other participants anticipate this moment and recognize the signs of its arrival: "He staggers, shrieks, sinks to the ground. . . ." All the while the other participants are on hand to aid his progress: "he rises again with the help of an assistant."

Finally, the ceremony reaches another crossroads: the possessed begins to speak. The musicians, who both guide and submit to the ebb and flow of the ceremony, set aside their instruments, as the servant of the *lwa* "improvises an air in honor of the god by which he is possessed." In this greatly anticipated moment, prophesies are uttered. Thus, just as the energy of collective performance facilitates the possession itself, the possession in turn lends "irrepressible" power to the ceremony: "According to the attributes of the god that dwells in him," the possessed subject "vaticinates [predicts in chanting style], prophesies, commands, prescribes imperatively."[94] The subject is granted the gift of prophetic language, which also empowers his audience. Indeed, in describing the ceremony Price-Mars's own language takes on a breathless, dramatic tone.

Although prophetic speech emerges as a significant outcome of Vodou possession, Price-Mars emphasizes that these momentary prophets are not great orators in their daily lives. Rather, they become attuned to an "internal voice" that urges them to say things that they would not normally say, that are foreign to them. Delivery ranges from inarticulacy to lofty, elevated speech: "Sometimes in this confusion of words there is a rough meaning which becomes all the more mysterious since it is obscure. Other times, the language is lively and colorful and the hyperdophasia of the subject becomes explicit in elegant terms, well-balanced phrases, even strange dialects, and all of it contrasts oddly with the habitual ignorance of the individual."[95] The "humble peasant" undergoes a ritual transformation, suddenly approaching an eloquence and authority that otherwise elude them. "The person possessed of voodoo, the humble unskilled worker of yesterday who has become suddenly the dwelling place of the Spirit, not only chides, reprimands, prophesizes, but what of the respect and the veneration by which he is heard, obeyed, feared by his entourage?"[96] Such a transformation, enabled by collective effort, provides Price-Mars with a bold vision of modern citizenship. Significantly, in contrast to models of authoritative leadership, Price-Mars provides a portrait of the peasant who "chides" and "prophesizes" while remaining accountable to the collective.

86

WRITING THE CROSSROADS

While Price-Mars is credited with attempting to legitimize Vodou, freeing it from the stigma that fueled imperial violence, here he does even more. His writings constitute an early archive of what Karen McCarthy Brown calls "possession-performances," indicating not a contrived quality, but a vital theatricality.[97] Price-Mars does not aim to decode the elusive practice of possession, but rather to elucidate its form: here, we have a choreography for Black living, where choreography is understood not only as the arrangement of bodies in space, but as a poetics of collective and self-invention. He emphasizes a dynamic interplay between individual and collective transformation, the paradox of intimacy and estrangement where one is both "home and not home" in the body. If, as Claudine Michel and Patrick Bellegarde-Smith write, "during the *sèvis* the invisible and visible interact with surprising intimacy," Price-Mars allows the two to mingle in his description.[98] This more dynamic and even volatile view of the folk ritual bears larger implications for Haiti's modernity and its active role in contemporary anti-imperial struggles.

STRANGE SCENES OF ECSTASY

Price-Mars's analysis goes beyond Haiti to propose a method of "comparative ethnography" for Black diasporic study. Later in the same chapter, he addresses spiritual ecstasy from an entirely different angle: his visit to a Black Baptist church in Washington, DC, in 1910. Led by "insatiable curiosity," Price-Mars recalls witnessing a "phenomenon of the same category" as the Vodou ceremonies that he had just discussed:

> Suddenly, the pastor with haggard eyes, earnest voice, pointed the right hand straight before him and cried out, "There is the Christ!" And the entire congregation turned instinctively toward the imaginary spot where the apparition seemed to be. Then one good woman got up, uttered plaints and lamentations, and danced and sang. Another followed her, another, still another. . . . Soon more than two thirds of the congregation were leaping around in a state of extraordinary exaltation, shouting at the top of their voice, "Oh Lord, have mercy!" But the pastor, who was himself silent during this whole strange scene, signaled that he had something else to say, and little by little calm returned to the flock. Then he extended his hands, implored the forgiveness of Christ for his flock of repentant sheep and the scene ended with a particularly expressive prayer. This lasted a good half-hour.[99]

Price-Mars pivots from Vodou trance to the "zeal of the revived Christian." Here, too, there are specific roles for the pastor and congregation, as well as a dynamic choreography that drives the ritual. All parties work together to assure its success. But despite these similarities, here Price-Mars more bluntly emphasizes his position as an outsider driven by "insatiable curiosity" to observe this scene of worship. Feeling at once out of place and curiously hailed by the performance, he experiences a palpable discomfort: "at the time we were both scandalized and moved by this show of foolery that so severely tried us before some of our American friends. One of them said to us, smiling, 'They were happy.' We only understood much later that our Baptists had been in a state of mystical delirium."[100]

Only in hindsight does Price-Mars fully understand that the worshippers "were happy," a colloquial term akin to "catching the spirit." He then classes them as mystics, putting the performance into the "same category" as the ritual possession that he had studied in Haiti.[101] Thus the strange is made familiar. Yet in his recollection of being "severely tried" in front of his "American friends," in feeling both "scandalized and moved," Price-Mars dramatizes his position as a racialized observer who nevertheless lacks, at least momentarily, the interpretive vocabulary to understand the "strange scene" of spiritual ecstasy. Racial kinship, he suggests, was not enough for him to *get* the performance; he needed a different interpretive framework to engage this provocatively opaque performance of Black spirituality. Certainly, Price-Mars's description of the Baptist service reveals the instability of ethnographic authority from one context to the next. In his momentary reversal of the gaze (he reads Christian "zeal," rather than Vodou, through the prism of strangeness), he might also be seen as providing an ironic critique of the U.S. visions of Haiti as exceptionally strange and primitive. But more than this, Price-Mars suggests that the connections between Afro-diasporic forms were not merely self-evident. They would need to be articulated with great care, often through moments of palpable discomfort.

Here, Price-Mars anticipates Hurston's description of the shouting rituals of the Sanctified church. Hurston draws an explicit connection between spirit possession and shouting: "Then there is the expression known as shouting which is nothing more than a continuation of African 'Possession' by the gods. The gods possess the body of the worshipper and he or she is supposed to know nothing of their actions until the god decamps. This is still prevalent in most Negro protestant churches and is still universal in the Sanctified churches."[102] Beyond an analysis of shouting's provenance,

Hurston offers a breakdown of its form: "broadly speaking, shouting is an emotional explosion, responsive to rhythm. It is called forth by: (1) sung rhythm; (2) spoken rhythm; (3) humming rhythm; (4) the foot-patting or hand-clapping that imitates very closely the tom-tom." Still, shouting may elude the observer's grasp because it is steeped in oppositions. It is both a "community thing" and "absolutely individualistic"; it is both "silent and vocal," choreographed and improvised.[103] Given its outburst at times of spiritual epiphany, shouting accompanies religious conversions and visions—the likes of which Toomer had imagined in *Cane*. Above all, Hurston tells us, shouting has become a form of "protest against the more highbrow church's efforts to stop it."[104]

By saying that shouting is "nothing more than a continuation of African possession," however, Hurston at once deems possession an Afro-diasporic phenomenon and detaches the practice from its historical, political, and regional specificity. In contrast to Price-Mars, she offers no moment of ethnographic hesitancy in classifying these possession performances. Yet she seems equally invested in the challenges of their unruly aesthetics. Having already explored spirit possession and "hoodoo" in the United States, Hurston only intensified her participation in anthropological debates about African retentions with her Caribbean studies. In her writings for the Florida Federal Writer's Project, she remarked that Caribbean migrants in the Gulf were closer to African traditions than their Black American counterparts: "The West Indian Negro generally has had much less contact with the white man than the American Negro. As a result, speech, music, dancing, and other modes of expression are definitely nearer the African."[105] Her transnational studies might be considered as part of her effort to test this theory. However, as we shall see in Hurston's work, Caribbean subjects' supposed mastery of African-derived cultural practices bore mixed implications for their agency and ultimately their citizenship.

"VOODOO AS NO WHITE PERSON EVER SAW IT!": HURSTON IN HAITI

In a 1936 letter to Alan Lomax, Hurston warned that "the Haitians say Seabrook is an awful liar." Hurston was referring to William Seabrook's *The Magic Island* (1929), a text that had "disgusted the Haitian government with Voodoo hunters." She was well aware of Haitian attitudes toward thrill-seeking U.S. travelers. Accordingly, she offered a word of advice to Lomax: "You will please have the Library, in your letters of introduction, ask permission for you to record some songs and not use the general term folk-lore or magic practices. If the letters are not specific, they may think you are another sensation seeker."[106] As Hurston observes in *Tell My Horse*, these suspicions were held not only by the government, but also by "the majority of the Haitian elite, who have become sensitive about any reference to Voodoo in Haiti. In a way they are justified in this because the people who have written about it, with one exception, that of Dr. Melville Herskovits, have not known the first thing about it."[107]

Such remarks are part of Hurston's effort to distance her own work from that of Seabrook and other writers in that sensationalist tradition. Unlike her predecessors, she was not another "sensation seeker," but rather a serious researcher. As she wrote in her proposal to the Guggenheim Foundation, her goal was to "make an exhaustive study of Obeah (magic) practices . . . to add to and compare with what I have already collected in the United States."[108] Hurston saw her fieldwork in Haiti as an extension of what she had accomplished with her first ethnography, *Mules and Men*. Traveling throughout the Gulf States to collect material for that volume, and later as part of her work for the Florida Federal Writers Project, she had observed and remarked upon the cultural influence of the Caribbean on U.S. Southern folk culture. From New Orleans to Key West, a West Indian element was "seeping into Negro folkways."[109] It is not surprising then that Hurston's travels to document folk culture would extend to the Caribbean itself. As Hazel Carby observes, "Hurston's work during this period . . . involves an intellectual's search for the appropriate forms in which to represent the folk and a decision to rewrite the geographical boundaries of representation by situating the southern, rural folk and patterns of migration in relation to the Caribbean rather than the northern states."[110] Hurston certainly had a wealth of material at her disposal. As she explained in a 1937 letter to Henry Allen Moe, "the task is huge, so huge and complicated that it flings out into space more fragments than would form the whole of any other area except Africa. . . . So you can see why a letter is difficult for me. It is like explaining the planetary theory on a postage stamp."[111]

Rewriting the "geographical boundaries of representation" also involved facing new representational challenges. Familiar questions of authority become especially urgent when Hurston faces her distance as a cultural outsider. The publicity for *Tell My Horse* attempted to erase this distance altogether. It exploited reader appetites for the exotic and primitive, while also establishing Hurston's authority as a racial insider. According to these advertisements, what made Hurston's volume distinct from previous studies of Haiti was its Black author. One sensational advertisement in the *New York Times Book Review* on October 23, 1928, exclaimed: "VOODOO as no WHITE PERSON ever saw it!" The ad referred to "the amazing experiences of an actual initiate of Voodoism, whose race enabled her to witness secret ceremonies seemingly incredible in these modern times."[112] Another publicity shot showed Hurston posed in front of a ceremonial drum (figure 2.2).

Unlike her white counterparts, Hurston's blackness presumably trumps her status as a foreigner and grants her unique access to the mysteries of Haitian "Voodooism," which she would then make accessible to white

FIGURE 2.2 Zora Neale Hurston, half-length portrait, beating the hountar, or mama drum, 1937.
Source: Library of Congress, Prints and Photographs Division, LC-USZ62-108549.

readers. Ironically, or perhaps appropriately, the advertisement also contains a statement of praise from Seabrook himself: "I must tell you how terrifically excited I am by this new book of Zora Hurston's," Seabrook gushes. "Papa Legba opened wide the gate for her—and Zora has come through as no white ever could."[113] Seabrook's reference to Papa Legba implies that Hurston is not only a racial, but also a *spiritual* insider. Papa Legba is the *lwa* who grants permission for humans to commune with the spirits at the opening of a Vodou ceremony. To claim that Legba "opened wide the gate for her" is to suggest that Hurston had been granted divine approval.

On the one hand, it is considerably ironic that this praise comes from Seabrook, whose work Hurston had privately criticized. On the other hand, in the pages of *Tell My Horse*, Hurston finds herself making similar claims. The title *Tell My Horse* invokes the signature utterance of an authoritative and subversive spiritual figure—a *lwa* named Papa Gede. In a similar fashion to Price-Mars's use of "so spoke the uncle," the invocation announces the fundamental truth of the pages therein. This approach becomes problematic with Hurston's foray into the realm of occupation politics. Whereas Price-Mars adopts the uncle's truth-telling authenticity to devise an argument against imperialism, Hurston melds folk authenticity with scientific authority to craft a redemptive narrative of the U.S. occupation.

"REBIRTH OF A NATION": HURSTON'S PARABLE
OF THE U.S. OCCUPATION

One hears resonances of Booker T. Washington in Hurston's chapter "Rebirth of a Nation."[114] Hurston's parable of ships describes the historical events that, in her analysis, "brought on" the American occupation: the government-ordered massacre of political prisoners at Port-au-Prince and the subsequent assassination of President Sam in June 1915. In Hurston's view, this disastrous event is the culmination of many years of political corruption and internal disorder. Hurston deploys brutal imagery not merely to document the violence, but to suggest that Haiti itself was like a fragmented, mutilated body, in need of being made whole again: "All that day of the massacre the families washed bodies and wept and hung over human fragments asking of the bloody lumps, 'Is it you, my love, that I touch and hold?' And in that desperate affection every lump was carried away from the prison to somebody's heart and a loving burial."[115] There is a palpable despair and helplessness in this characterization: it is a scene worthy of pity. The Haitian people issue a desperate plea for help that is answered, at long last, by the arrival of white troops in Haiti. Hurston figures the landing of the ship in the language of biblical salvation, with the white U.S. forces cast in a messianic relationship to the Black masses: "One Black peasant woman fell upon her knees with her arms outstretched like a crucifix and cried, 'They say that the white man is coming to rule Haiti again. The Black man is so cruel to his own, let the white man come!' With the bodies in the earth, with the expectation of American intervention, with the prong of such cries in their hearts, the people moved toward the French legation."[116] Hurston imagines that Haitians remain literally and figuratively in this posture of supplication until a symbol of salvation appears: a black plume of smoke on the horizon. It is as if a prophecy had been fulfilled. As Hurston writes, "a prophet could have foretold [peace] was to come to them from another land and another people utterly unlike the Haitian people in any respect. . . . Wait for the plume in the sky."[117]

As it turns out, the plume is a column of smoke emanating from the American battleship U.S.S. *Washington*:

> They were like that when the black plume of the American battleship smoke lifted itself against the sky. They were like that when Admiral Caperton from afar off gazed at Port-au-Prince through his marine glasses. They were so engaged when the U.S.S. *Washington* arrived in the harbor with Caperton in command. When he landed, he found the head of Guillaume Sam hoisted on a pole on the Champ de Mars and his torso being dragged about and worried by the mob. . . . But it should be entombed in marble for it was the deliverer of Haiti. L'Ouverture had beaten back the outside enemies of Haiti, but the bloody stump of Sam's body was to quell Haiti's internal foes, who had become more dangerous to Haiti than anyone else. The smoke from the funnels of the U.S.S. *Washington* was a black plume with a white hope. This was the last hour of the last day of the last year that ambitious and greedy demagogues could substitute bought Caco blades for voting power. It was the end of the revolution and the beginning of peace.[118]

Scholars have appropriately critiqued Hurston's profound misreading of Haitian history and the politics of the occupation. However, her argument remains familiar: Haiti's distress came from "internal foes"; ambition and greed had caused so much corruption among leaders that the only hope for a peaceful future would come from without. Of course, this is a racialized narrative. The saviors would have to be "utterly unlike the Haitian people in any respect"—that is, they would be civilized, devoted to principles of democracy, and (perhaps above all) white. Perhaps the most telling phrase of the passage is its final sentence: "It was the end of the revolution and the beginning of peace." Ironically, peace would be delivered to Haiti via militarization: an American battleship and armed U.S. forces.

No matter how accustomed one is to the engrossing contradictions in Hurston's oeuvre, such a passage is jarring. While *Mules and Men* offered little political commentary, here Hurston supplies both historical narrative and political analysis in a tone of prophetic wisdom. Hurston exhorts readers to imagine that if a "prophet could have foretold" the events that led to the U.S. occupation, that prophet would have been (and in fact *is*) Hurston herself. To perform such omniscient authority, however, Hurston must make herself disappear. Eschewing the first person, this account instead adopts a style of biblical inevitability. Hurston the field worker—a necessarily biased source with her own set of subjective opinions—recedes from view. As she attempts to balance so-called authentic folk wisdom with anthropological objectivity, a third voice emerges—a prophetic one that merges the fundamental truths of the former with the authoritative distance of the latter.

Hurston dramatizes this tension through her well-known metaphor of the "spy-glass of anthropology," which operates, in Autumn Womack's terms, as a "technology of both subjection and elucidation."[119] In the introduction to *Mules and Men*, Hurston admits that although she enjoyed the distinct insider advantage of having been born and raised in the Eatonville community in which she intended to collect folklore, it was "fitting me like a tight chemise. I couldn't see it for wearing it."[120] Thus, she needed to look through the "spy-glass of anthropology" to make full sense of the material that she encountered. While her background granted her closeness to her subjects, her training under Franz Boas provided an interpretive lens and the appropriate critical distance required for legitimate scientific study. Of course, as Karen Jacobs indicates, a spyglass signals "not just the penetrating male gaze of science but the imperial white gaze of colonialism, both of which inform the ambiguous history of anthropology and its consolidation as a discipline in the 1920s and 1930s."[121] The maritime telescope figures remarkably in Hurston's tale of the occupation's onset, in which "Admiral Caperton from afar off gazed at Port-au-Prince through his marine glasses." Beyond embodying the distant imperial gaze, the spyglass here is a tool of militarization. Even as an instrument of observation, the vision that it enables is far from objective: it allows perspective but can be used only "from afar off," and its lens necessarily distorts and limits what is seen.

In her writings on U.S. Black culture, Hurston negotiates the limits of anthropological distance by providing evidence of her participation in the communities that she studies. While it was important to be able to "stand off and look at [her] garment," her construction of authenticity hinged on her ability to reinhabit that cultural garment when the need arose. Such a negotiation enables the double vision that is Hurston's hallmark, which allows her to spy from above while keeping her feet on the ground. Although this duality was part and parcel of the participant-observer method that was becoming widespread by the 1930s, Hurston prided herself on being a step closer to her subjects than her counterparts in the field, who were traditionally white and male. However, her Caribbean studies raised a new challenge. In view of the considerable cultural, national, and linguistic differences that separated her from her subjects, she could not claim the same kind of membership in Haitian folk community as she had in her Eatonville studies. Ifeoma Kiddoe Nwankwo notes that "Hurston's (re)representations of the Caribbean in *Tell My Horse* reflect, belie, and magnify the tensions between community membership, anthropological voice, and cultural and geographical proximity or distance that surface in *Mules and Men*."[122] Because Hurston "explicitly names familiarity as an impetus for her anthropology at home," the question arises of what approach she takes "when that driving force of familiarity is not available to her."[123] Nwankwo observes that in contrast to the largely "dialogic," folksy style of *Mules and Men*, the tone in *Tell My Horse* is "didactic" and "detached," suggesting a "distance from the subject(s) of the Caribbean project."[124] While I agree with Nwankwo that part I of *Tell My Horse*, which begins with a survey of the Jamaican landscape, "recalls traditional anthropologist-as-outsider and objective observer approaches," I argue that the beginning of part II, on Haiti, aims to do something more. Hurston's tone in "Rebirth of a Nation" is not merely didactic and detached—it attempts to merge the storytelling power of the folk and the authoritativeness of ethnographic narrative into a single, prophetic voice.

Such stylistic choices build upon Haiti's mythical status in the Black literary imagination. Haiti's revolutionary history and its epic struggle to achieve nationhood and recognition as the first Black republic in the Western Hemisphere were legendary throughout the diaspora. A special kind of voice was needed as a point of entry into the lofty Haitian story. Hurston crafts a narrative of the U.S. occupation that makes its advent seem inevitable, as much a part of Haiti's destiny as the revolution of 1804. Equally important, "Rebirth of a Nation" also dehistoricizes the U.S. occupation, replacing specificity with timeless universality. As a result of such strategies, Haiti becomes more accessible and malleable to Hurston as both storyteller and researcher, smoothing her own messy entry into a cultural and political sphere that was less familiar to her. Thus, what Hurston wrote about the protagonist of her 1938 novel *Their Eyes Were Watching God* (also written in Haiti) rings true for Hurston herself: "[H]er old thoughts were going to come in handy now, but new words would have to be made and said to fit them."[125]

In the subsequent chapter "Politics and Personalities in Haiti," Hurston sheds her prophetic voice to ask, "So where does [Haiti] go from here?" This open question allows her to speculate on the state of Haitian politics—past, present, and future. Turning to the issue of Haiti's leadership, she remarks, "In the past, as now, Haiti's curse has been her politicians," who are full of "political tricks" and believe "that a national election is a mandate from the people to build themselves a big new house in Pétionville and Kenscoff and a trip to Paris."[126] Hurston's analysis of Haiti's deeply ingrained political corruption does a great deal to reinforce the narratives of salvation. Unlike imperialist rhetoric, however, Hurston also turns to the problem of Haiti's "Race Men," launching a critique of Black leadership that goes beyond Haiti to encompass the United States. Aside from the blatantly corrupt, Haiti had suffered from:

Another internal enemy. Another kind of patriot. . . . The bones of L'Ouverture, Christophe and Dessalines were rattled for the poor peasants' breakfast, dinner and supper, never mentioning the fact that the constructive efforts of these three great men were blocked by just such "patriots" as the present day patriots. . . . These talking patriots, who have tried to move the wheels of Haiti on the wind from their lungs, are blood brothers to the empty wind bags who have done so much to nullify opportunity among the American Negroes. The Negroes of the United States have passed through a tongue-and-lung era that is three generations long. These "Race Men's" claim to greatness being the ability to mount any platform at short notice and rattle the bones of Crispus Attucks; tell what great folks thirteenth and fourteenth amendments to the constitution had made out of us; and *never* fail to quote, "We have made the greatest progress in sixty years of any people on the face of the globe. . . . It made us feel so good that the office-seeker did not give out any jobs."[127]

Hurston objects to a certain brand of "patriot," who built political platforms by invoking the ghosts of Haiti's long-dead revolutionary heroes. However, what bothers her most is not that these patriots have debased the legacy of Haiti's heroes. Rather, she feels disturbed by the prevalence of empty oratory. Although Hurston privileges the oral mode, she makes a distinction between innovative uses of language and the rhetoric of "empty windbags" and "tongue-and-lung" leaders. Such talk was useless because it did not have the power to be transformative: none of this "bone rattling" had served to improve the material conditions of the masses. "What happened in 1804 was all to Haiti's glory," she intones, "but this is another century and another age. . . . The peasants of Haiti are so hungry, and relief would not be difficult with some planning." Broadly, such passages evince Hurston's critique of what Erica Edwards calls Black male charismatic leadership. In her reading of Hurston's 1939 novel *Moses, Man of the Mountain*, Edwards contends that "Hurston uses the literary text to critique common notions of modern black leadership—to contest charisma as a structuring paradigm for Black politics—showing the production of charismatic authority to be a spectacle."[128]

Hurston's comparison of Haitian politicians to "Race Men" in the United States also shows her impatience with narratives of progress. She regards the landmark legislation of the Thirteenth and Fourteenth Amendments as the achievement of a bygone time. It is significant that Hurston singles out these Reconstruction-era amendments mandating emancipation and citizenship, for it was precisely these principles that had been upheld in articulations of resistance to the occupation. The division that she imposes between social equality and economic advancement is reminiscent of Booker T. Washington, even as he too is implicated in her critique of "Race Men." Applied to Haiti, such a division makes it possible for Hurston to view the country's struggle for self-determination as separate from "public education, transportation, and economics," which she claims were improved by the occupation. In the spirit of Washington's imperative to "cast down your buckets where you are," Hurston urges compromise: "So far there has been little recognition of compromise, which is the greatest invention of civilization."[129]

Whereas Price-Mars had warned of the price of compromise years before, Hurston's rewriting of occupation history results in a narrative that Carby labels "reactionary, blindly patriotic, and consequently superficial."[130] Calling attention to the racial dimension of this patriotism, Nwankwo describes Hurston's use of "binaristic blackness," a strategy in which African Americans are raised up and Haitians are concomitantly lowered.[131] Such a tactic is evident in Hurston's bold declaration that, unlike their Haitian counterparts, American leaders were learning to move past empty talk into the realm of action: "But America has produced a generation of Negroes who are impatient of the orators. They want to hear about more jobs and houses and meat on the table. They are resentful of opportunities lost while their parents sat satisfied and happy listening to crummy orators. Our heroes are no longer talkers but doers."[132] However, Hurston does briefly praise a few promising young leaders among the ranks of the Haitian elite. Haiti's potential lay with "a group of intelligent young Haitians grouped around Dividnaud [sic], the brilliant young Minister of the Interior.[133] These are young men who hold the hope of a new Haiti because they are vigorous thinkers who have abandoned the traditional political tricks."[134] Such intellectuals included Louis Mars, Price-Mars's son, and others who were helping to transform the field of ethnography in Haiti. These were men who, as Hurston observes, "admire France less and less, and their own native patterns more."[135] However, these intellectuals had invoked these "native patterns" to oppose the occupation—a point of divergence that Hurston does not address. It was precisely this group to which Price-Mars appealed, and who he hoped would be the key voices of resistance to foreign intervention.

In contrast to Price-Mars's optimism about the power of such a group to change the face of Haitian politics, Hurston ultimately concludes that such intellectuals are scarce, and moreover, "these few intellectuals must struggle against the blind political pirates and the inert mass of illiterates."[136] The description of the Haitian majority as "blind" and "inert" is strikingly reminiscent of the kneeling slave at the feet of Booker T. Washington in the famous statue at Tuskegee. In Hurston's narrative, the duty to lift the veil of ignorance lay not with young Haitian intellectuals (who, she suggests, were not yet as advanced as their American counterparts), but rather with the wise purveyors of American democracy. Hurston seems to align herself with the latter. Again, such alignment reflects as much a rhetorical strategy as Hurston's political views. While she upholds the as-yet-unrealized potential of the Haitian elite, her text is careful not to cede too much authority to them. And this caution does not come from lack of familiarity. As Duck observes, Hurston was "unquestionably acquainted" with prominent figures of the movement, including Price-Mars and Dorsainvil, who "are featured repeatedly as sources in Herskovits's *Life in A Haitian Valley*, which Hurston cites approvingly."[137] At the time of Hurston's visit, Price-Mars's ideas were still being widely discussed and would have been accessible to Hurston, despite the fact that *So Spoke the Uncle* had not yet been translated into English. Yet Hurston does not explicitly reference him, despite the fact that many of the youths she describes were his protégés. Doing so would have troubled the dichotomy that she draws between "vigorous" intellectual energy and anti-imperial resistance.

Instead, Hurston uses another tactic to address the anti-imperial perspective, reconstructing a conversation with an anonymous Haitian man who stands in for all attitudes of opposition to the occupation. The man complains, "We never owed any debts. We had plenty of gold in our bank which the Americans took away and never returned to us. . . . But what can a weak country like Haiti do when a powerful nation like your own forces its military upon us, kills our citizens and steals our money?"[138] After recording a few of these statements (which constitute, as it so happens, an accurate précis of American intervention), Hurston seizes narrative authority, informing the reader that "every word of it was a lie." She goes on to remark that "his statements presupposed that I could not read and even if I could that there were no historical documents in existence that dealt with Haiti. I soon learned to accept these insults to my intelligence without protest because they happened so often."[139]

Hurston's invocation and dismissal of a native informant returns us to Trouillot's inquiry about the value of native discourse: "Anthropology has yet to reach a consensus on both the epistemological status and semiotic relevance of native discourse anywhere. Is native discourse a citation, an indirect quote, or a paraphrase? Whose voice is it, once it enters the discursive field dominated by the logic of academe? Is its value referential, indexical, phatic, or poetic?"[140] Although Hurston dismisses the nameless man's comments as patently untrue and tinged with "self-pity," it is clear that she sees his views as a challenge to her status as an intellectual, which here is inextricably bound up with literacy. Indeed, she holds her ability to read historical documents as a key qualification for discerning truth. This literacy automatically grants her authority in a nation where "so few of the . . . population can read and write." Such an idea appears a surprising reversal of Hurston's usual privileging of orality, local knowledge, and cultural memory. Here, she invites readers to privilege her own written text, not the oral narratives that she records. Among the documents to which Hurston might have referred are the writings of Price-Mars or James Weldon Johnson. By attributing some of their arguments to an anonymous and presumably illiterate informant, Hurston effectively silences interlocutors who might seriously challenge her narrative.

One cannot attribute Hurston's tendency to suppress narratives of resistance to the occupation only to her nationalism or her Americanness. As Duck observes, Hurston's fiction "began to explore the possibility that folklore could be used by corrupt politicians to win the allegiance of persons they plan only to exploit."[141] In particular, she questioned the fitness of the elite to lead the masses, often viciously parodying the self-serving tactics of this very group. At the root of the satire was a sincere doubt that the leadership of a privileged few could ever work toward the best interests of the masses. Such a perspective certainly could have shaped Hurston's view of Haitian politics. However, as I have suggested, I am interested in how this critique is also a part of Hurston's struggle for authority against voices that threaten to silence her.

Stepping into a political arena dominated by male "talk," deploying the tools of a traditionally male discipline, and unable to claim the cultural insidership of a native son, Hurston seems especially anxious about ceding narrative authority. Such a risk crops up in her conversation with a "very intelligent young Haitian woman":

> She asked me if I knew the man I was going to study with. I said no, not
> very well, but I had reports from many directions that he was powerful . . .
> she said I was not to go about trusting myself to people I knew nothing
> about. Furthermore it was not possible for me to know whom to trust without
> out advice. . . . She was as solemn and specific about the warning as she was

vague about what I was to fear. But she showed herself a friend in that she introduced me to an excellent mambo (priestess) whom I found sincere in all her dealings with me.[142]

Although this passage has been read as indicative of Hurston's dramatization of her own vulnerability in the face of "voodoo's potential for malevolent activity," I would posit that the true danger is the reliance on untrustworthy, yet powerful male guides.[143] After learning that Hurston was on her way to the mountains to study Vodou practices with a powerful priest, the woman redirects her by referring her instead to a *manbo*, a female Vodou priestess. By referring Hurston to someone who she knows will be "sincere in all her dealings," the woman "showed herself a friend." This exchange is a departure from the encounters with men that Hurston records throughout the text—which set her up for "lies," "self-deception," and "insults to [her] intelligence."[144] Above all, these encounters threaten to consume her narrative voice. In contrast, Hurston makes sure to note that she and the young woman "had come to be very close to each other. We had gotten to the place where neither of us lied to each other about our respective countries. . . . We neither of us apologized for Voodoo. We both acknowledged it among us, but both of us saw it as a religion no more venal, no more impractical than any other."[145] Basing their talk on honesty and reciprocity, the women develop a level of intimacy akin to the relationship between Janie and Pheoby in *Their Eyes Were Watching God*, which Hurston wrote in Haiti. It is such intimacy—as much as the true religious cross-fertilization between the United States and the Caribbean—that allows Hurston to claim Vodou as her own. Surely, Hurston's attitude toward Haitian religious practices sharply diverges from her grim appraisal of Haitian politics. Contrary to many American assessments of the country's ills, Hurston's narrative contends that "voodoo is not what is wrong with Haiti."[146] I would infer that part of the reason for the difference between Hurston's critique of local politics and her praise of local culture is her awareness that women are excluded from the former and central to the latter. In contrast to the initial chapters that document a largely corrupt, male-dominated political arena, the remainder of her text maps a cultural terrain in which women play pivotal and often subversive roles. It is on such grounds that Hurston finds her footing, uncovering alternative sites of resistance that she had previously seemed to foreclose.

"TELL MY HORSE": SPIRIT POSSESSION AND
CULTURAL AGENCY AT THE CROSSROADS

"What is the truth?" Hurston's chapter "Voodoo and Vodoo Gods" opens
with this sweeping question. By way of an answer, she refers to "a Voodoo ceremony in which the Mambo, that is the priestess, richly dressed is
asked this question ritualistically. She replies by throwing back her veil and
revealing her sex organs. The ceremony means that this is the infinite, the
ultimate truth. There is no mystery beyond the mysterious source of life."[147]
In a dramatic departure from the first part of the text, Hurston's discussion
of Vodou begins, quite literally, with a display of femininity. To be sure,
such a description essentializes the feminine by locating authenticity in the
body, particularly in the ability to give birth to life and truth.

But the passage moves beyond upholding the importance of the essential "truth" to highlight the practical role of women in Vodou ritual. The
mambo is not merely the object of the ceremony; she also controls it. The
mambo holds the power to commune with the *lwa*, to welcome worshippers or to send them away, to either encourage spirit possession or to
check its progress to keep the ceremony on task. Far from being inherent,
such gifts result from years of careful study and practice. The photographs
in the book tell a similar story. Of the individual portraits in the text, all
but one feature women—mostly Vodou priestesses or participants in ceremonies. Over the course of the text, Hurston takes pains to show how these
priestesses are respected, if not revered, for their wisdom and expertise. All
but invisible in the first part of the text, here women play a central role.
(Hurston also dedicates quite a bit of space to describing the importance
of women within the Vodou pantheon itself, especially Erzulie Frieda,
the "pagan goddess of love.")[148]

Hurston also seems interested in the ways in which Vodou ritual—particularly possession—could also empower women who were not Vodou
priestesses. As Price-Mars explains, possession held the power to transform
any worshipper into the "temporary dwelling place of the Spirit."[149] Like
Price-Mars, Hurston allows us to imagine an arena in which the empow-
erment of these women and men is enabled through collective effort. As
Samantha Pinto notes, "No easy community, the possessive audience is
shown to labor before, during, and after a possession, in order to create the
very circumstances of the performance."[150] Hurston lingers on the figure of

Papa Guedé, a humble yet powerful *lwa* who wears tattered clothing and requires no sacrifice other than roasted peanuts and clairin, a locally made rum. Like Uncle Bouqui, the folk hero of Price-Mars's text, Guedé is singled out for praise precisely because he resembles and empowers the people who created him. Unlike Uncle Bouqui, however, the figure of Guedé also holds the potential to transcend gender. Although Guedé is male, women are equally likely to be possessed by him. In turn, they are able to possess some of the truth-telling authority normally granted to men. This concept bears direct implications for Hurston's own narrative authority, as the utterance associated with Guedé *"parlay cheval ou"* ("tell my horse")—becomes the title and guiding trope of the text.

Although *Tell My Horse* abounds with descriptions of *lwa* and instances of spirit possession, Hurston's chapter on Papa Guedé provides the most sustained example of spirit possession as a form of compelling insinuation. She claims that Guedé is "the one *lwa* who is entirely Haitian" and he "sprang up or was called up by some local need." Unlike the other *lwa*, Guedé requires no elaborate ceremonies and no *ounfort* (temple) for his worship. His offerings are humble: "Guedé eats roasted peanuts and parched corn like his devotees. He delights in an old coat and pants and a torn old hat." Smoking a cigar, Guedé cavorts about, drinking and talking. However, his true hallmark is freewheeling speech. Created by the people, he speaks through them and on their behalf: "One can see the hand of the Haitian peasant in that boisterous god, Guedé, because he does and says the things that the peasants would like to do and say." Although invisible, Guedé "manifests himself by 'mounting' a subject as a rider mounts a horse, he then speaks and acts through his mount. . . . Under the whip and guidance of the spirit-rider, the 'horse' does and says many things that he or should never had uttered unridden."[151]

Once Guedé's presence is announced, a stream of derisive speech is sure to follow: "'*Parlay cheval ou*' ('tell my horse') the *lwa* begins to dictate through the lips of his mount and goes on and on. Sometimes Guedé dictates the most caustic and belittling statements concerning some pompous person who is present. A prominent official is made ridiculous before a crowd of peasants."[152] Requiring neither a special ceremonial atmosphere nor the cover of night, Guedé's speeches frequently take place in broad daylight and on the busy city streets where he can find a large and receptive audience. Clearly, this *lwa* is "a deification of the common people of Haiti,"

created by the peasants because "they needed a spirit which could burlesque the society that crushed him."[153] Accordingly, Guedé's favorite object
of critique is the Haitian elite, who frequently attempted to suppress Vodou
worship and looked down on the masses. Guedé belongs to the workers,
the "uneducated Blacks," the folk. And crucially, he also belongs to *women*,
who are otherwise relegated to silence in their everyday lives: "you can
see him in the market women, in the domestic servant who now and then
appears before her employer 'mounted' by this god who takes occasion to
say many stinging things to the boss. You can see him in the field hand, and
certainly in that group of women about a public well or spring, chattering,
gossiping and dragging out the shortcomings of their employers and the
people like him." According to Hurston, "this manifestation comes as near
a social criticism of the classes by the masses as anything in all Haiti."[154]
Nowhere else in the pages of Hurston's text are the masses granted such
agency and subversive speech power.

Hurston coined the term "compelling insinuation" years before her
encounter with Guedé in Haiti. And yet, as Anthea Kraut describes, Hurston's preoccupation with the *lwa* in *Tell My Horse* "reflects an ongoing
interest in the marriage of suggestive embodiment and provocative speech
that she had honed in the various stagings of her musical revue the 'Great
Day.'" Kraut elaborates that Hurston's "staging of choreographed movement
constituted a crucial aspect of her approach to representing the folk."[155]
Hurston framed such choreographic interest in decidedly transnational
terms. For instance, "The Great Day" incorporated a Bahamian fire dance.
Kraut's work urges us to explore how choreography functions broadly in
Hurston's ethnography and fiction. Indeed, Hurston took interest not only
in choreographing the folk, but also in documenting folk culture's various
choreographies in each of the research contexts in which she moved.

Certainly, the "god of derision" offers much in terms of choreography.
Guedé is known for the provocative gyrations of his hips and raucous,
gravity-defying movements. Guedé spirits "stumble but do not fall. Performers catapult themselves in space, plummet toward the ground but
always tilt vertically and stabilize themselves."[156] Because Guedé's jarring
movements often accompany "caustic speech," he emerges not as a mere
folk hero, but also a source of discomfort and reminder of difference.
Representations of Guedé spirits appear often in the Caribbean folkloric
dance repertoire of the 1940s, especially in the choreography of Jean-Léon

Destiné, Geoffrey Holder, and Katherine Dunham.[157] In *Island Possessed*, Dunham recalls being profoundly unsettled by the antics of Guedé, who, on one memorable evening, had chosen as his mount a *mambo* named Téoline, whom Dunham had heretofore regarded as a nurturing teacher and mentor: "I had only once seen her in bad humor. On second thought it wasn't even Téoline, because Guedé was in her head and Guedé and I had never gotten on well together," Dunham recalls. On that occasion, Dunham remembers being accosted by the mount, who used profanity, "smoked a cigar[,] and rudely blew billows of smoke into my face," and most offensively, demanded that she remove her blue corduroy skirt: "Why should I have something better than the others? If I thought myself a *blanc* I shouldn't be there." Dunham's hunch that the spirit possession actually masked the woman's covetous intentions toward her wardrobe ("Now I remembered Téoline fingering my skirt, asking about the material and if such a thing could be found in Haiti") is also, in fact, in keeping with Guedé's purpose: to prompt uncomfortable reflections on one's subject position relative to structures of power.[158]

If Guedé spirits are a site of subversive choreographic possibility in *Tell My Horse*, they live in striking counterpoint to the zombies in the chapter that precedes it. Zombification, Hurston explains, is the process by which normal human beings are reduced to "unthinking, unknowing" shells. Lacking "consciousness of his surroundings and conditions and without memory of his former state" the zombie is also reduced to permanent silence: "He can *never speak again*, unless he is given salt."[159] Only able-bodied victims are chosen since the main motivation is labor. Victims are forced to toil "ceaselessly in the banana fields, working like a beast . . . like a brute crouching in some foul den in the few hours allowed for rest and food."[160] From the perspective of the masses, it was not the zombie that was to be feared, but rather the structures of power that reduced one to such a state. Zombification represented the ultimate threat to subjectivity and agency. Rather than attributing zombie tales to superstition, Hurston's text affirms the existence of these "living dead" and suggests that the masses in general, and women in particular, were especially vulnerable. Hurston even includes a photograph of Felicia Felix-Mentor, an "authentic case." The analogy to chattel slavery is obvious. But modern-day Haitians would have found a contemporary analog not only in the persistence of the plantation labor, but also in the *corvée*, the outdated road labor system revived by the U.S. military during the occupation. In many accounts, the *corvée* represented a form of "zombification" in which the zombie is not a victim of some dark magic, but rather, as Tavia Nyong'o observes, a figure "crushed by the everyday weight of reproducing social life under capital."[161] Despite Hurston's own refusal to critique U.S. intervention, she offers spirit possession as a form of resistance to the zombifying logic of occupation, precisely because it provides its own logic of occupying the body and occupying space and place.

Annette Trefzer avers that spirit possession takes on new significance in light of the imperial drive to zombify populations and "possess" Caribbean territory: "Historically and politically oppressed by Euro-American colonizers, [Haitians] are not only victims but also masters of 'possession.' The performative function of spiritual possession 'frees' Caribbean subjects from their colonial enslavement and imperial surveillance."[162] Furthermore, as Hurston explains, possession by Guedé was especially transformative because it offered not only spiritual affirmation, but also "social consciousness, plus a touch of burlesque and slapstick." In this way, possession is a strategic method of social critique, employed so often and with such zeal that it functions for Hurston as an important form of everyday signifying: "That phrase 'Parlay cheval ou' is in daily, hourly use in Haiti and no doubt it is used as a blind for self-expression.... So one is forced to the conclusion that a great deal of the Guedé 'mounts' have something to say and lack the courage to say it except under the cover of Brave Guedé."[163]

As Mary Renda observes, it might also be said that the phrase "tell my horse" serves as a blind for *Hurston's* self-expression, through which she announces and legitimates her own critique of the political arena in Haiti.[164] Political leadership, in Hurston's view, is marked by "empty talk," "crummy orators," "self-deception," and flat-out lies. There is no concept of majority rule since (according to Hurston) the majority—an "inert mass"— are as yet too ignorant to voice political opinions. Furthermore, unable to read or write, they "have not the least idea of what is being done in their name."[165] It is this prevalence of "empty speech," more than corruption, historical disadvantage, or foreign interference, that Hurston links to Haiti's presumed failure of leadership. In contrast, spirit possession unleashes devastating revelations and "absolutely accurate" readings of the past and future. Political lies explode as Guedé "covers up nothing," considering it his mission to "expose and reveal." Guedé enables a critique of Haiti's class divisions, empowering the masses by allowing them to humble their "betters."[166] Hurston's stance in *Tell My Horse* rests on a telling contradiction: by dismissing the majority as an "inert mass" on one hand and valorizing their folk cultural practices on the other, she constricts the parameters of their resistance.

But as Trefzer contends, "possession as protest definitely works within limits."[167] This scope is nowhere clearer than in Hurston's devastating example of a Guedé possession:

> A tragic case of a Guedé mount happened near Pont Beudet. A woman known to be a Lesbian was "mounted" one afternoon. The spirit announced through her mouth, "Tell my horse I have told this woman repeatedly to stop making love to women. It is a vile thing and I object to it. Tell my horse that this woman promised me twice that she would never do such a thing again, but each time she has broken her word to me as soon as she could find a woman suitable for her purpose. But she has made love to women for the last time. She has lied to Guedé for the last time. Tell my horse to tell that woman I am going to kill her today. She will not lie again." The woman pranced and galloped like a horse to a great mango tree, climbed it far among the top limbs and dived off and broke her neck.[168]

Hurston recounts this story without further comment. But the deadly tale (and Hurston's silence) haunts the remainder of the chapter, naming an ironic and devastating contrast between Guedé's liberating and transgressive performance of sexuality and gender and the limited conditions of possibility for Black queer life in the public sphere. As Omise'eke Natasha Tinsley illustrates, Vodou is a religion that is "radically inclusive of creative genders and sexualities," exemplified not only by Guedé spirits, but by Ezili, the "*spirit of women who love women.*"[169] Given this possibility, where does one place the lesbian in Hurston's text who appears "only at the moment of her death or sacrifice," and with her final breath adopts the speech of the masculinist, heteronormative structures that oppress her?[170] Hurston's designation of the tale as a "tragic case" does not necessarily imply a critique of the circumstances that led to the woman's death. Her words—like Guedé's—are a form of compelling insinuation that hides even as it exposes. And yet at the heart of this story lies an unspoken question: What kind of rupture occurs when folk culture itself becomes a vehicle of coercion and violence, even as its very existence is made possible by nonnormative, transgressive bodies and ways of being?

As Renda observes, even if *"Guedé pas dras"* (Guede is not a sheet), "Guedé's words in Hurston's title may cover up quite a lot, even if they reveal a critical, subversive voice in her text."[171] Unlike Price-Mars, Hurston does not link folk culture to anti-imperial resistance. Indeed, Hurston seems more doubtful that subversive folk practices might lead to political participation, enfranchisement, and ultimately self-determination—especially for the most vulnerable. Ultimately, then, what does compelling insinuation tell us about the potential for social justice, sovereignty, and the simple act of everyday living? If we are to follow Hurston's claim that compelling insinuation is only one part of an unfinished act, a call for the spectator to carry out the suggestions of the performer, then folk culture's transformative or destructive potential depends largely upon its interpretation and use—or, as would become evident in the years that followed, its tragic misuse.

When "Papa Doc" Duvalier rose to power in the 1950s, he exploited the folk cultural aesthetics of Vodou to bolster his authority. As Paul Christopher Johnson notes, "Duvalier's very physiognomy, accoutered in black hat, glasses, and cane as a *Gede*, a member of the spirit family that guards the borders between life and death, and even in speaking in that spirit's typical nasal tones, was a bridge that linked representations of religious power and national authoritarian power."[172] In effect, Duvalier harnessed cultural resonance of the Guedé spirits, while simultaneously suppressing their challenges to power, their unwieldiness, and their queerness. Specifically, Duvalier fashioned himself after Baron Samedi, the leader of the Guedé group of spirits—an austere, exacting, fatherly figure who stood in contrast to the raucous figures that Hurston describes. Having studied as an ethnologist, Duvalier also sought to bolster his scholarly authority by appropriating the teachings of Price-Mars—including his valorization of Vodou and folklore, as well as his anti-imperial politics. In an essay tellingly entitled "Jean Price-Mars, un intellectuel en otage" ("Jean Price-Mars, an Intellectual Held Hostage"), the Haitian novelist Dany Laferrière recalls how *So Spoke the Uncle* was branded in the 1960s by *"les jeunes loups du duvaliérisme"* (the young wolves of Duvalierism). In the hands of Les Griots, which included "Papa Doc" Duvalier, Laferrière recounts, the formulation of a singular, authoritative folk voice became a justification for a dictatorship:

> *Le livre n'avait pas changé d'un iota, mais ses nouveaux lecteurs pensaient y avoir trouvé l'argument majeur pour implanter une dictature en Haïti. Ils faisaient dire au livre de Price-Mars que, d'une certaine manière, un monarque noir valait toujours mieux qu'un colon blanc. En fait, on ne veut ni de l'un ni de l'autre.*

> The book had not changed one iota, but its new readers thought to have found in it a serious argument for implanting a dictatorship in Haiti. They made Price-Mars's book convey that, in a certain manner, a black monarch was always worth more than a white colonizer. In fact, one wants neither one nor the other.[173]

Here, Lafferière conveys a timely reminder that valorization of blackness and folk culture offers no intrinsic guarantee of social liberation. But equally important, he wants to revive the potential in Price-Mars's work (and also, I would add, in Hurston's) for an ethics of collective participation grounded in the practices of folk culture and mass-based resistance. Citing Aimé Césaire's famous figuration of Haiti as the country where *"la négritude se mit debout pour la première fois et dit qu'elle croyait à son humanité"* (Négritude stood up for the first time and said that it believed in its humanity),[174] Laferrière asserts that the Haitian struggle is no narrative of singular mastery but an *"extravagante épopée qui nécessita une participation collective"* (an extravagant epic that requires collective participation).[175]

Neither Hurston nor Price-Mars resolves the significant tensions in their work. On the contrary, their writing registers the difficulties of practicing the kind of collective participation that Laferrière describes. However, in their compelling engagement with spirit possession, we find provocative potential for *rasanblaj*, a Kreyòl term that, as Gina Athena Ulysse explains, is "defined as assembly, compilation, enlisting, regrouping (of ideas things, people, spirits. For example, *fè yon rasanblaj*, do a gathering, a ceremony, and protest), *rasanblaj*'s very linguistic formation resisted colonial oppression." Citing Article 16 of the French Code Noir, which "forbade slaves of different masters to gather at any time under any circumstances," Ulysse asserts the continued significance of *rasanblaj* as a decolonial, interdisciplinary act in the present. Above all, she casts *rasanblaj* as a provocation to "reframe discursive and expressive practices in the Caribbean and diasporas. . . . It calls upon us to think through Caribbean performance and politics, recognizing the crossroads not as destination, but as a point of encounter to then move beyond."[176] *Rasanblaj* usefully extends compelling insinuation, enacting the collective forms of performance implied by Hurston's theory. Crucially, it contains an expression of intent, or as Ulysse frames it, an "awareness of self / position / agenda," the very kind of awareness that authoritative regimes attempt to suppress. As a "point of encounter to then move beyond," it would call for an ongoing reevaluation of the uses of folk culture and the various possibilities that might emerge from it—including possibilities of upheaval and disruption.

The implications of *rasanblaj* for forms of collaboration, translation, and performance are taken up in the second half of this book. In part 1, I have turned to folk culture as a catalyst for literary form through which writers reshape the logics of imperialism. In part 2, I deepen my analysis of embodied practices, poetics, and anti-imperial politics by exploring what happens when Black writers take to the stage or radio themselves. I show how writers and performers such as Eusebia Cosme, Langston Hughes, Nicolás Guillén, Sylvia Wynter, and others gathered in Havana, New York, and London to craft new forms of Black social life centering around their engagements with folk culture. Here, I suggest a mutually constitutive relationship between Black writing and the midcentury performance archive. My use of archival materials and published writings enables a layered approach to performance, showing how discourses of folk culture are advanced, revised, and destabilized by the ephemeral traces of unruly Black bodies.[177]

PART II

Performing the Archive

Chapter Three

"CUBAN EVENING"

Embodied Poetics of Translation in the Work of
Eusebia Cosme, Nicolás Guillén, and Langston Hughes

In February 1946, the dancer, choreographer, and anthropologist Katherine Dunham wrote Langston Hughes with an urgent message: "It is very important for me to see you as soon as possible regarding our forthcoming Cuban affair. Miss Eusebia Cosme and I are anxious to get it started right away."[1] Dunham was eager to forge ahead with preparations for "Cuban Evening: The Poems and Songs of Nicolás Guillén," to take place May 29 at the Dunham School at 220 West 43rd Street. The bilingual program of song, poetry, and dance starred Hughes and Cosme, the acclaimed interpreter of Afro-Cuban poetry. Cosme and Hughes took turns reciting works from the oeuvre of the Cuban poet Nicolás Guillén, with interludes featuring the vocal stylings of Eartha Kitt. "Cuban Evening" played a key role in the promotion of *Cuba Libre*, Hughes's forthcoming translation of Guillén's poems.

But the event also served to showcase the talent of Cosme, who was in the midst of a remarkable run in the United States. Already famous in the Caribbean, she made a splash in 1938 when she performed before a packed audience at Carnegie Hall in New York. The *Pittsburgh Courier* exclaimed, "Harlem's Spanish Section Raves about Cuba's Premier Dramatic Artist, Eusebia Cosme," praising her "interpretive recitals in costume, featuring the work of Negro poets. Critics assert that she runs the entire gamut of human emotions and is proficient in all."[2] The *Chicago Defender* dubbed

her "The Soul of the Tropics," declaring that "you just like to look at her
and hear the sounds whether you know any Spanish or not. She can be
saucy or sad, heartbroken or gay, a slave mother crying for her daughter or
a rhumba dancer, and you're bound to 'catch on.'"[3] Both reviews disavowed
the importance of language, touting the ability of sound and spectacle to
directly transmit an Afro-Cuban or "tropical" experience.

In reality, the racial and cultural significations of Cosme's performances
were far more uncertain. What precisely did it mean to embody the "soul
of the tropics," which by the 1940s had become the subject of countless
exoticized representations on stage? How did Cosme's reception as a Black
performer in the United States compare with her reputation in Cuba, where
her performances came to signify what the anthropologist Fernando Ortiz
called her "*nueva mulatez afirmativa*," her presumed ability to embody
a culturally hybrid national identity?[4] And how might these perceptions
have shifted when Cosme performed alongside Hughes, a celebrated poet-
translator who was becoming known for performative recitations in his
own right? Rather than merely projecting an authentic blackness that tran-
scended language, her recitals show audience and performer engaged in
mutual acts of cultural, linguistic, and formal translation—an ultimately
imperfect process that reveals the unwieldiness of the Black performing
body. Hughes and Cosme's collaboration for "Cuban Evening," therefore,
was not merely a vehicle for the promotion of Hughes's written translations.
Rather, the event compels us to ask about the role of performance in the
linguistic, cultural, and aesthetic work of translating blackness.

This chapter reads Cosme alongside Hughes and Guillén in order to
attend to the intersection of folk culture, performance aesthetics, and
translation in the work of all three artists. Guillén and Hughes, who met in
1930 during Hughes's historic visit to Cuba, are now a familiar and important pairing in work on diaspora and translation.[5] Shortly after their meeting, Hughes published translations of Guillén's poems in journals such as
Opportunity, *The Crisis*, and the *Negro Quarterly*. He also included them
in *The Poetry of the Negro, 1746–1949*, an anthology on which he worked
with Arna Bontemps. In 1948, Hughes and the Howard University professor of Spanish and travel writer Ben F. Carruthers published *Cuba Libre:
Poems by Nicolás Guillén*. The collection incorporated fifty translations,
including Guillén's famous *Motivos de son* in a section titled "Cuban Blues."
Hughes recited these translations with Cosme on at least two occasions:

at the Dunham School for the 1946 "Cuban Evening," and again in 1948 at an event at the Schomburg Library to promote *The Poetry of the Negro*, an event Hughes nostalgically called "a flashback to the twenties."[6] Guillén and Hughes met again in Cuba in 1931, in battle-torn Spain during the Spanish Civil War, and once again in New York in 1949. Throughout his career, Guillén wrote several essays and poems about Black life in the United States, especially in Harlem. And when Hughes died in 1967, Guillén published "Recuerdo de Langston Hughes," an essay in remembrance of his artistic legacy, as well as their friendship.

Here, I build on the work of critics who, turning to Hughes's written translations, have illuminated the challenges and rewards of translating race and anti-imperialist politics across Cuban and U.S. contexts. The Hughes-Guillén pairing finds robust treatment in the work of Vera Kutzinski, who regards *Cuba Libre* "as the literary culmination of the two poets' long-standing friendship" and a "key chapter in the history of hemispheric cultural relations."[7] Deepening our knowledge of the way that "blackness travels" in interwar literature, Ryan Kernan astutely argues that "the work of these authors exemplifies how Guillén and Hughes created a poetics by being put in conversation with each other and is illustrative of how diasporic poetics develop intertextually."[8] What would it mean to read the 1946 program "Cuban Evening" as a different kind of artistic culmination—one that helps us attend to what we might call the "poetic performance of translation"?

Considering performance alongside written translation, this chapter moves beyond the Hughes–Guillén pairing to reveal a larger circle of collaborators, including artists such as Cosme, whose work limns the performative dimensions of the literary movement known as *afrocubanismo*. Cataloguing the salient poetic figures of that 1930s literary movement, the poet Nancy Morejón states, "There wasn't a woman, with the exception of the reciter and actress Eusebia Cosme."[9] However, if Morejón's words indicate the scant opportunities for women on the literary scene, they are also a reminder of the ways in which *Afro-Cuban* poetics extended beyond print culture. During the 1930s and 1940s, live recitation served as an important vehicle for the dissemination and translation of Hispanophone poetry. As Licia Fiol-Matta observes, "Afro-Antillian poetry was written with performance in mind, to be executed by black diseurs and diseuses who could supposedly convey authenticity because, being black, they were taken to be more proximate to the poetry (the two most famous were the Puerto Rican Juan Boria and the Cuban Eusebia Cosme)."[10] As we shall see, what it meant to "convey authenticity" was often also gendered, and furthermore, highly contingent upon the racial and cultural definitions held by performers and spectators. Attending to the fact that poetry was "written with performance in mind"—and not merely inspired by performance—requires very specific attention to the poem's complicated life beyond the page.

To begin our inquiry with "Cuban Evening" is first to read poetic recitation as a *specific mode* of performance—one that more directly reveals the provocative tensions between page and stage. Of course, this event is only one of several points of entry into the poetics and politics of performance. In a broad sense, performance was a hallmark of the work of both Hughes and Guillén. Soon after his meeting with Hughes in 1930, Guillén published *Motivos de son* (*son* motifs), a book of eight *criollo* poems written in Cuban vernacular and in the spirit of the *son*, the popular Afro-Cuban dance music that began in the late 1800s but spread internationally in the 1930s. The book thrust him into national prominence, causing—as he writes with evident satisfaction in one letter to Hughes—"*un verdadero escándolo*" (a veritable scandal) in Havana.[11] Some critics too hastily attribute the conception of Guillén's debut effort to Hughes's "immediate" and "transcendent" influence[12] as a blues poet from Harlem, perhaps echoing Guillén's contemporary Gustavo E. Urrutia, who hyperbolically assured Hughes that Guillén's *son* motifs "are the exact equivalent of your blues."[13] While such statements of equivalence attempt to establish the music of the masses as the common ground of this Harlem–Havana encounter, they also erase key differences between the technical aspects of the two genres, their performance, and their literary adaptation.

However, there is another significant difference between Guillén's and Hughes's poetic influences and impact: in 1930s Cuba, the Spanish Caribbean, and Latin America at large, *poesía negra* began to be supported by a tradition of *declamación*, with no precise equivalent in the United States. As Jill Kuhnheim explains, *declamación* is "not simply recitation . . . but the physical and aural enactment of written poems."[14] A formal discipline linked to theater and music that often incorporates movement, gesture, and elaborate costuming, *declamación* allowed performers to shape the meanings of the poems they recited—indeed to translate them into a different medium. Thus, while Guillén was influenced by the rhythms of *son* and the cadences of *criollo* (creole) speech, his work was in turn interpreted by reciters in elite venues far removed from the streets of Havana. Cosme was the most famous of these performers. In several interviews, she frames her discovery of Guillén's work as an artistic epiphany. She notes that in her early career, "I was reciting white poetry; until one day when a book of *poemas negros* by Nicolás Guillén fell into my hands, and, upon reading them, I felt as if something that had been silenced, dormant for centuries, was suddenly awakened inside of me. Since then I have been decidedly inclined toward this literary genre."[15]

Through a U.S. racial lens, it would be easy to misconstrue Cosme's juxtaposition of "*poesías blancas*" and "*poemas negros*." Many authors of *poemas negros*—a transnational genre characterized by the use of racialized themes and forms—were in fact white, and some of them, such as the Puerto Rican poet Luis Palés Matos, continued to be a staple of Cosme's repertoire. Thus, this anecdote does not merely recall her fortuitous discovery of her roots, but rather her conscious decision to participate in a literary movement. Although framed in personal terms, Cosme's reference to "something that had been silenced" must also be viewed in a broader social context—in light of a public sphere that had historically criminalized Afro-Cuban artistic expression. In the late nineteenth through the early twentieth centuries, *son* music was a source of enormous controversy, prompting not only the public disdain of the elite classes, but also legislation banning its playing in public. Special ire was reserved for its key instrument, the *bongó* drum. In 1900, for example, a Havana mayoral decree prohibited the public playing of drums of African origin, and in 1929, the Cuban government condemned the *bongó* specifically. These bans emerged partly in response to the musical activities of the *cabildos de nación*, African mutual aid societies that emerged during slavery and whose customs were increasingly adopted by Cuban whites, to the dismay of many Cuban leaders.[16] Reporting approvingly on the 1929 ban, the *New York Times* warned of the *bongó's* role in a dangerous and elusive "jungle wireless" system. *Son* came to represent an integral, yet disavowed presence in Cuban culture: a disruptive sonic reminder of Cuban blackness.

By the 1930s, however, the use of Afro-Cuban forms as inspiration for literature was far from unusual. Race was becoming a regular (if controversial) part of public discourse, thanks to the contributions of Guillén and others to the column "*Ideales de una raza*," edited by Urrutia, which appeared in Havana's leading daily newspaper, *Diaro de la Marina*. What is remarkable about Cosme's "discovery," then, is the role that she imagines for herself as a Black woman. Cosme's turn to *declamación* also reflected her limited options in Cuba where, as Magali Roy-Féquière bluntly states, "to become a serious actress in the theatre arts one had to be white."[17] Cosme also recalls how, as a child, she enjoyed assisting the dramatic productions that came to her neighborhood in Santiago de Cuba, aspiring to someday grace the stage herself. However, she remembers thinking that "being a *niña negra*, I'd never be able to step onto those stages."[18] While Cosme ultimately emphasizes her triumph over circumstance, her comment registers her awareness of the limited opportunities available to Black women in the dramatic arts. However, far from being a lesser alternative to a career in drama, *declamación* offered her unique opportunities to shape the dissemination of Afro-Cuban poetry. More than simply amplifying the words of the male poets in her repertoire, Cosme's work makes salient the gendered dimensions of poetic translation and performance in ways that disrupt masculinist narratives of transnational poetics.

Cosme's international reputation in *declamación* made her a natural choice to appear in "Cuban Evening" alongside Hughes, who by the 1940s had also adopted recitation as an important part of his poetic practice. A playwright and songwriter, Hughes not only looked to Black folk performance—particularly blues, jazz, and vernacular speech—as formal and thematic inspiration for his poetry. He also famously recited his poetry to the accompaniment of jazz bands. Meta DuEwa Jones deftly explores "the critical role of vocal instrumentality and performance for assessing the nuances in the gendered, racialized, and sexualized innovations evident in [Hughes's] blues and jazz aesthetic."[19] Hughes collaborated with jazz musicians, performing selections from *The Weary Blues* and *Ask Your Mama: 12 Moods for Jazz*. But what was the relationship between Hughes's interest in poetic recitation and his translation work? What dynamics and considerations were at play when he recited his translations of Guillén's poems, and how did Hughes's more subdued performance style compare to Cosme's dramatic recitations? Finally, how did recitations of Guillén's poems—performed by Cosme, Hughes, and himself—shape understandings of Guillén's oeuvre across space and time?

To address these questions is also to acknowledge the asymmetry of the comparison at hand, and to address the silences in the archives of midcentury Black performance. Juxtaposing Cosme, Hughes, and Guillén raises certain methodological challenges. Unlike Guillén and Hughes, Cosme did not leave a substantial written archive (of her own publications), and there are few extant recordings of her early work. We are left instead with what Antonio López (citing Édouard Glissant) terms *fragments arrachés* that, in the absence of a definitive master object of critical attention, make the enterprise of writing about her both a challenge and rewarding."[20] López's chapter is one of the most comprehensive treatments of Cosme's professional trajectory, and scholars such as Takkara Brunson, Viviana Gelado, Jill Kuhnheim, and Emily Maguire also play a key role in her recuperation. I join in these recuperative efforts by piecing together details of Cosme's collaboration with Hughes and Guillén from fragments in the archive. One such fragment is "Cuban Evening," which has received only passing mention in previous scholarship. While there are no existing recordings or reviews of the event, I turn to correspondence, the event program, and importantly, to the repertoire of poems recited both in Spanish and in English by Cosme and Hughes.

By turning to this fleeting moment in literary and performance history, I excavate a poetics of *interruption*. I borrow "interruption" from Guillén's sweeping, satirical poem about exploitative sugar plantation labor and tourism in the wider Antilles, "West Indies, Ltd."[21] Halfway through Guillén's caricature of political corruption, racial hypocrisy, and ravenous tourists who "*Viene comerse el cielo azul / regándolo con Bacardí*" (Come to munch our blue sky / and wash it down with Bacardi) (41–42), a voice intervenes, disrupting the flow of the poem: "*Cinco minutos de interrupcion. La charanga de Juan el Barbero toca un son*" (Five minutes of interruption. The band of Juan the barber plays a *son*). This italicized announcement reads like a musical cue signaling a radical change in form:

De la caña sale azúcar,	From cane comes sugar,
azúcar para el café;	Sugar for coffee;
de la caña sale azúcar,	From cane comes sugar;
azúcar para el café:	Sugar for coffee:
lo que ella endulza, me sabe	That which it sweetens, [tastes] to me
como si le echara hiel.	Like they've put in bile.

This expression may very well be the same voice from the cane fields that sounds earlier in the poem, where, "*de entre la oscura / masa de pordioseros que trabajan,/surge una voz que canta,/brota una voz que canta/sale una voz llena de rabia,/se alza una voz antigua y de hoy,/moderna y bárbara:/Cortar cabezas como cañas,/¡chas, chas, chas!"* (From among the dark/mass of paupers who work,/surges a voice that sings,/sprouts a voice that sings/comes a voice full of rage,/rises a voice ancient and from today,/modern and barbaric:/Cut heads like cane stalks,/chas, chas, chas!). As a counterpoint, or perhaps a compliment to this militant eruption, the *son* that follows approaches the melancholy of blues:

Me matan, si no trabajo	They kill me, if I don't work
y si trabajo, me matan:	And if I work, they kill me:
siempre me matan, me matan	They're always killing me, killing me
¡siempre me matan!	They're always killing me!

The interruption occurs three times, serving to bring about the poem's climax, in which (as an "American Union cruiser" looms offshore) "a clear, a clear and lively/*son* of hope erupts over the land and ocean." Rather than reading this line as a triumphant ending, in which the *son* serves as a harbinger of revolutionary hope, I would like to focus on the more modest and elusive function that it serves in the poem as Guillén labels it: an "interruption," an interlude not unlike the narrator of Ralph Ellison's *Invisible Man* experiences when, without warning, he descends into the "silence of sound," guided by Louis Armstrong's voice.[22] In both instances, the significance of the interruption lies in the music's ability to alter the time space of the narrative, introducing other forms of subjectivity and ways of knowing—however ephemeral this moment may be.

Such an interruption is all the more potent due to the ways that Cuban music and *son* in particular has circulated both as a commodity in the United States and a sign of racial harmony within Cuba itself. Attending to a poetics of interruption compels us to listen again—to hear the cry of rage and taste the bitterness of the music, confronting the very forms of subjectivity that are threatened by erasure not only by dubious interests, but sometimes by the very act of translation itself. Guillén's poetics of interruption is an apt figure for the modes of poetic and performative intervention that I highlight in this chapter. The *son* affects what Kandice Chuh calls the "interruptive function of aesthetics," in which sound interrupts the social order, causing familiar tropes—in this case, those of tourism and American

commerce—to veer momentarily off course.[23] Locating a poetics of interruption in Black sonic culture, Andrew Brooks argues that "an interruption
is a cut or break that produces a movement toward disequilibrium and
change. While an interruption might occasionally produce a spectacular
rupture that commands attention, more often than not it passes unnoticed,
a fleeting interference that is felt without being consciously registered."[24]
"Cuban Evening" serves as one such "fleeting interference" into the literary
historical record—an ephemeral yet significant interruption of the familiar
narrative of Guillén and Hughes's collaboration, as well as of masculinist
narratives of diasporic collaboration more generally. "Interruption" might
also describe ways that recitation and *declamación* disrupt poetic meaning, leading to more nuanced understandings of Cuban poetics. Whereas
the interrupting voice in "West Indies, Ltd." is male (as *soneros* traditionally are), the performances of Cosme in particular and women reciters in
general interrupt the very understandings of collaboration, authenticity,
and race that spectators and critics brought to their work. Rather than
merely amplifying the voices and politics of the male poets whose work
she recited, Cosme's performances serve as acts of translation that produce
a "movement toward disequilibrium," disrupting what we think we know
about the archives of Black internationalism.

"Cuban Evening" provides a valuable lens through which to glimpse the
interplay between performance and translation in the careers of Cosme,
Guillén, and Hughes. In distinct ways, each artist attends to the translation of Black folk culture—or as Guillén phrased it, interpreting "*asuntos
de los negros y del pueblo*" (the affairs of Blacks and the people).[25] If, as
Brent Hayes Edwards posits, "The cultures of black internationalism can
only be seen *in translation*," then to what extent does performance further
extend or disrupt this process of linguistic and cultural exchange?[26] Here, it
is necessary, as Edwards suggests, to "differentiate among *kinds* of translation, with the understanding that any and all may be at work in any given
instance under analysis."[27] For Cosme and Hughes especially, translation
was not only linguistic and cultural, it was also a matter of form—as evident in the interpretive shift from embodied performance to the printed
page and back again.

A provocative example of various forms of translation simultaneously
at work appears in "Conversación con Langston Hughes" ("Conversation with Langston Hughes"), an interview conducted and published

by Guillén in *Diario de la Marina* during Hughes's visit in 1930. Guillén suddenly interrupts Hughes's lengthy description of his recent literary activities to ask about the race problem in the United States. " '¿Cómo ve usted'—le pregunto—'el problema de razas en los E.U., en lo que toca a la negra? ¿Se adelanta en la solución? Me gustaría conocer lo que usted opina.' " ('How do you perceive'—I asked him—'the race problem in the United States, as far as it concerns the Negro? Is a solution close at hand? I want to know your opinión.')[28] This interruption is the only formal question in Guillén's published interview. Hughes takes his time to respond to Guillén's inquiry:

> The poet smiles. He fingers his school ring with its shining emblem, and finally responds: "Look, I'm not a social scientist. I've never studied for that. I'm simply a poet. I live among my people, I love them; every blow that is dealt them hurts me as well and I sing their pain, translate their sorrows, give flight to their worries. All this I do in the manner of the people, with the same ease with which the people have done. Do you know that I've never been preoccupied with studying the rules of classical verse? I am sure that I've never written a sonnet, you know? What I write comes from within. I don't study the Negro, I feel him."[29]

What is perhaps most remarkable about Guillén's description of Hughes is what remains unsaid. Guillén lends irony to Hughes's hyperbolic disavowal of classical verse, as well as his claim that he does not "study" the Negro by describing Hughes's shining university ring. Contrary to Hughes's self-fashioning as a poet of the people, such a gesture in fact suggests a distance from his subject and hints at the ways in which artists are in fact students and producers of culture. Guillén's subtle framing encourages us to read Hughes's connection to the Black masses not as merely organic, but as an articulated connection that must be spoken and written into existence—in short, one made possible through acts of translation.

Indeed, Hughes's own phrase "translate their sorrows" (*traduzco sus tristezas*) emphasizes a process of interpretation. For Hughes, to translate is not merely to represent, but rather to transform (in this case, into another medium). As William Scott phrases it, "Hughes wants to rethink expression as a dismantling of representationality."[30] Indeed, even Hughes's imperative to "sing their pain" and "give flight to their worries" veers away from straightforward representation and instead approaches a politics of translation, where the very act must be understood as marking a transformative nonequivalence with the original. In more than one sense, Hughes's poetic vision concerns attending to that which cannot be represented—whether it is the "pain" of the people or, as Hughes's reframing of Guillén's question shows, the "race problem in the United States." This passage allows us to regard Hughes (and ultimately Guillén and Cosme) not merely as authentic ambassadors of the Black masses, but rather as interpreters who made specific choices as they carried meanings from one context to another.

"Conversación con Langston Hughes" thus suggests the mediated nature of all literary depictions of folk culture—which also was a salient point of Hazel Carby's well-known critique of the politics of authenticity in Zora Neale Hurston's work.[31] But what is at stake in framing these depictions as translations: reading a *son*-poem as a translation of a of an Afro-Cuban musical form, or understanding poetic recitation as a translation of a poem that relies on visual and sonic cues as much as it does the words on the page? In the case of Hughes, I hope to show how these cultural and formal modes of translation are intertwined with the linguistic choices that he made as he sought to translate Guillén's poetry from Spanish to English.

This chapter approaches translation first in a linguistic sense: comparing Hughes's translations with Guillén's Spanish originals to provide insight into the politics of race, gender, and anti-imperialism that informed Hughes translation practice. However, unlike previous discussions, I mainly limit my focus to the poems that Hughes recited during "Cuban Evening." The fact that Hughes saw "Cuban Evening" as connected to his forthcoming volume of translations is evident in his handwritten notes in the draft of the manuscript, in which he marks poems "used on Katherine Dunham program" (figures 3.1–3.2).[32] The subtle changes between these drafts and the final versions suggest that Hughes's live recitations served, quite literally, as one forum for the rehearsal of his developing translation aesthetic.

Cosme, who interpreted Guillén's poems before U.S. and Latin American audiences, was no less engaged in acts of translation. Just as Guillén's anecdote shows how a simple gesture—such as the fingering of a university ring—can suggest a different meaning from the words that Hughes uttered, Cosme's embodied performances produced new poetic meaning.

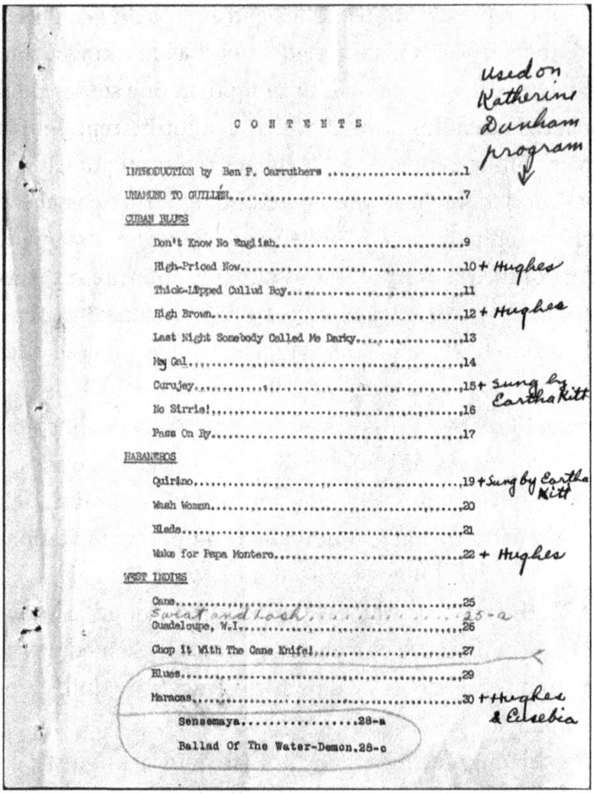

CONTENTS

Used on Katherine Dunham program

FIGURE 3.1 *Cuba Libre*, selection of poems used for Katherine Dunham "Cuban Evening Performance," 1946. *Source*: Langston Hughes Papers, James Weldon Johnson Collection in the Yale Collection of American Literature, Beinecke Rare Book and Manuscript Library, Yale University, New Haven, CT.

Here, I do not take for granted the ability of performance to transcend language, as many of Cosme's reviewers suggest. On the contrary, in many cases, the nuances of the language—that is, its social and historical resonances—would have been lost in translation. However, exploring the ways that Cosme interpreted a sense of so-called Afro-Cubanness or tropicality before various national audiences reveals much about how concepts of Cubanness circulated and changed, especially through the voices and embodied performances of women. As I will argue, the juxtaposition of Hughes and Cosme on the "Cuban Evening" program attunes us not only to linguistic difference, but also contrasting ways of representing the Black voice and body.

KATHERINE DUNHAM

Stages a Cuban Evening

STARRING EUSEBIA COSME AND LANGSTON HUGHES •
WITH SONGS BY EARTHA KITT • DANCES BY LUCILLE
ELLIS AND TOMMY GOMEZ • MUSIC BY CANDIDO, JULIO,
LA ROSA AND REYES • SETTINGS BY ELSA KULA — TO
PRESENT THE POEMS OF NICOLÁS GUILLÉN.

NICOLÁS GUILLÉN

Nicolás Guillén, Cuban poet, friend of the Gypsy, Garcia Lorca,
is highly regarded wherever Spanish is spoken. Spanish and
Cuban critics find in him a creative genius who makes vivid the
folklore of Cuba and protests the wrongs inflicted on common
people. A vigorous writer fighting against vapidity, Guillén has
put iron into Cuban literature. Afri-Cuban poetry is meant to
be read aloud and that of Guillén is brilliantly recreated by
Eusebia Cosme.

EUSEBIA COSME

Eusebia Cosme has dedicated herself to interpreting the rhythmic,
sultry, sometimes acid verse of her Cuban countrymen. She is
widely appreciated in Cuba and has triumphed in Puerto Rico,
Santo Domingo, Venezuela and Mexico. In the United States
she has appeared in New York, Chicago and Washington. Radio
and motion pictures take most of her time but she is at her
best before a visible audience. Wednesday night she is assisted
by Langston Hughes.

LANGSTON HUGHES

Langston Hughes, poet, is the author of Fine Clothes to the Jew,
The Weary Blues, Shakespeare in Harlem, The Dream Keeper,
The Ways of White Folks, Not Without Laughter, The Big Sea.
Mr. Hughes is ". . . one of the few young writers in America
whose work has kept pace with a growing reputation." Together
with Ben Frederic Carruthers, Langston Hughes has translated
into English selections from the poems of Nicolás Guillén.

8:30 WEDNESDAY EVENING, MAY 29
220 WEST 43rd STREET — TELEPHONE LO 5-0013

Program

KATHERINE DUNHAM

presents

Cuban Evening

The Poems and Songs of Nicolás Guillén

EUSEBIA COSME
Balada de los dos Abuelos
José Ramón Cantaliso
Balada del Guije
Sensemtro de la mujer de Antonio

LANGSTON HUGHES
Song of the Bongo
Wake for Papa Montero
Sabas
Maracas

EUSEBIA COSME
Maracas

CANDIDO, JULIO, LA ROSA and REYES
RICHARDENA JACKSON
Maracas—Santiago de Cuba............Music by Marcedo

INTERMISSION

LANGSTON HUGHES
Little Ode to a Cuban Negro Boxer
WALTER NICKS
Diablitos—Cuban Ritual
EUSEBIA COSME
Simón Caraballo
Pregón
Sensemayá

LA ROSA
The Novice Is Possessed by a Snake
EARTHA KITT
Quirino . . . .] Music by Greuet
Curujey . . . .]
EUSEBIA COSME and LANGSTON HUGHES
Mulata—Langston Hughes
Bucaté Plata—Eusebia Cosme
Me Vendo Caro—Langston Hughes
Bito Manué—Eusebia Cosme

Settings by Elsa Kula

FIGURE 3.2 "Cuban Evening" program. *Source:* Eusebia Cosme Papers, Schomburg Center for Research in Black Culture, New York.

"CUBAN EVENING"

If Dunham's correspondence with Guillén is any indication, "Cuban Evening" was a resounding success. As she explains to Guillén on June 18, 1946, she became familiar with his works through Hughes's cotranslator, Ben F. Carruthers, who was then serving as a Spanish instructor on the faculty of the Dunham School's Cultural Studies Division. (Following Dunham's philosophy of holistic dance education, all students observed an academic curriculum.)[33] Guillén's works, Dunham writes, "impressed my [sic] deeply since I am concerned with bringing Cuban culture and folklore to the institution of which I am founder. So deeply impressed, in fact, that I staged a 'Cuban Evening' here in one of the studios and because of the many request [sic]

I received, I repeated the affair with equal success."[34] Indeed, "Cuban Evening" was staged twice at Dunham's Broadway studio, debuting on May 17 and with an encore on May 29. Although Dunham's work had long centered on Caribbean themes, Cuba was not originally on the itinerary of places that she visited when doing ethnographic research in the 1930s.[35] During a later trip, the anthropologist Fernando Ortiz introduced her to the Cuban percussionists La Rosa Estrada and Julio Mendez.[36] Estrada and Mendez joined the "Cuban Evening" program, along with the drummer Cándido, dancers Lucille Ellis and Tommy Gomez, and finally, the singer Eartha Kitt, who was then a student at the Dunham school. Later that year in Bal Nègre, Dunham's company, backed by the music of the Cuban composer Gilberto Valdés, performed the suite "Motivos," which included the numbers "Rhumba" and "Son."

Given Dunham's interest in Cuban folk culture, spirituality, and music, her turn to the poetry of Guillén (and her recruitment of Hughes and Cosme) made a great deal of sense. The event was one of several collaborations between Hughes and Dunham. In a 1941 letter to Carl Van Vechten, Hughes confides: "Did I tell you I did a libretto of THE ST LOUIS BLUES for Katherine Dunham? A danceable story woven around the song? Hope she uses it. But she rather thinks she ought to do Latin American things— Cuba, Brazil, etc. Easier to sell to concert managers and to Hollywood."[37] Among the factors at play in Dunham's development of a "Latin American" repertoire was the simple matter of marketability. Like other Black artists of the era, Dunham participated in what Shane Vogel calls the "Caribbean faddishness occupying Manhattan supper clubs, U.S. airwaves, and Broadway stages."[38] At the same time, Vogel argues, Dunham often "tried to transform a stock bit of Broadway exotica by bringing to it some anthropological detail and Caribbean movement (by which I mean Caribbean history)."[39] Dunham's stagings resulted from what VèVè Clark has termed Dunham's "research-to-performance" method—an approach that involved extended fieldwork, participation in local rituals, and collaboration with Caribbean artists prior to their incorporation in choreography.[40] However, Dunham did not aspire to merely duplicate the folk forms that she observed. Rather, Dunham sought to produce "stylized depictions" of Black life, adaptations that showed her own choreographic imprint.[41]

Dunham's company set the tone for the interplay of poetics, music, and embodied performance in "Cuban Evening." But the event differed from others in the school's repertoire, in that poetic recitation took center stage. Guillén's poems did not function as a backdrop or an interlude between acts, but rather as *the* featured element of the performance. Indeed, the staging of the event encouraged the audience to regard poetic recitation as embodied performance and of equal theatrical importance to the dance and song numbers alongside it. It was fitting, then, that Cosme would be a star of the evening. Although Hughes is often credited with introducing American readers to the work of Guillén, Cosme had introduced Guillén to even broader audiences in her critically acclaimed performances throughout the United States, Europe, and Latin America, as well as on her 1940s CBS radio broadcast "The Eusebia Cosme Show," in which she also read works by Hughes and Paul Laurence Dunbar translated into Spanish. Cosme and Guillén also remained close personal friends. Guillén had dedicated his poem "Balada del Guije" ("Ballad of the Water-Demon") to Cosme, and when she returned to Cuba in 1952, having been established as one of the most sought-after interpreters of *la poesía negra*, he published "Regreso de Eusebia Cosme" ("The Return of Eusebia Cosme"), an essay marking the occasion. To "Cuban Evening," then, Cosme lent international fame as well as a rigorous work ethic honed from her theatrical training. As costume designer (and Dunham's husband) John Pratt informs Hughes matter-of-factly, "Eusebia Cosme has decided to have sort of final rehearsal and run-through Thursday evening at 9:00 o'clock."[42]

Another key figure in the conceptualization of "Cuban Evening" was Carruthers. While Dunham credits Carruthers with introducing her to the work of Guillén, he also enthusiastically promoted the work of Cosme, who had been the subject of several of his published and unpublished writings. Carruthers wrote the biographical notes that appeared in the program, which were largely drawn from a November 1945 essay in *Theatre Arts* entitled "Eusebia Cosme and Nicolás Guillén." While he begins by calling Guillén a "great revolutionist in Spanish West Indies verse," he soon pivots to the importance of performance: "Afro-Cuban poetry such as Guillén's is meant to be recited aloud—dramatized; and his poetry nowadays creates a sensation wherever it is read, especially in those places where it has been recreated by Eusebia Cosme, high priestess of poetry recitals, who has dedicated her career to interpreting the rhythmic, sultry verse of her countrymen."[43] Cosme did not merely recite, but "dramatized," "recreated," and "interpreted"—phrases that point to a translation aesthetic, where translation might be understood as both a linguistic and an expressive act. In the "Cuban Evening" program, Carruthers changes the phrase to "interpreting the rhythmic, sultry, *sometimes acid* verse of her countrymen" (emphasis mine), hinting, perhaps, at the acerbic tone of some of the selections for "Cuban Evening." He makes a similar addition to Guillén's introduction, adding that Guillén "put iron in Cuban literature," a phrase that indicates more hardness than harmony.

For his part, Hughes was eager to promote his forthcoming translation of Guillén's poems, *Cuba Libre*, on which he had been working, with the aid of Carruthers, for more than a decade. The program was ambitious. In the first half of the affair, Cosme and Hughes took turns reading in Spanish and English, respectively, while a musical interlude (featuring percussion followed by orchestral music) led into the intermission. The second half featured dance numbers; two poems, "Quirino" and "Curujey," set to music by the Cuban composer Eliseo Grenet and sung by Kitt; and a finale entirely in Spanish—in which Hughes and Cosme alternated reciting poems in Cuban vernacular.

Cosme opened with *"Balada de los dos abuelos"* ("Ballad of the Two Grandfathers"). It was a selection that she performed often at her U.S. engagements. As the *Amsterdam News* misleadingly declared of her 1939 performance at Town Hall, "she opened her bill with 'Balada de los dos abuelos' in which the poet recalls his grandfathers, one white and one colored, and sings a hymn to racial tolerance and amity."[44] What the *Amsterdam News* calls "racial tolerance" was more precisely cultural hybridity, as symbolized by the tearful embrace of the two grandfathers at the close of the poem. However, the core of the poem is less harmonious, featuring a stanza invoking the Middle Passage and the specter of the sugar plantation:

¡Qué de barcos, qué de barcos!	So many ships, so many ships!
¡Qué de negros, qué de negros!	So many Negroes, so many Negroes!
¡Qué largo fulgor de cañas!	What a vast glow of cane fields!
¡Qué látigo el del negrero!	What a whip has the slave trader!
Piedra de llanto y de sangre,	Blood? Blood . . . Tears? Tears.
venas y ojos entreabiertos,	Half-opened veins and half-opened eyes,
y madrugadas vacías,	And empty mornings,

y atardeceres de ingenio,	And sunsets at the sugar mill,
y una gran voz, fuerte voz,	And a great voice, a strong voice,
despedazando el silencio.	Bursting the silence.
¡Qué de barcos, qué de barcos,	So many ships, so many ships,
qué de negros!	So many Negroes!

(TRANSLATION BY HUGHES AND B. F. CARRUTHERS)[45]

Far from serving as evidence of a painful past now long over, the imagery of ships (*barcos*) and cane (*cañas*) in this stanza also invokes the contemporary reality of U.S. imperialism in the Caribbean. The embrace of the grandfathers at the end of the poem is less a moment of racial transcendence than a hard-won expression of revolutionary possibility. The *Amsterdam News*'s reading of the poem as "a hymn to racial tolerance and amity" thus affects a blunting of Guillén's racial politics typical to U.S. reception of his work. Significantly however, their review of Cosme's recitation places racial reconciliation in the embodied performance of a Black woman. It is imaginable that the performative content of the poem offered a built-in stage direction for Cosme to enact: the grandfathers are tired, they weep, they sing, they embrace. Even non-Spanish-speaking audiences may have perceived the poem's racial content—as evident in the unmistakable exclamations of the word "*negros.*" Whether one perceived the poem as a catharsis, a resolution, or a call to arms, Cosme's performance raised the fraught question of women's roles in the narration and embodiment of Cuban racial history. As "Balada de los dos abuelos" drew to a close, "Cuban Evening" already stood on complicated ground.

The rest of the program similarly centered on themes of race and embodiment. Cosme recited "José Ramon Cantaliso," "Balada del Guije," and ."Secuestro de la mujer de Antonio" ("The Kidnapping of Antonio's Wife"). Hughes read his translations of "Song of the Bongo," "Wake for Papa Montero," and "Sabás." But one poem, "Maracas," stands out. The title appears three times on the program, right before the intermission. Hughes read an English version of the poem (translated by Carruthers), immediately followed by Cosme's Spanish recitation and a dance number of the same name—a rumba—composed by Don Marzedo. Taken from Guillén's 1934 volume *West Indies, Ltd.*, "Maracas" comments on the vexed politics of spectatorship and performance:

De dos en dos	Two by two
las maracas se adelantan al yanqui	Maracas approach the Yankee
para decirle:	Asking him
—¿Cómo está usted, señor?	Sir, and how are you?
Cuando hay barco a la vista,	When a ship comes into sight,
están ya las maracas en el puerto,	Maracas are ready at the dock,
vigilando la presa excursionista	following the tourist trade
con ojo vivo y ademán despierto.	with lively eye and wakeful pose.
¡Maraca equilibrista,	Equilibrist maracas
güiro adulón del dólar del turista!	flattering seekers of tourist cash!
Pero hay otra maraca con un cierto	But there's another maraca, with a certain
pudor que casi es antiimperialista:	Modesty which is almost anti-imperialist:
es la maraca artista	It's the artist's maraca
que no tiene que hacer nada en el puerto.	that has nothing to do with docks.
A ésa le basta con que un negro pobre	Satisfied it is that a poor Negro
la sacuda en el fondo del sexteto;	shakes it at the back of a sextet;
riñe con el bongó, que es indiscreto,	Disputing with the indiscreet bongo,
y el ron que beba es del que al negro sobre.	and the rum it gets is what the Negro leaves.
Ésa ignora que hay yanquis en el mapa;	It doesn't know there are Yankees on the map;
vive feliz, ralla su pan sonoro,	lives happily, cuts its sonorous bread,
y el duro muslo a Mamá Inés destapa	while Mama Inez' hard hip rolls
y pule y bruñe más la Rumba de oro.	burnished and brighter than a rumba of gold.

(TRANSLATION BY B. F. CARRUTHERS)[46]

To the U.S. audience, the title "Maracas" may have signaled a celebration of rhythm, centered on the gourd instrument that vocalists often shake ostentatiously in Latin music. But in the actual text of the poem, Guillén sardonically critiques the touristic consumption of Cuban music, and further, the complicity of Cuban performers themselves. Guillén's approach is oblique—the instrument itself metonymically represents the musical tourist trade. "Maracas" approaches the *yanqui* (the American tourist): it greets, performs, flatters, caters to the tourists with an "equilibrist" balancing act of appeasement. "Maracas" recalls Guillén's caricature of the ravenous sightseers in "West Indies, Ltd.," who "Come to munch our blue sky, / and wash it down with Bacardi" (*Viene a comerse el cielo azul, / regándolo con Bacardí*) (41–42). In both poems, the dock—or, more accurately, the port (*puerto*)—is a portal to the Caribbean Sea and simultaneously a site of commerce, artistic exchange, and rife exploitation.[47] But in "Maracas," the critique shifts to Cuban participation in the tourist economy, raising questions about the politics of performance in the context of U.S. hegemony in Cuba.[48]

The poem, it should be said, bears no trace of admiration for these musical hustlers. But the third stanza of the poem strikes a different tone. There is another maraca, "with a certain / modesty which is almost anti-imperialist." If Guillén's oddly tentative phrase "modesty (*pudor*) which is *almost* anti-imperialist" falls short of the militant posture of his other poems, it nevertheless signals a politics premised on understated artistry rather than spectacle. Furthermore, this "artist's maraca" has a specific race and class inflection: it is shaken by a "*negro pobre*" (poor negro) at the back of a *son* sextet (typically bongos, double bass, claves, guitar, maracas, and *tres*). It is granted a spiritual offering of rum. Its subtle echo "disputes" the "indiscreet bongo," an instrument whose "*profunda voz*" (deep voice) Guillén elsewhere establishes as the most subversive and African-inflected of instruments.[49] Ultimately, however, the relative freedom of the "artist's maraca" seems to hinge on a kind of naiveté: "it doesn't know there are Yankees on the map," and therefore it declines to perform for them. By the final stanza, the iconic figure of Mama Inéz—"that prototypical signifier of African slavery"—is invoked, and the poem ends with a rumba.[50]

The context of the performance amplified the poem's many tensions. How was this invocation of American imperialism received in a concert premised on U.S. enjoyment of "authentic" Cuban culture? Did the audience feel implicated in the poem's repetition of "Yankee?" Did the performance itself engage in a kind of self-referential critique? How did the two recitations change the way that the audience experienced Marzedo's upbeat rumba, "Maracas"? Rumba was an appropriate accompaniment to Guillén's seaside scene since this dance music, as Ned Sublette explains, "has always been associated with manual laborers, particularly with dockworkers."[51]

While there is no definitive way to answer these questions, it is clear that the program was deliberately structured to accentuate this recitation: "Maracas" was the only poem recited in both English and Spanish. Regarding the original alongside Carruthers's translation above—which Hughes recited—underscores the tensions between the two versions. Spanish and English speakers alike may have noted the presence of rhyme in the Spanish version, which lends the poem a musicality not present in the English. But there are other meaningful (and perhaps perplexing) differences. In the English version, maracas are at the dock "following the tourist trade," a phrase with a much more subdued connotation than the Spanish "*vigilando la presa excursionista*," which more literally translates to "watching or guarding the excursionist *prey*." Such language goes a step further than the opportunism suggested in the English, casting "maracas" in a decidedly predatory light. Guillén also introduces another instrument—the *güiro*, a hollow gourd that produces sound when its ridges are rubbed with a stick. Carruthers's choice to omit Guillén's reference to the lesser-known instrument may seem inconsequential. However, in naming two percussion instruments commonly played by vocalists, Guillén also implies the centrality of the *voice* to the tourist economy that he describes.

Indeed, perhaps the most significant contrast between the two readings involved the voices of Hughes and Cosme themselves. To begin with, their performance styles could not have been more different. As evident in his recorded collaborations with musicians, Hughes often favored understatement and a slow, methodical delivery. Furthermore, as Jones notes, "Despite the poet's many decades as Harlem's celebrated resident and 'voice,' the nasal Midwestern drawl evident in his enunciation register his Joplin origins and his upbringing in Kansas and Ohio."[52] Hughes's style, carriage, and accent seemed to deny audiences the performative "folksiness" that they often anticipated, given his material.

And yet in the context of this 1946 performance, Hughes's "drawl" subtly introduced the Black Midwest (along with New York City and Havana) as unexpected coordinates in the transnational landscape of "Cuban Evening." We can surmise from the program that Hughes read at least two works in Spanish: Guillén's dialect poems "Mulata" and "Me Bendo Caro."

While there is no recording of the event, recordings of his later work, the long poem *Ask Your Mama: 12 Moods for Jazz*, provide a clue to the sonic dynamics of Hughes—Harlem's Midwestern-born poet laureate—reading in Spanish.[53] One might consider, for instance, Hughes's reading of this stanza from the second section (or "mood') of the poem:

IN THE QUARTER OF THE NEGROES
TU ABUELA, ¿DONDÉ ESTÁ?
LOST IN CASTRO'S BEARD?
TU ABUELA, ¿DONDÉ ESTÁ?
BROWN SKY BY MONT PELÉE
¿DONDÉ ESTÁ? ¿DONDÉ ESTÁ?
WAS SHE FLEEING WITH LAMUMBA?[54]

In the refrain "*Tu abuela, dondé está?*" (Your grandmother, where is she?), Hughes invokes the common trope of a hidden Black ancestor (usually an *abuela*) tucked away in the kitchen—a figure often seen in Guillén's work. To hear Hughes read in Spanish is to confirm Guillén's observation that "Mr. Hughes' Spanish is not very rich, but he makes marvelous use of it" (*El castellano de Mr. Hughes no es muy rico. Pero él lo aprovecha maravillosamente*).[55] That is to say, the heaviness of Hughes's American accent, his lack of mastery of an "authentic" Cuban or Antillean inflection, is actually a valuable part of his bilingual poetics. Hughes's lapse into Spanish here does not signal an assumption of Afro-Cuban identity (and Cuba *is* one possible setting here, as the reference to Castro implies); rather, it attunes us to diasporic difference. While Hughes's "quarter of the Negroes" spans multiple Black geographies, from the United States, to Cuba, to Mont Pelée of Martinique, to the Congo, its expansive possibilities are encapsulated in a voice that bears traces of home.

Cosme provided a counterpoint to Hughes. This was not merely because her Cubanness meant that she was closer to the material, but also due to her training in *declamación*, her use of props and backdrops crafted by herself, and above all her costume (figure 3.3). A typical Cosme recital included several changes of costume, including, as Carruthers describes, the dress of "the *rumbera*—tight fitting organdy from the shoulder to the thigh—then flaring out with yards of ruffles and a long, ruffled train."[56] Although there are no photographs of the event, one can imagine Cosme donning such a gown for "Cuban Evening." (In contrast, Hughes's "costume" consisted

FIGURE 3.3 Eusebia Cosme, 1930. *Source*: Cuban Photograph Collections. University of Miami Digital Collections. Photo is signed, *"Para Ignacio Rivero, muy afectivamente, Eusebia Cosme."*

simply of a dinner jacket.) Indeed, in his draft of the program, Hughes scribbles a cue for music to be played at the end of Cosme's recitation of the poem.

In contrast to Hughes's reading, Cosme's performance elevates the tensions of the poem by raising questions about the status of women's bodies and performances in the tourist economy that Guillén describes, even as the audience was invited to gaze upon her performance in real time. Recited by Hughes, the lines "Mama Inez' hard hip rolls / burnished and brighter than a rumba of gold" encouraged the audience to imagine a rumba performer. Recited by Cosme, however, this utterance would have suggested her own embodiment of such a figure. Such a fact renders the discrepancy between the English and Spanish endings even more fascinating. The final lines more literally translate to "the maraca lives happily, cuts its sonorous

bread / and uncovers the hard thigh of Mamá Inés / and polishes and bur-
nishes the Rumba of gold." Thus, in the Spanish version, the maraca, not
Mamá Inés, is the subject of the sentence and its main agent. Here, the
exposed thigh of Mamá Inés (who is most certainly a Black woman) serves
as sensual inspiration for a golden rumba. What did it mean for Cosme to
utter lines that implied her own sexualization while also wielding a performative agency that cast her as far more than a muse? While critics have persistently (and not without reason) imagined the persona of Guillén's poems
as male, Cosme's performances allow us to consider the role of female artistic agency in the shaping of poetic meaning.

The contrast between Hughes and Cosme also raises questions about
what López calls the "embodied vocality" of Black performance. Indeed, a
1938 review by Andrés Ituarte offers a representative description of Cosme's
voice and accent:

> La poesía antillana sale de sus labios en un español típicamente cubano, en un
> deseo alegre y vivo, con unas vocales abiertas, unas jotas imperceptibles y unos
> finales de palabra y de frase desmayados, con un ritmo nuevo que es la aport-
> ación del negro y del mulato a la lengua castellana. No únicamente es Eusebia
> Cosme muy dueña del espíritu de los poemas de tema negro que recita sino,
> dentro del acento y la cadencia cubana, un ejemplo de la dicción del español
> en las Antillas.

> Antillean poetry leaves her lips in a Spanish typically Cuban, in happy
> and vibrant desire, with open vowels, imperceptible "j's," and the ends of
> words and phrases dropped, with a new rhythm that is the contribution of
> the negro and the mulatto to the Castilian language. Not only does Eusebia
> Cosme own the spirit of the negro themed poems that she recites but also,
> within Cuban accent and cadence, is an example of the diction of Spanish
> in the Antilles.[57]

Ituarte refers to a "typically Cuban" Spanish, including, for example,
dropped consonants at the ends of words that give the Spanish version
a clipped, percussive feel, an almost abrasive word-music largely lost in
English. However, the review was more explicitly referring to a *Black*
"accent and cadence," which he attributes to Cosme's embodied experience
as an Afro-Cuban woman. But this emphasis on innate ability seems to

downplay Cosme's studied attention to Guillén's poetics: indeed, Cosme emphasizes these speech effects not simply because they come naturally to her, but because Guillén often attempted to reproduce them on the page, as in the poem "Búcate Plata" (which Hughes and Carruthers translate to "No Sirrie"):

Búcate plata,	Git some cash,
búcate plata,	Git some cash,
poqque no doy un paso má	'cause I ain't takin' another step
etoy a arró con galleta,	Rice and crackers all I get.
na má.	
yo bien sé cómo etá to,	I know how it is,
pero biejo, hay que comé:	But, Daddy, I got to eat!
búcate plata,	Git some cash,
búcate plata,	Git some cash,
poqque me boy a corré.	Else jes' watch my feet!

The elided consonants (*"búscate"* becomes *"búcate,"* *"por que"* becomes *"poqque,"* *"más"* becomes *"má,"* *"estoy"* becomes *"etoy,"* etc.) and accents mimic *son*'s instrumentation. (I have placed the Guillén and the Hughes versions side by side to highlight some of the challenges of translating Cuban vernacular to African American vernacular, which incidentally, also bring into relief some of the poem's central tensions.) Cosme's successful performance of the poem (a complaint from a woman to her broke lover) was not merely due to an extension of her native speech patterns, but rather her mastery of poetic form and sensitivity to the written text.

It is useful to keep in mind Cosme's careful artistry when considering her performance of "Maracas." As Tom McEnaney observes, "Cosme's sonic performance succeeds not because she speaks with some impossibly authentic voice. Rather, it is precisely the high artificiality, the academic training, and the aesthetic labor of this joint venture that makes the poems a popular and critical success."[58] To note Cosme's "high artificiality" is not to diminish the value of her performances. If Hughes's and Cosme's recitations offered two different ideas of what it meant to "sound" Black, the poem ("Maracas") itself was a reminder that such effects could indeed be *performed*.

Ultimately, "Cuban Evening" comprised less a straightforward celebration of Cuban culture than a meditation on the politics of performance.

And yet the program (including the selections that followed "Maracas") raised more questions than it answered about how, if at all, performers might disentangle themselves from the problematics of cultural consumption. Despite the poem's triumphant ending, there were in fact "Yankees on the map" and in the audience. And any calls for African American and Cuban cultural exchange would have to consider the pervasive presence of the United States on the island, and indeed throughout the Caribbean. While it is a largely forgotten episode in Black diasporic literary and performance history, "Cuban Evening" remains emblematic of the questions that would occupy Cosme, Hughes, and Guillén throughout their careers: What might an anti-imperial poetics look like, and how might it sound?

WHO IS EUSEBIA COSME? INTERRUPTING MYTHS OF CUBAN NATIONAL IDENTITY

For Guillén, an anti-imperial poetics was above all a *mestizo* poetics. *Mestizaje* resists translation into U.S. racial vocabularies according to which, as Hughes explained, "the word 'Negro' is used to mean anyone who had *any* Negro blood at all in his veins."[59] But beyond its translation to a U.S. context, Guillén made a stark contrast between *mestizo* poetics and *poesía afrocubana*. On one noteworthy occasion, he framed this strategic disavowal in relationship to Cosme herself. In an essay entitled "Regreso de Eusebia Cosme" ("The Return of Eusebia Cosme"), written on the occasion of Cosme's return to Cuba in 1951, Guillén declares sardonically, "*¿Poesía 'afrocubana,' música 'afrocubana,' arte 'afrocubano?' ¿Qué quiere decir esto? A mi juicio, perdón, señores especialistas, no quiere decir nada*" (Afro-Cuban poetry, Afro-Cuban music, Afro-Cuban art? What is that supposed to mean? In my judgment, pardon me, sir specialists, it means nothing).[60]

He continues: "I don't believe—I have never believed—that there exists among us a manner of being Afrocuban, apart from the essential Cubanness."[61] Despite being hailed as a principal figure of *afrocubanismo* (he, along with Cosme, Amadeo Roldán, and Alejandro García Caturla, joined the Sociedad de Estudios Afrocubanos, which had been founded by Ortiz in 1937), Guillén frames the term as a sociological imposition that had been falsely applied to Cosme's work, as well as his own.[62] Instead, he stresses a "vast process of *mestizaje*, still unfinished." Cuban identity, Guillén explains, is forged of a (profound union of two bloods) "*estamos hechos de una unión profunda de dos sangres.*" There is "the blood, culture and spirit of Spain . . . in many spaces this Spanish blood is mixed with the indigenous; in others, scrambled with that of slaves."[63]

Such a statement is consistent with Guillén's articulation of a *mestizo* poetics in his other prerevolution writings, including the famous prologue to his 1931 collection *Sóngoro cosongo*, in which he plainly states that the "spirit of Cuba is mestizo":

> *No ignoro, desde luego, que estos versos les repugnan a muchas personas, porque ellos tratan asuntos de los negros y del pueblo. No me importa. O mejor dicho: me alegra. Diré finalmente que éstos son unos versos mulatos. . . . Opino por tanto que una poesía criolla entre nosotros no lo será de un modo cabal con olvido del negro. El negro—a mi juicio—aporta esencias muy firmes a nuestro coctel . . . Por lo pronto, el espíritu de Cuba es mestizo. Y del espíritu hacia la piel nos vendrá el color definitivo. Algún día se dirá: "color cubano." Estos poemas quieren adelantar ese día.*

> I'm not unaware, of course, that these verses will disgust many people because they deal with Negroes and the people. It doesn't matter to me. Or better said: It makes me happy. I will say finally that these are mulatto verses. . . . I further believe that a creole poetry here would not be complete if one forgets the Negro. The Negro—in my judgment—brings very strong essences to our cocktail. To begin with, the spirit of Cuba is *mestizo*. And from the spirit through the skin will emerge a definitive color. Someday we'll say: "Cuban Color." These poems seek to bring forth that day.[64]

Guillén's prediction that his verses would disgust "many people" implicitly referred to what he saw as the haughty prejudice of the Cuban middle class toward Blacks and the masses. But beyond deploying blackness as a mode of provocation and discomfort in his readers, he insists that an understanding of Cuban culture is incomplete without acknowledgment of Black vernacular production, and conversely, that blackness could not be understood apart from Cuba's *mestizo* heritage.

The implications of a *mestizo* poetics are not straightforward, however, given its variable translations within Cuba itself, not to speak of its circulation throughout the Caribbean and Latin America. As Kutzinski explains, "*Mestizaje* can variably be translated as miscegenation, racial

amalgamation (as in *blanqueamiento*, whitening), creolization, racial mix-
ing, inter-transculturation. It is perhaps best described as a peculiar form of
multiculturalism—one that has circulated in the Caribbean and in Hispanic America . . . as a series of discursive formations tied to nationalist interests and ideologies."[65] Cuba's nationalist articulations of *mestizaje*
often worked to bury divisive social realities beneath a rhetoric of racial
unity. As insinuated by the related term, *"blanquemiento*," *mestizaje* is often
deployed coercively, as assimilation to a white standard. During Guillén's
youth, racial conflict—exemplified by the massacre of members of the
Partido Independiente de Color (PIC) in 1912, as well as the often vigorously enforced color line in Cuba—supplied ample evidence that injus-
tices continued to persist. Furthermore, the struggle against racism and
imperialism was not a twin mission for all members of Cuban society, as
authorities could be vehemently anti-imperialist even as they took measures to reinforce the color line. But most relevant to my purposes are the
ways in which, alongside this wide-scale disenfranchisement, vernacular
culture and performance became central to the definition of *mestizaje*, as
"syncretic forms of Afro-Cuban popular music and dance became the new
signifiers of a desire for cultural and political independence."[66] As Maguire
notes, poetry inspired by these forms has been used to bolster claims Cuba
had achieved a "racially harmonious society."[67]

And yet, as a series of "discursive formations," which by definition
resist stability, *mestizaje* is perhaps best understood in terms of its uses—
the specific kind of political, cultural, or epistemological work that it performs in any given instance, including differences between the work of
authors as well as within a single author's work. Guillén's specific articulation of *mestizaje* in "Regreso" takes shape in relationship to Cosme,
particularly in light of her long absence from an island that had changed
drastically since her departure in 1938. The intervening years had seen
the closure of the local performance venues in which Cosme had gained
notoriety, as well as the contrasting explosion of an international market for all things Afro-Cuban. Guillén felt that the culture industry had
become decontextualized from the everyday realities of Cuban life, and
furthermore that the poetic sphere was rife with a "literary opportunism that presents to us a touristic, superficial, stupid negro."[68] Eager to
rescue Cosme from such caricature and misappropriation, Guillén's essay,
as Maguire observes, "performs a gesture of reincorporation. No longer a

racialized exile, Guillén's article returns Cosme to Cuba in both a physical and a cultural sense."[69]

But at base, Guillén's gesture of reincorporation is also a *gesture of containment*—one that in many ways is exemplary of the way that women's bodies and performances were, as López puts it, "configured to Cuban discourses of *mestizaje*."[70] In seeking to correct misapprehensions about Cuban national identity, Guillén's essay betrays anxieties about Cosme's divergent approach to inhabiting and performing blackness. If, as Vogel observes, "the disavowal is a *process* that retains an idea even as it rejects it," then paradoxically Guillén's descriptions of what Cosme's performances are *not* raises into view a possible alternative vision of Cosme's lifework.[71] This was not the racist caricature that Guillén feared, but an artist who felt comfortable away from Cuba for years at a time, reciting poetry for the "*colonia latina*" in New York and spending evenings in Harlem *charlando* with Bola de Nieve and Langston Hughes.[72]

At stake in Guillén's effort to "impose nationalist ethics" on Cosme is also a sense that her art was an extension of his, and thus should reflect his own politics and artistic sensibilities.[73] Such a view was proffered by various male critics, and it was one that Cosme herself occasionally perpetuated. In an interview with the Puerto Rican journalist Julia de Burgos, Cosme declares her appreciation of the poets who constitute her repertoire: "It is for [through] them that I am. And it is for them that I live" (*Es por ellos que soy. Y es por ellos que viven*).[74] Burgos reads this declaration as evidence of Cosme's modesty, a quality that Cosme's interviewers often juxtaposed with descriptions of her larger-than-life stage persona. However, Cosme's words register her awareness that *declamación* was her only point of entry into a male-dominated literary world. At the same time, *declamación* expanded the geographical and temporal reach of a movement that some believed was in decline by the 1930s. Thus, if Cosme "lives" for her poet contemporaries, her performances also extended the life of their works. The Cuban poet Félix B. Caignet expressed such a sentiment, writing to Cosme, "ninety percent of the myth of my verses is in your interpretation. . . . My poetry exists only when you perform it!"[75]

Beyond expressing admiration, Caignet's phrase "the myth of my verses is in your interpretation" foregrounds the ways in which Cosme's performance and body were presumed to encapsulate myths of Cuban identity. The *negra* and *mulata* were ubiquitous tropes in *poesía negra*, and audiences may have perceived that Cosme's performances brought those images to life. But Cosme's body and performance also posed a conundrum: bodies are in fact unruly, and performance, with its emphasis on liveness, ephemerality, and shifting meanings, meant that the racial meanings that audiences perceived were neither stable nor definitive. Yet in dozens of reviews (written mainly by men), the unwieldy question of Cosme's blackness was managed through gestures of containment—rhetorical moves that must themselves be considered performative.

One early example of this politics of containment concerns Cosme's breakthrough performance at the Havana Lyceum on July 23, 1934, where she was introduced by Fernando Ortiz. The address, published as "La poesía mulata: presentación de Eusebia Cosme, la recitadora" in *Revista Bimestre Cubana*, introduced the then up-and-coming Cosme to the members of the Lyceum, an elite social club whose members consisted mainly of white women. Excerpts from Ortiz's speech would later be quoted in Cosme's programs, continuing to frame audience reception for years to come. The address also reinforced Ortiz's authority as an expert on Afro-Cuban performative culture, or more specifically what he called "*poesía mulata*," "a new movement in the history of the aesthetic expressions [*expresiones estéticas*] of our people."[76] Ortiz would not officially introduce the influential concept of "transculturation" (denoting a complex process of cultural convergence) until the publication of *Cuban Counterpoint* in 1940. However, the seeds of these ideas are present in his introduction, where they converge, problematically, in the body of Cosme herself.

Ortiz begins with the question, "*Quién es Eusebia Cosme? Intentaré decírselo a los socios del Lyceum, que para esto me invitan. Acaso tenga que decírselo a ella misma, cuya propia sinceridad ella siente, sabe y vive sin poderla explicar*" (Who is Eusebia Cosme? I will try to explain it to the members of the Lyceum, since this is why they invited me. Perhaps I will have to tell it to her [Eusebia] herself, whose own sincerity she feels, knows, and lives without being able to explain it). With a flourish of intellectual authority, Ortiz not only announces his intention to introduce Cosme to the members of the Lyceum, but also, "in a revealing, condescending gesture," as López phrases it, professes even to introduce Cosme to herself. Ortiz continues, "Eusebia Cosme is an artist of true and beautiful speech, [*decir*] who feels and makes her art; the art of reciting verses and poetry of mulatto soul, rhythm, and sometimes, even melodies." By implying that Cosme's art is the result of pure, intuitive feeling rather than intentional practice (and that he is in a better position than she is to apprehend her own art), Ortiz rehearses a common script in appraisals of women performers: she does not merely recite mulatto verses, but rather *embodies* the mulatto spirit of Cuba. In making this claim, Ortiz elides Cosme's blackness and denies the ways in which her art is an act of labor, and indeed translation.

In fact, in Ortiz's address, translation functions as a tragic event. After detailing the distinct historic struggles of the *"negro"* and the *"blanco"* in Cuba, he declares that the *"mestizo,"* crushed by the "centrifugal pressure" of two racial worlds, has suffered most of all. The "mulatto soul," Ortiz posits, "has had obstacles, forced as it was to translate itself [*traducirse*], to transfer itself to another language not totally its own, and in the process of this instrumental change to lose not a little of its spontaneity, its intimate essence and its morphological liberty."[77] Ortiz uses the verb *"traducir"* (to translate) as an analogy for racial disavowal. The mulatto falsely assumes the expressive "language" and essence of Black or white without truly embodying either. If "translation" is a form of falsification and inauthenticity, Ortiz assures his audience that Cosme's art is in fact, the *opposite* of translation: it is a pure expression of the soul.

Cosme's gift, Ortiz insists, is to *"recoger las bellezas de la nueva poesía y trasmitirlas puras a la multitud. Esta es su aportación a la historia del arte cubano"* (collect the beauties of the new poetry and transmit them pure to the multitude. This is her contribution to the history of Cuban art).[78] Here, "transmit" implies a direct, if somewhat mystical process that erases the mediated nature of all interpretation, as well as the individual choices of Cosme as a performer. However, in another respect, Ortiz's use of the word was prescient: anticipating Cosme's radio show in which she would "transmit" her poetic recitations to the masses.

Cosme's debut, according to Ortiz, signaled the culmination of a sweeping saga of racial struggle and transcendence, the dawning of a new "poetic fluency" that is not *negra*, but *mulata*: *"No creo que esta reciente fluencia poética que mana de lo hondo de nuestro pueblo sea negra, sino sencillamente mulata, hija de un abrazo inextricable de África y Castilla en la emoción, en el ritmo, en el vocablo, en la prosodia, en la sintaxis, en la idea, en la tendencia"* (I don't believe that the recent poetic fluency that flows from the depth of our people is *negra*, but rather it is simply *mulata*, daughter of an inextricable embrace between Africa and Spain in emotion, rhythm, vocabulary, prosody, syntax, ideas, tendency).[79] As Maguire notes, "Ortiz characterizes Cosme as a cypher whose significance he can read, but it appears that he does not, in fact, see her at all. . . . Ortiz merely uses her as a signpost towards racial harmony."[80] Thus, Ortiz squeezes Cosme's performance into a framework of racial transcendence in which her blackness is "safely incorporated into the broader (read: whiter) Cuban society."[81]

"Presentación" is as much a vehicle for Ortiz's ideological musings on Cuban cultural identity in general as it is an introduction of Cosme. To name both Guillén's and Ortiz's writings as gestures of containment is not to equate their views and politics. Whatever Guillén's critique of the terminology of *afrocubanidad*, he does not attempt to erase her identity as *"una negra venida del oriente de la Isla"* (a Black woman from the west of the island).[82] Nevertheless, both writings betray anxieties about what Daphne Brooks calls a "performative threat": the challenge that Cosme's performance and physical body posed to a definition of *poesía negra*.[83]

In drawing upon such accounts, I do not mean to suggest that the significance of Cosme's performances is predetermined by her male critics. Rather, I hope to highlight what Brooks calls the "electrifying dialectic" between the accounts of "confused white spectators" and the "dissonant gestures of performers embedded within that same review that sometimes tell a different story of the event in question."[84] Dissonant gestures might also be discursive. In one 1936 interview, the Cuban journalist Juan Bonich refers to Cosme as *"la negra que tiene el alma blanca"* (the Black woman with the white soul), a phrase meant to reassure audiences of Cosme's delicate sensibilities despite her lack of phenotypical whiteness.[85] But in the same interview, Cosme sounds a dissonant note by exalting the entertainer Josephine Baker: "she spoke to us of Josephine Baker, the black Venus who one day became an idol in Paris and she told us how then, in her childhood, in the first years of her childhood, she dreamed of achieving a shred of [Josephine's] glory." Cosme not only signals her admiration of Baker's international fame, but she also identifies with Baker's experiences as a Black woman performer who was engaged in the precarious work of translating race for her audiences. Read alongside Cosme's oft-repeated claim that "as a black girl, I could never reach [the] stages" that were only open to white performers in Cuba, Cosme's invocation of Baker serves as an act of intentional, strategic affiliation that positioned her work and her aspirations in relationship to other Black performers.[86] Her repeated references to her childhood as a "*niña negra*" resist attempts to transform her into "*mulatica*" ("little mulatta," to quote Ortiz), a term that she never used, even figuratively, to refer to her own racial identity.

Such dissonant gestures might turn our attention toward other ways that Cosme framed her performances. One such vehicle was her CBS radio program "The Eusebia Cosme Show," which aired from 1943 to 1947 on Cadena de las Américas. As López observes, "the *Cosme Show* was also an instance of U.S. 'Good Neighbor' ideology," a range of policies, rhetorical gestures, and cultural programs designed to frame the U.S. imperial project in terms of neighborly relations with Latin America.[87] However, if the show was one of the many cultural endeavors framed as part of this dubious agenda, the actual content of the program performed subversive cultural and political work. Alongside the rest of her repertoire, the "Cosme Show" offered an expansive understanding of blackness—one forged through a range of transnational coalitions and acts of translation. Beginning each broadcast with a quote from the Venezuelan writer Miguel Otero Silva, who had been ejected from the United States due to his communist leanings, Cosme recited a range of material, including works in translation (enlisting the work of a translator named Enrique Portes). She thus expanded her repertoire beyond the *poesía negra* for which she was known. In a radio script dated August 25, 1944, Cosme introduces her poetic project by quoting Langston Hughes's most translated poem in Latin America, "I, Too, Sing America":

> *Les habla Eusebia Cosme. Les traigo mis anitguos poemas y muchos otros que he encontrado en el camino. El arte es interpretarlos y comunicarles a ustedes la emoción que yo siento. Pues, como ha dicho el poeta, . . . Yo también soy América, soy el hermano negro.*

> Eusebia Cosme speaking. I bring you my old poems and many others that I have encountered along the way. My art is to interpret them and to communicate to you the emotion that I feel. Since as the poet has said, . . . I, too, am America, I am the Black brother.[88]

The original version of the poem reads: "I am the darker brother. / They send me to eat in the kitchen / When company comes, / But I laugh / And eat well / And grow strong."[89] But Portes translates Hughes's phrase "I am the darker brother" as "*soy el hermano negro*," rather than the more literal "*soy el hermano más oscuro*." Such a choice was not anomalous. As Kutzinski explains, "In Fernández de Castro's 1928 version, the added 'negro' already appears in an emphatic position at the end of the preceding line."[90] But here Cosme does not recite Hughes's words as a translated poem, but rather as an attempt to frame the scope of her own broadcast (figure 3.4). While "I, Too" had circulated in Latin America as an anti-imperialist creed, here it functions as a way of speaking to *afrodescendientes* in the diaspora.

In another broadcast, Cosme recites a translation of Paul Lawrence Dunbar's "Little Brown Baby" ("*Morenito mío de brillantes ojos*"): "*Morenito mío de brillantes ojos / Acércate a papá, sube a sus rodillas / ¿Qué cosas hacías? ¿Tortillas de lodo? Mira este babero. Qué sucio. Dios Mío*" (Little brown baby wif spa'klin' eyes, / Come to yo' pappy an' set on his knee. / What you been doin', suh—makin' san' pies? / Look at dat bib—you's es du'ty ez me). The

FIGURE 3.4 Salas photo, and Langston Hughes. *LH at Tuskegee Airfield with Eusebia Cosme. Source*: Langston Hughes Papers, James Weldon Johnson Collection in the Yale Collection of American Literature, Beinecke Rare Book and Manuscript Library, Yale University, New Haven, CT.

radio script indicates musical accompaniment to punctuate the playful arc of the poem, in which the speaker jokingly chides the child for playing in mud, threatens him with the bogeyman, then concludes with a reaffirmation of the child's beauty: "short chords suggesting danger as background. Remember 'el duende' or the bogeyman is being called to act." There are "sharp chords suggesting a wild animal" and finally a "lullaby," all of which suggest a performative ground for Black childhood that emphasized the playfulness, innocence, and beauty not often afforded to them in the mainstream. What is lost, of course, is the dialect of Dunbar's original, here not translated to the kind of Cuban vernacular that was present in Guillén's *criollo* poetry. What marks the poem differently is the term *"morenito mío,"* which might function ambiguously as either a term of endearment or condescension. Here, it is placed firmly within the context of Black family ties.[91]

The "Eusebia Cosme Show" thereby enacted a transnational poetics of racial affiliation that is ultimately irreducible to a single national project—even as it reflected Cosme's perspective as a Cuban subject. The show might serve as what Brent Hayes Edwards calls a "framing structure" for Cosme's own version of a transnational poetics, a medium for "imagining its scope of implication, its uses, its 'future.'"[92] The show thus extends the work of her live performances, allowing Cosme considerable autonomy not only to broaden her repertoire, but also to alter its form.

NEGRO DE VERDAD

One final interruption is worth recounting. In "Conversación con Langston Hughes," Guillén recounts Hughes's desire to visit *"un cabaret de negros"* during his visit to Havana in 1930. Along with Gustavo Urrutia and José Fernandez de Castro, Guillén escorted Hughes throughout the city, providing a kind of access that Hughes may not have experienced otherwise. It was not Hughes's first trip to Cuba. He had traveled there in 1927 as a mess boy aboard a ship bound for Havana from a port in New Orleans. He documents the trip in a travel journal entitled "1927 Trip South," a notebook in which he sketches details of his travels to New Orleans, Mobile, and Tuskegee.[93] The fact that Hughes considered Havana a stop on his journey "South" not only highlights the geographical proximity of Cuba to the United States; it also suggests a linkage between the southern United States and Cuba in Hughes's regional conceptualization of the South. Indeed,

Hughes hoped that like the South of his own country, Cuba would provide a rich field of folk material. He returned to Cuba in 1930 with the
express purpose of seeking a Black composer with whom to write a folk
opera "using genuinely racial motifs," a premise that his sponsor, Charlotte Osgood Mason, backed wholeheartedly. Hughes would later write
that Mason's insatiable hunger for all things "primitive" fueled her enthu-
siasm.[94] "I am to go to Havana for rest, new strength, and contact with the
song," he writes.[95] However, as Hughes recalls in *The Big Sea*, his meeting
with the Cuban composer Amadeo Roldán proved disappointing when the
Cuban insisted that "he wasn't a Negro":

> That winter I had been in Cuba looking for a Negro composer to write an
> opera with me, using genuinely racial motifs. The lady on Park Avenue
> thought that Amadeo Roldán might do, or Arturo Caturla. I could not find
> Caturla, and Roldán said he wasn't a Negro. But Miguel Covarrubias had
> given me a letter to José Antonio Fernandez de Castro, person extraordinary
> of this or any other world.
>
> And José Antonio saw to it that I had a rumba and a good time and met
> everybody, Negro white and mulatto, of any interest in Havana—from the
> drummers at Marianao to the society artist and editor of *Social*, Masaguer.
> But I came back to New York with no Negro composer who could write an
> opera.[96]

Hughes's encounter with Roldán hints at the tension between U.S. and
Cuban understandings of race, as well as the simple fact that most members of the *afrocubanista* movement would not have identified as "Negro."
Whatever the details of this meeting, however, Roldán was not in fact averse
to so-called racial motifs and soon endeavored to set Guillén's *Motivos de
son* to music, with a concert premiere in New York in 1934, the same year
that Cosme had her breakthrough performance at the Havana Lyceum.

But Hughes's visit took another productive turn, away from the music
of the concert hall and toward Cuban street music and nightlife. The daily
record of his activities in Havana reveals an itinerary of meetings with
various writers and artists by day; sumptuous dinners, rum, and Cuban
dance halls at night. "To a fiesta in a private house with Mike and Guillén,"
Hughes records in his journal. "The rumba again. . . . To bed at three."[97]
Cuban nightlife and performance made a major impact on Hughes's overall

impression of Havana. While Hughes frames his turn to Cuban nightlife as a natural expression of his populist sensibilities, his fluid movement throughout Havana—from high-society affairs to dances for the "poor and declassé"—was also a function of his class, color, and U.S. privilege, and the social caché that he absorbed through his affiliation with prominent members of the Cuban literati.

As Guillén tells it, Hughes's wish to see *negros* takes on the quality of obsession: "*¿Vienen negros a este café? . . . ¿En esta orquesta no admiten negros? ¿No hay artistas negros aquí? ¡Me gustaría ir a un cabaret de negros en La Habana!*" (Do negroes come to this café? Do they not admit negroes in this orchestra? Aren't there negro artists here? I would like to go to a negro cabaret in Havana!). Guillén obligingly escorts him to an *academia de baile*, "*de esas que sólo danzan los individuos de nuestra raza*" (of the kind in which only dance those of our race).[98] It was there that Hughes heard rumbas and *sones*, which he admiringly describes in his autobiography as "hip shaking music, of Afro-Cuban folk derivation, which means a bit of Spain, therefore Arab-Moorish, mixed in. The tap of the claves, the rattle of gourds, the dong of iron bells, the deep, steady roll of drums speak of the earth, life bursting warm from the earth, and earth and sun moving in steady rhythms of procreation and joy."[99] Hughes's fascination with the *son* was stoked by his interest in the cultural production of the Afro-Cuban masses, whom he deemed as a unique lens into Cuban experience. But one moment in Guillén's narration of the cabaret scene deserves further comment: as the tale goes, Hughes stood captivated for a long time next to the band, which was furiously playing a *son*. As the music "[spread] its green smoke," Hughes—"his breath faltering with emotion"—strained to follow a rhythm that was "new to his spirit." Finally, after gazing with wonder at the *bongosero*, he exclaimed with an air of longing: "*Yo quisiera ser negro. Bien negro! Negro de verdad!*"[100]

Critics have read Hughes's outburst ("I'd like to be Black. Really Black. Truly Black!") as suggestive of his racial essentialism and romanticized desire for access to a more authentic blackness. However, more pertinent to my analysis is Guillén's strategic narration of the scene. By framing the American poet's visit as a quest for authenticity that culminates in his encounter with the *son*, Guillén initially appears to suggest the music's ability to encompass the "truth" of Afro-diasporic blackness. Complete with beating drums and mysterious "green smoke," the scene sounds like the primitivist descriptions of jazz clubs in Harlem Renaissance literature in which music unearths repressed racial memories of Africa. However, read in the context of Guillén's oeuvre, the phrase *"negro de verdad"* is provocatively open-ended rather than a definitive statement on blackness. What, in the context of international collaboration, does it mean to be *"negro de verdad"*? To what understanding of blackness does music—or performance in general—provide access?

Although it comes at the end of Guillén's piece, Hughes's outburst is an interruption, or put more precisely, an interjection: signaling a break in continuity between ideas of race and blackness. As both Keith Ellis and J. Patrick Leary note, "Conversación con Langston Hughes" was not the first time that the phrase *"negro de verdad"* appeared in Guillén's writing in relation to Hughes. It is also the last line of Guillén's 1929 poem "Pequeña oda a un negro boxeador cubano," which Hughes translated as "Little Ode to a Negro Cuban Boxer." Written for the popular Cuban featherweight boxer Eligio Sardiñas, also known as Kid Chocolate, who arrived in New York in 1928, the poem critiques the voracious U.S. and European consumption of Cuban blackness in general and Black male physicality in particular. Long after their meeting, Hughes not only would translate "Little Ode" for *Cuba Libre* (archival records show that it is one of the poems that Hughes translated on his own), but he would also recite it at "Cuban Evening" after Cosme's rendition of "Maracas." Here, I place the version of the translation that Hughes edited for "Cuban Evening" alongside Guillén's original. The key phrase appears in the final stanza, which reads:

Y ahora que Europa se desnuda	Now that the white world
para tostar su carne al sol,	toasts its body in the sun
y busca en Harlem y en La Habana	and looks for rumbas
jazz y son,	in Havana, shine in your
lucirse negro mientras aplaude	blackness, kid, while the crowd
el bulevar,	applauds—
y frente a la envidia de los blancos	and, envied by the whites,
hablar en negro de verdad.	speak for the blacks indeed![101]

Among the most obvious differences between the two versions is Hughes's replacement of "Europa," which undresses to toast its meat (*carne*)

in the sun, with "white world," a change that generalizes Guillén's more specific critique of the colonial and neocolonial presence of Europe in Cuba.
Furthermore, in the original poem, "Europa" searches for *jazz and son* in
Harlem and Havana, and not merely *rumbas* in Havana. Indeed, Guillén
places Harlem alongside Havana to signal the fraught politics of cultural
consumption in *both* locations; we are asked to consider jazz and *son* not as
equivalent artistic forms, but as mutually subject to touristic appropriation.
In excising Harlem and jazz, Hughes displaces Guillén's critique of tourist
consumption in New York itself, appearing to name a dynamic that is hap-
pening farther away.

Finally, while the lines *"y frente a la envidia de los blancos / Hablar
en negro de verdad"* may basically translate to "And facing the envy of
the whites, speak truly black," Hughes's variation, "envied by the whites,
speak *for* the blacks indeed" inserts an additional layer of meaning: the
boxer is not only "speaking Black," he also speaks *for* Blacks.[102] This rendering may compare to the final lines of another translation by Roberto
Márquez and David Arthur McMurray, which jubilantly reads: "Let the
envy of the whites / know proud, authentic black!"[103] While both of these
translations end on a triumphant note, with the latter also implying
recognition on the part of whites, the original poem remains far more
equivocal about the prospect of transcending the white gaze. Indeed, the
"boulevard" applauds, but does not truly understand the athlete, and we
are left wondering if his defiant speech-act (*hablar en negro de verdad*)
will be heard at all.

Alongside Guillén's account of Hughes listening to *son* in Havana, the
poem invokes, as Leary contends, a "deep skepticism about the cultural
enterprise of Black internationalism itself."[104] Leary asks, "[I]s Hughes, in
consuming the *son* of Havana to reaffirm his own connection to black Cuba,
simply behaving like the European tourists of the 'boulevard' who search
for jazz and authenticity on upper Broadway?"[105] Put more broadly, to what
extent do African Americans participate in the project of U.S. imperialism,
even as they seek solidarity with Black people abroad?

Whether Guillén was making a pointed allusion to his earlier poem or
was merely being faithful to Hughes's words, the echoes are nevertheless
striking: the original version of the poem, published in *Diario de la Marina*
in 1929 before Guillén's and Hughes's initial meeting, contained this sly reference to Hughes:

De seguro a ti

no te preocupa Waldo Frank ni Langston Hughes

(el de "I, too sing America.")

No doubt you

Are not worrying about Waldo Frank nor about Langston Hughes

(He of "I, too sing America.")[106]

   While Hughes's poem referenced the U.S. relationship to its darker subjects, the poem also circulated as an allegory for the U.S. relationship with the rest of the Americas. Both interpretations could apply to Kid Chocolate, who is marginalized both at home and abroad. Here, Guillén preserves the English title—rather than the Spanish "Yo también soy América"—emphasizing the poem's U.S. authorship and offering a taste of the bilingual poetics that would become Guillén's favorite vehicle for sardonic critiques of the United States. Of course, the point is that although the message of Hughes's poem may be relevant to the boxer's situation in *theory*, the athlete is too occupied with negotiating his own survival in a ruthless industry to worry about the flourishing of literary modernism that both Waldo Frank and Hughes represent. Although Guillén removed the stanza in a later version of the poem (perhaps due to his friendship with Hughes), the original indicates a distance between Hughes's poetry and the everyday folk whom he claims to depict, as well as the limits of transnational affiliation.

   It is both ironic and fitting, then, that Hughes recited "Little Ode" at "Cuban Evening," some sixteen years after the incident that Guillén recounts. In keeping with other selections for the event, the poem effects resonances between musicianship and sports and their connection to gesture, performance, spectatorship, and the oppressive expectations for authenticity that brutalize Black subjects. Like "Maracas," which immediately preceded it on the program, "Little Ode" invited the audience to meditate on the implications of their spectatorship. Furthermore, the poem's intimate knowledge of the racial geographies of New York City—its references to Broadway, for instance—would have resonated all the more strongly due to the Dunham School's location in the heart of the theater district. Hughes's live recitation amplified the connections between performance, sports, Black male physicality, and desire that already were present in the poem. In this context, Hughes's role shifts: as the speaker of the poem, he is no longer the tourist in search of authenticity; instead, he is the poetic persona who exposes the problematics of the gaze. He gives advice; he observes; he admonishes; he goads. Of course, by inhabiting this role, Hughes does not transcend the problematics exposed in the poem. On the contrary, embodying the contradictions of transnational blackness in his very performance, Hughes is in fact both spectator and dissenting voice, both tourist and comrade.

While Cosme, Dunham, Hughes, and Guillén were collaborating on "Cuban Evening," a young Sylvia Wynter was prepared to make her own contributions to postwar Caribbean performance and literary culture. Building on this chapter's method of reenvisioning events from fragments in the archive, the next and final chapter of this book recuperates Wynter's early career in dance and radio as the basis for her transformative theories of folk culture, sovereignty, and the human.

Chapter Four

REINTERPRETING FOLK CULTURE
AT THE "END OF THE WORLD"

Sylvia Wynter's Dance and Radio Drama

> We shall take this old world up
> We shall turn it upside down
> And remake it as our own
>
> —SYLVIA WYNTER, *MASKARADE*

On November 12, 1958, Sylvia Wynter wrote to Laurence Gilliam, a producer for the drama department of BBC Radio, announcing her intent to collect and record folk songs, folktales, and dialect during an upcoming trip to British Guiana and the West Indies. Wynter had worked with the BBC since 1956 as an occasional commentator and writer of radio plays and short stories that aired on the shows *Third Programme* and *Caribbean Voices*. Along with her then-husband, the novelist, playwright, and poet Jan Carew, Wynter was part of a group of London-based Caribbean creatives who endeavored to transmit Caribbean culture over the airwaves. She explains, "My husband and I have for years been transposing West Indian and Guianese dialect into a literary language and using it in plays and stories. This dialect, essentially the language of an illiterate people, is compressed, epigrammatic, and full of sensuous images." Adding to this repertoire of folk language, Wynter proposed undertaking a project for the BBC Features Department that would include:

1. The recording of folksongs, river chanties and work songs in the interior of British Guiana, the Maroon Country of Jamaica and some of the remote Country districts of the Easter Caribbean Islands . . .

2. The recording of English dialect as spoken by the Negroes, East Indians, Europeans, Chinese and South American Indians, and also the creoles who are descendants of these recent racial groups . . .
3. The collection of folk tales.

Like many collectors of folk culture, Wynter framed the trip as a preservationist endeavor, showing a genuine concern for the continuity of cultural forms, as well as a savvy awareness that conveying urgency was necessary to secure funding and support. She warned that "there is a danger of much of what is authentic to the multi-racial peasant culture of this area disappearing." However, Wynter's goals would ultimately prove more transformative than guarding against the threat of obsolescence. She was also engaged in the work of "transposing" folk forms—transferring them to a different place or context—into a literary language (or in musical terms, into a different key) to be used in her own creative work. Indeed, Wynter's description of a folk language that was "compressed, epigrammatic and full of sensuous images" offers a key to the poetics that she was then developing in her dramatic works and short stories, several of which were broadcasted over BBC Radio in the 1950s.[1] Such collected material may have supplied the folk songs that sound throughout her 1959 radio play *Under the Sun*, which contained traditional music with lyrics revised, arranged, and sometimes sung by Wynter herself.

Written five years after she earned an MA in Spanish at King's College in London, this correspondence reveals a nuanced version of Wynter as a traveling collector of folk materials who sought to enrich her own creative practice by immersing herself in the everyday speech, storytelling, sonic, and embodied practices of the folk. By 1958, Wynter was not only an emerging cultural critic, but also a playwright, actor, and member of an acclaimed Caribbean dance troupe. As she recalls, "When I went to London, there was a group from Trinidad led by Boscoe Holder. Of course, we all wanted to be a part of this dance troupe, because at the time everything Caribbean was still new, still to be done."[2] Wynter approached Caribbean culture not just as raw material on which to theorize, but rather as part of an ever-evolving creative praxis that was always "still to be done." This correspondence with Gilliam also shows Wynter, like the Jamaican writer and producer Una Marson before her, navigating the "conservative and cautious" institution of the BBC in the 1950s. Like Marson, Wynter deployed the technologies of empire to subvert it from within, reinterpreting Caribbean culture along the way.[3]

Returning to this book's opening meditation on folk practices that "turn the world upside down," I approach Wynter's multifaceted repertoire as part of an anticolonial practice that she termed "reinterpretation." As she states in "We Must Learn to Sit Down Together and Talk about a Little Culture," "to reinterpret reality is to commit oneself to a revolutionary assault against it. For me then, the play, the novel, the poem, the critical essay, are a means to this end. Not ends in themselves."[4] Wynter's statement about the transformative politics of Black literary production at large might just as easily be applied to her own creative practice. On the one hand, reinterpretation is a project of historical revision: throughout her work, Wynter reinterprets the colonial condition, the pernicious legacy of the plantation system, and Western conceptions of humanity. Folk culture remains the lens through which Wynter glimpses an "alternate way of apprehending reality," not due to its access to organic truths or more authentic forms of blackness, but because it might serve as a "focus of criticism against the impossible reality in which we are all enmeshed."[5] In other words, Wynter is interested in how everyday folk navigate and theorize the paradoxes of what Cedric Robinson calls "racial capitalism."[6] But Wynter also reinterprets the *form* of folk culture itself, "transposing" it across genres and media, incorporating folklore and song into her prose, and in the case of her radio work, adapting its sound. Wynter's praxis of reinterpretation—a critical and aesthetic process that seeks to reinvent the very form of politics—is the focus of this chapter.

This chapter considers Wynter's creative work in London during the 1950s—first as a student and dancer, and then as a playwright and commentator with the BBC—alongside her early criticism, including her unpublished manuscript *Black Metamorphosis: New Natives in a New World*, to deepen an understanding of Wynter as an artist who developed her ideas and craft over a variety of genres and media. In addition to Wynter's own recollections culled from interviews, I examine Wynter's unpublished plays, radio commentaries, and short stories, which are housed at the BBC Written Archives Center in Caversham, United Kingdom. Such works constitute a vital phase of Wynter's artistic and intellectual development, particularly around themes of embodiment, orality, and ceremony.[7] Furthermore, looking at Wynter's performance and broadcasting career reveals her connection to figures such as Katherine Dunham, Marson, Boscoe Holder, and others alongside whom she is not commonly considered. Here, I explore what it would mean to regard Wynter's practices of collecting, transposing, performing, and broadcasting not merely as a prelude to her scholarship, but rather as its foundation.

While "We Must Learn to Sit Down" proposes a politics of reinterpretation for cultural criticism, such revelations can take place in the street, onstage, or as Wynter recalls in one anecdote from her London years, in the discounted gallery seats of a concert hall:

> When [Katherine Dunham] came to England, I remember sitting up in the gallery right at the top, the cheap seats, and I could almost have fallen out. I had never heard such rhythm in my life and the power of that rhythm. That was a powerful influence in my life and that was why dancing was just part of my whole life that I was living at the time.[8]

Framing the experience as an awakening, Wynter insists that she "could have fallen out," in the colloquial sense of feeling viscerally overwhelmed by "the power of that rhythm." Wynter elaborates, "[Dunham] went all over the new world finding the relics of the music and the things that have been carried on from Africa and also from Latin America—from the indigenous peoples of the Americas."[9] Being a Caribbean student in London meant not only getting a formal education at King's College, but also enjoying the theater, in the "cheap seats," witnessing Dunham's stylized reinterpretations of folk dance that Wynter frames as "part of the anticolonial struggle." It is also in London that Wynter was introduced to pan-Caribbean carnival traditions that imagine "the end of the world, the overturning of the [imperial] order."[10] Taking on renewed urgency in the context of the colonial uprisings of the 1950s and 1960s, such enactments of the "end of the world" also invoke the recurring process of upheaval and inversion that Wynter theorizes in her later works. Thus, she retained from her London years the idea that dance and other embodied practices can spark transformative insights about the nature of being, beyond the constraints of reality. As Aaron Kamugisha observes, "beyond coloniality does not exist in a future theory or a future heaven. It exists in the creative self-activity of the African diasporic masses."[11]

Here, I build on several important readings of Wynter's creative oeuvre.[12] Carole Boyce Davies's preface to *The Caribbean Woman Writer as Scholar* illuminates the figure of the creative-theoretical, whose critical work is "intimately connected to the imaginative."[13] Davies's recent discussion of Wynter's 1970 musical play *Maskarade* further displays this intimate connection.[14] Similarly, in "Rebellion / Invention / Groove," Katherine McKittrick attends to descriptions of performance in *Black Metamorphosis*, contending that "what [Wynter] begins to open up, then, is the perceptive and groundbreaking claim that *making black culture reinvents black humanity and life*."[15] Broadening her expansive engagement with Wynter's oeuvre, McKittrick proposes a mode of reading that is as attentive to Wynter's accounts of quotidian performance as it is to her sweeping critiques of Western modernity.

Sonya Posmentier takes up such a method of reading in *Cultivation and Catastrophe*, where she highlights Wynter's persistent turn to performance even in works that appear to privilege other genres. For example, "Novel and History: Plot and Plantation" links indigenization to prose narrative, which has prompted critics to read the essay as a framework for Wynter's own novel. Indeed, Wynter explains that while "the planters gave the slaves plots of land on which to grow food to feed themselves in order to maximize profits," enslaved subjects transformed such plots into "the locus of resistance to the market system and market values" through cultivation, ritual, and performance.[16] However, as Posmentier observes, the essay takes a "curious turn" when Wynter states that "the plot has its own history, a secretive history expressed in folk songs."[17] Concluding "Novel and History" with excerpts from these songs and chants, she amplifies the sonic trace of the "secretive history" of indigenization. The presence of such gestures, Posmentier argues, attunes us to the possibility that "what Wynter calls the indigenization of Caribbean literary culture takes place not through the novel but through other genres and potentially other media."[18] Indeed, Wynter's practice of inviting songs, epigrams, and chants to "ventilate" her prose—to borrow a term that Nathaniel Mackey uses in reference to Jean Toomer's *Cane*—remains a key part of her aesthetic.[19] Such strategies command attention to the various forms through which Wynter theorizes.

Following Posmentier's call to examine "Wynter's thinking of the provision ground in relationship to performance," I elucidate a creative repertoire that encompasses both Wynter's performance practices and her writerly interventions.[20] While Wynter's essay "Jonkonnu in Jamaica: Towards the Interpretation of Folk Dance as a Cultural Process" is indeed an inaugural effort to forge a "comprehensive theorization" of Caribbean culture, it is also an accumulation of the knowledge and experience that she gained during the previous decade that she spent as a performer.[21] For instance, an earthbound, dancerly sensibility shows up in the essay's descriptions of indigenization. Drawing from Jean Price-Mars, Wynter describes indigenization as a process through which Black subjects "humanized the landscape by peopling it with gods, and spirits, with demons and duppies, with all the rich panoply of man's imagination."[22] She sees it in the signifying spectacle of the Christmas Jonkonnu performances, particularly in the dances performed by enslaved and free women. She uncovers it in the transformative practice of spirit possession, in which the individual is elevated and the community edified. And finally, it is present in spiritual ceremonies in which "dance turns world upside-down, liberating participants."[23] In all of these examples, as Elizabeth Maddock Dillon notes, "the deinstrumentalization of both man and earth brings into visibility a set of relations that are social and reproductive—relations that slavery seeks to eradicate."[24] To acknowledge that Wynter approaches this work not only as a theorist and playwright, but as a dancer and actor, is to invite a more sustained engagement with Wynter's own artistic practices and the experiences that informed her writing.

Intent on revealing the "cultural-historical continuity" between different flash points in Black hemispheric modernity across time, Wynter reinterprets and subsequently transmutes the unruly forms of folk culture that I have discussed in the previous three chapters of this book.[25] Her project concerns, as Yomaira C. Figueroa-Vásquez maintains, "the labor of imagining other ways of being human in the modern/colonial and settler colonial world."[26] But it also entails envisioning the "end of the world," the "reversal of the order of power and authority."[27] Most saliently, her engagement with Price-Mars reveals a persistent drive to consider folk culture in comparative terms, as an asymmetrical yet complimentary process that transforms the landscape of the Americas.[28] This is the Black metamorphosis that Wynter speaks of in the manuscript of the same name: "the extra-African's cultural response to the dehumanizing alienation of the capitalist plantation system of the New World was to reroot himself, making use of the old cultural patterns which had undergone a true sea-change, in order to create the new vocabulary of the new existence."[29] Wynter locates this new vocabulary of existence in an ever-evolving repertoire of Black cultural practices to which she bears witness as well as performs.

TOWARD AN EARTHBOUND VOCABULARY OF MOVEMENT: DANCE AT THE END OF THE WORLD

David Scott's magisterial interview with Sylvia Wynter, "The Re-Enchantment of Humanism," contains several striking photos of Wynter midperformance.[30] In one image, taken in Rome during the 1950s, she flourishes a Spanish fan and dons a head-wrap, gold hoops, and twirling skirt as one leg pushes forward in a sambalike movement. In another photograph, she reclines, resplendent in a fringed gown, fishnet stockings, and peep-toe heels, one arm extending toward a dapper partner as she gazes in the opposite direction. A third photograph shows Wynter at the center of a group of gesturing actors, at a staging of her play *Shhh, It's a Wedding* in Jamaica in 1961.

How might these images allow us to picture Wynter more dynamically? To return to her time as a student and dancer amid the creative and political ferment of London in the late 1940s and early 1950s is to assert the importance of embodied practice and sociality to her theories of Black expressive culture and anticolonial resistance. Wynter left for London in 1947 on a Jamaican Centenary scholarship to attend King's College, where she majored in romance languages with a minor in English, eventually earning a master's degree in Spanish in 1953.[31] The timing was fortuitous: Wynter arrived on the front end of what would come to be called the Windrush Generation, an influx of some half million migrants who traveled from the British West Indies to London between the years of 1948 and 1962 to fill labor shortages after World War II, changing the cultural and political landscape of Britain. As J. Dillon Brown and Leah Reade Rosenberg explain, "Among the metropolitan migrants of these early, exciting postwar years were a remarkable number of authors: for literary critics, Windrush now also denotes a generation of particularly productive and visible West Indian writers who migrated to Great Britain to ply their trade at this time."[32] Wynter stood in the company of many emerging figures of Caribbean thought, including the novelist Jan Carew (whom she married in 1958), Wilson Harris, George Lamming, Roger Mais, and others who explored the topic of coloniality, exile, and self-determination. As Scott proposes in his conversation with Wynter, "so there is in the 1950s, for your generation in London, a very self-conscious effort to transform the imagination."[33]

However, when Scott asks whether Wynter was "hooked into a circuit of Caribbean writers and scholars," she replies: "as a student, I think I was more hooked into the dancers. I was part of Boscoe Holder's dance troupe. My central interest there was in the dancing and that was far more my world." That statement indicates neither a disavowal of the Caribbean literary circuit nor of writing in general, but rather an insistence on the foundational significance of dance as a mode of cultural transformation and embodied knowledge. As Wynter elaborates, "The idea of the dance at that time was so powerful because I think it bridged the divide in the Caribbean between the literate written tradition and the stigmatized yet powerful undertow of African religions and their cultural seedbed that had transformed itself into a current that was now *neoindigenous* to the Caribbean. And this was what was being resurrected."[34]

The idea of dance as a *bridge* between literate and folk tradition, public and submerged culture, and perhaps most urgently, between Caribbean subjects themselves defines this early phase of Wynter's work and study. Her involvement in dance connects her to a range of figures apart from the canonical writers typically associated with Windrush. One of those figures, of course, was the Trinidadian choreographer and painter Boscoe Holder. Born in 1921 in Trinidad to parents from Barbados and Martinique, Boscoe and his younger brother, the dancer, actor, and artist Geoffrey Holder, worked across a variety of media. When U.S. military forces were based in Trinidad during World War II, the elder Holder hosted a radio program called *Piano Ramblings*. He started a dance troupe in the 1930s, taught dance at the Katherine Dunham School in 1947, and traveled to London in 1950. One of his concerts, *Bal Creole*, aired on BBC television on June 30, 1950. Holder, often credited with introducing the first steel drum band to London, also collaborated with the calypsonian Lord Kitchener, who had sailed to London on the *Empire Windrush* in 1948. His company, Boscoe Holder and his Caribbean Dancers, performed at the coronation of Queen Elizabeth II in 1953, and they toured the continent afterward.[35]

A photograph of Wynter performing in Rome in 1950 suggests that she joined the company for at least part of their travels.

In an oral history interview, Holder recalls his efforts to develop a "vocabulary of movement" involving a range of pan-Caribbean styles and techniques that would serve as the foundation of his dance pedagogy. His methods were gleaned from his observations of Caribbean folk ritual, particularly Trinidadian Shango and limbo, as well as the beguine, which he observed on a pivotal 1946 trip to Martinique (the birthplace of his mother), when he also met the sisters Jeanne and Paulette Nardal, two architects of the Négritude movement.[36] Holder makes an appearance in Earl Leaf's 1948 book *Isles of Rhythm*, in which Leaf recalls a rain-soaked pilgrimage to the ceremonial hut of a Shango *Ogun* featuring Holder and the Trini dancer Beryl McBurnie. Leaf also included a photograph of Holder with the dancers Irma Jarrett and Percy Boarde with the caption: "West Indian dances, some true reproductions and others interpreted and rearranged for public performance."[37] By making a distinction between "true reproductions" and those choreographies that were "interpreted and rearranged," Leaf places Holder's dances on a spectrum of authenticity according to their presumed proximity to the original. And yet even the term "true reproductions" suggests a process of mediation. For his part, Holder seemed little interested in proclaiming the authentic folksiness of his work: "I wasn't folk people; I was a middle-class colored person. My contribution was proper artistic education on how to present something from there on stage."[38]

Indeed, it was Holder's middle-class status that afforded him the privilege of travel, enabling him to tap into the vogue for all things tropical in London. Shane Vogel's claim that Geoffrey Holder developed a repertoire that involved the "choreographed abstraction of folk movement" could also apply to his older brother, Boscoe.[39] Rather than directly corresponding to the folk dances that Boscoe Holder observed in the field, these interpretations, rearrangements, and abstractions constituted their own genre of Black dance. The settings in which these dances were performed were just as important to this process of abstraction as the choreography. From the concert stage to the nightclub, Caribbean dance (often with exoticized costuming, setting, and props) remained a hallmark of London performance and nightlife.

Two documentary films, produced not for educational purposes but to promote London night culture, illustrate this point. A short clip from the

1953 documentary *Tonight in Britain* shows Holder and his troupe performing "Tropicana" at Churchill's club. Backed by a full orchestra, the dancers whirl about in a carnival-like procession holding parasols (the likes of
which would also appear in Boscoe's paintings). A 1956 video recording
called "Drum Dance" shows Holder and a smaller ensemble of four members of his troupe—three female dancers and a male bongo drummer and
vocalist—performing on a tiny stage at the Cote d'Azure Club. Save for one
enthusiastic spectator, the white audience watches the ensemble with stoic
amusement. "An exhibition of native dancing," declares the voiceover narration. Two female dancers, kneeling, wave their arms and sway backward
in mock possession. Eventually, Holder is the only dancer on stage. At over
six feet, he cuts an imposing figure as he performs a series of leaps. The long
lines of his body defy the constricting space. In the final moments of the
performance, he lifts the bongo while it is still being played by the drummer, who rises from a seated position as the two move in a circle. For a
split second, they exchange a conspiratorial look before moving offstage.[40]

Holder and his contemporaries performed during a time when, as
Anthea Kraut contends, the "trope of black primitivism functioned as
the primary lens through which Caribbean dancing was read."[41] As these
recordings illustrate, Holder capitalized on tastes for Caribbean culture,
while also subversively altering the visual, sonic, and embodied landscape
of a conservative 1950s artistic sphere in London. But the work of Holder
and his dancers was significant not merely because it presented Caribbean
movement to white British audiences. Rather, its greatest value was in serving, again, as a bridge, as Wynter phrases it, connecting Caribbean subjects
gathered in the metropole. As Wynter suggests in a 2017 oral history interview, the gesture of "bridg[ing] the divide" was encapsulated in the act of
leaving her college lectures to "go across" to Holder's nearby dance studio,
a physical and conceptual crossing that Wynter recalls as a point of entry
into the anticolonial movement:

> Dancing and singing was part of my life growing up. But what happened that
> was sort of formal was as part of the anti-colonial movement. I went to the
> University of London. In London there was a famous dancer called Boscoe
> Holder [Arthur Aldwyn Holder]. He came—like his brother, Geoffrey [Geof-
> frey Lamont Holder] who came to United States and became famous—they
> came from Trinidad. Trinidad had carried on the tradition of the carnival

and that tradition is actually universally applicable—sort of the end of the world, the overturning of the order. As you know, we still have it in New Orleans and Brazil so on and so forth. So he had a dance company. I would leave my lectures at King's College and go across to his studio and begin to dance with him, right. That's how I came into dancing.[42]

In the physical gesture of going across, Wynter bridges her academic studies and her dance training, experiencing such activities not just in terms of contrast, but rather connection. In performing such a gesture, Wynter became what Stefano Harney and Fred Moten call a "subversive intellectual," who "disappears into the underground, the downlow lowdown maroon community of the university . . . where the work gets done."[43] As Wynter asserts, to invoke *marronage* is not to suggest a retreat to a "political and cultural cul-de-sac," nor is it a kind of heroic individualist work.[44] Rather it invokes a stealing back and forth common to the practice of *marronage* in the Caribbean; it is the recursive work of forging new collectivities.

Such movement would become important to Wynter's lifework. Writing about the Cuban singer Graciela Pérez, who in the 1930s during the repressive Gerardo Machado regime "slipped out the back door" of the University of Havana to join a band of female musicians, Alexandra Vazquez reminds us that "subversive intellectuals do not, cannot, work alone."[45] What Wynter most emphasizes about her time in Boscoe Holder's dance company is the cultivation of a collective sense of West Indianness, forged not only in lecture halls and literary cafés, but also in other ephemeral moments of embodied sociality. On more than one occasion, she recalls such a fleeting moment: "We met Trinidadians there, and the Trinidadians brought calypso, and I remember one Christmas dancing out into the snow in a low-cut dress and ending up with pneumonia."[46] While it is easy to pass over such an anecdote (or to disregard, to return to a previous example, the conspiratorial look that Holder briefly shares with his fellow dancer), Wynter emphasizes the ways that dance forged new forms of sociality and togetherness—performing an anticolonial labor from within the heart of empire.

In exploring the subversive potential of dance aesthetics, I draw upon Vogel's notion of "working against the music," a phrase that he borrows from Boscoe Holder's brother Geoffrey. As Vogel recounts, when a rather clueless interviewer inquired about Holder's approach to dancing to the airy classical score of Giuseppe Verdi's opera *Aida*, Holder replied, "I worked against it. Against the music. You see the music is all flowery and all in the air, but I had to be the earth beneath it." As Vogel explains, Holder's concept is both technical and metaphorical, describing a "choreographic tension between relatively more formal and rigid forms of European dance and relatively more earthbound, bent-knee African movements that were performed across the Caribbean." Working against the music is thus not only "an aesthetic principle but also an act of labor that finds productive force in an oppositional stance."[47]

Attentive to Wynter's position as a student of dance and literature in the European metropole, I would add to Vogel's framework another possible notion of "working against" Western aesthetics and thought, where the word "against" implies not only opposition, but also physical contact, a pressing against, as with an interface. Here, "against" implies contiguity and even entanglement—a conceptual manifestation of the "choreographic entanglement" of which Holder speaks. Put another way, as Wynter acknowledges, such continuity might describe the Caribbean relationship to Western thought: " I study the West from a place outside, though I am in it as well."[48] This paradox of being both outside and inside, working in opposition to but also in fraught proximity with Western systems of knowledge, offers an expansion of Holder's notion of working against the music. Such a practice of working right up against empire defines the work of Caribbean subjects like Wynter who lived, worked, and studied in the "belly of the beast."[49] It is from this practice of working against / up-against Western value systems that Wynter believes that one might invent new genres of being human.

How might these early experiences as a dancer in the metropole have afforded Wynter with, to borrow Holder's phrase, a "vocabulary of movement," an expressive and critical language rooted in the embodied practices of Black life? Such a vocabulary might usefully frame a discussion of the earthbound aesthetics and politics that form a consistent thread through Wynter's work, particularly her claim in "Jonkonnu" that "the dance was an expression of, and a strengthening of Man's relation with the Earth."[50] Drawing from a Caribbean vocabulary of movement and relation, Wynter names and enacts what McKittrick, invoking Édouard Glissant, has called "a poetics of landscape," through which "expressive acts, particularly the naming of space—regardless of expressive method and technique—is also a process of self-assertion and humanization, a naming of inevitable black geographic presence."[51] Writing about the function of the landscape (*la fonction du paysage*) in the development of Caribbean national literatures, Glissant argues that "the relationship with the land, one that is even more threatened because the community is alienated from the land, becomes so fundamental in this discourse that landscape in the work stops being merely decorative or supportive and emerges as a full character."[52] As McKittrick writes, "the poetics of landscape, then, comprises theories, poems, dramatic plays, and historical narratives that disclose black women's spaces and places. They comprise an interdisciplinary and diasporic analytical opening, which advances creative acts that influence and undermine existing spatial arrangements."[53]

To recall that Wynter develops a poetics of landscape as a practitioner of dance as well as a critic provides insight into the ways that an earthbound orientation might provide the substance of both a politics and a creative praxis. Earthbound subjects are not merely bound to the earth in a restrictive sense (although Wynter certainly explores this meaning in her description of bondage). They are also bound to the earth in the sense of moving toward, as well as in the other sense of "bound": to leap upward, "to walk or run with leaping strides."[54] Earthbound aesthetics thus function simultaneously as a choreographic principle, a historical process of labor and ritual, and a metaphor for mass-based resistance. Across the various media in which she was engaged, Wynter theorizes culture and modernity by staying close to the ground (with special attention to the earth and land) and working from the bottom up, an anticolonial practice akin to what Mimi Sheller has called "citizenship from below."[55]

As I suggest, landscape "emerges as a full character" across Wynter's various works both in and beyond her dance practice. It appears in the dynamic that she describes between the plot and the plantation, between the natural world and the domestic sphere, between "ruinate and cultivate," as one character phrases it in *The House and Land of Mrs. Alba*, Wynter's earthy adaptation of García Lorca's *La casa de Bernarda Alba*.[56] As Wynter elaborates in "Novel and History: Plot and Plantation," indigenization transformed the "plot": small areas of land granted to the enslaved for food cultivation, or designated areas in maroon settlements where "crops [were] cultivated, and religious feasts celebrated with song and dance," and continues in the festival and carnival culture of the Caribbean, in Black music forms, and language. It also appears in everyday choreographies of ritual and gesture in which the body, as Mayra Rivera observes, is both vehicle and product of transformation.[57] Beyond dance, such can be glimpsed in Wynter's rich descriptions of embodied practices, which Koritha Mitchell (drawing from Diana Taylor) broadly defines as "any bodily act that conveys meaning."[58] I turn to Wynter's dance work as a reminder that whenever Wynter turns to the landscape, the Black body is present.

But the development of Wynter's earthbound sensibility was not forged in a straight line from her dance work to her cultural criticism. In the 1950s, she continued her interest in performance while expanding into different media, writing radio plays and short stories for the BBC. In stories such as "Bat and Ball" and "Paramour" and plays such as *The Barren One* and *Under the Sun* (on which her novel *The Hills of Hebron* is based) Wynter thematizes the relationship between the body and the land. While she later argues that the "plot system, was, like the novel form in literature terms, the locus of resistance to the market system and market values," Wynter took a more multigenre approach to form in the years leading up to the publication of her novel.[59] Using both the stage and the radio, she theorized the relationship between embodied knowledge, writing, and ontological sovereignty.

TRANSMITTING CULTURE: WYNTER AT THE BBC

Wynter's turn as a dancer was part of larger ambitions for the stage as an actor in the theater and film. She auditioned for roles, but she recalls, "I could never get a part for myself. Either I was not black enough, or sometimes Americans would put make-up on you and transform you into this or that. For example, I was one of Pharaoh's concubines in the film *The Land of the Pharoahs*! So I started to write parts for myself. Then I found I was more interested in the writing than in the parts themselves."[60] This recollection reflects the challenges of seeking performance work as a Black woman in 1950s London, where imperial racism, both British and American, ever loomed.

In the 1950s and 1960s, Wynter entered an active period of writing and producing plays for stage, radio, and television. In 1958 and 1959, respectively, *Under the Sun* and *The Barren One*, Wynter's adaption of Federico García Lorca's *Yerma*, were broadcast on BBC's *Third Programme*. Also in

1959 came *Miracle in Lime Lane*, which she wrote and produced with her then-husband, Jan Carew, followed by the musical *Shh, It's a Wedding* in 1961. These were followed by a series of dramatic works produced after Wynter's return to Jamaica. While any of these endeavors would be a fruitful point of entry, I focus on a select portion of Wynter's radio work from the 1950s, including her play *The Barren One*, her literary commentary setting criteria for early West Indian writing, and her short stories about Black girlhood, "Bat and Ball" and "Paramour." These early works have gone undiscussed by critics in part because they were not composed for print publication, but rather for BBC Radio's *Caribbean Voices* and *Third Programme*. The recordings have been long lost, and they exist now only as radio scripts accessible at the BBC Written Archives. As James Procter notes, "Most of the sound archive from this period has been wiped—destroyed decades ago when the tight budgetary constraints of the Overseas Service and the relative expense of recording technologies made the costs impossible to bear. But thankfully many of their scripts still survive, preserved in silence at the BBC Written Archives in Caversham."[61] Procter's poetic phrase "preserved in silence" suggests the loss that exists even in preservation. And as Procter also observes, the archive's location in a quiet suburb of Reading, far from the din and buzz of London, further effects this sense of quiet.

What does it mean to encounter Wynter's voice—and Caribbean voices more broadly—in radio scripts rather than audio recordings?[62] Because sonic media transmits meaning differently than written text, one certainly loses a sense of the aural texture of these works. And yet, building upon the method I employed in chapter 3 to describe Eusebia Cosme's and Langston Hughes's recitations, I approach this archive attentive to its traces of sound and embodiment: to "sensuous" dialogue, to musical cues and stage directions written into the lines of her scripts, and finally, to the persistent presence of the body.

It is also necessary to account for the material and social conditions under which Black contributors worked at the BBC. For Wynter, the partnership served both artistic and practical purposes, allowing her to hone her creative skills as well as simply to "make a living."[63] Such a beginning was not unique among such artists. As Peter Kalliney observes, "many West Indian writers cut their teeth at the BBC, eventually making their way onto *Third Programme*. During the 1950s, getting aired on *Third Programme* was generally recognized as an unequivocal stamp of approval from the highbrow world."[64] Since its inception in 1946, *Third Programme* styled itself as an elite purveyor of culture. Training a wary eye on the cultural ascendance of the United States, it advanced the BBC's aim to use "high-cultural objects as instruments of imperial didacticism."[65] Yet such an aim stood in tension with the varying political attitudes of the BBC's West Indian contributors, who in turn participated in, openly contested, or quietly subverted its aims. Although radio served as an imperial technology of containment, the technology itself could not be contained. The voices of Black authors appraising their own literature and politics were suddenly able to reach a much wider audience. As Kalliney observes, "as a consequence of the extensive reach of radio broadcast, a nascent Anglophone Caribbean literature was made more accessible regionally than any published book, magazine, journal, or newspaper could have achieved at that juncture in the region's cultural development."[66]

The groundwork for Caribbean participation in *Third Programme* was laid by *Caribbean Voices*, a literary series that ran from 1943 to 1958 and that first gained notoriety under the production of the Jamaican poet, playwright, and activist Una Marson. Initially, Marson was hired in 1941 to work on *Calling the West Indies*, a wartime broadcast to the colonies. *Caribbean Voices* was born when Marson decided to curate a weekly literary segment featuring poems, fiction, and guest interviews with Caribbean authors such as Edward Kamau Brathwaite, Sam Selvon, Derek Walcott, George Lamming, and V. S. Naipaul. A sonic literary journal, *Caribbean Voices* provided a forum to discuss a nascent Caribbean literature, as well as a vehicle for broadcasting that literature to audiences that it might not otherwise have reached. As James Procter notes, Marson's tenure at the BBC showed that "old-fashioned imperial racism and enlightened thinking circulated in the same units and corridors of the corporation."[67] After Marson's departure in 1946 (which by many accounts was a fraught parting), production was taken over by Henry Swanzy, who later was successed by Naipaul.

During the final two years of *Caribbean Voices*, Wynter made periodic appearances as a commentator and fiction author, supplementing her work in radio drama on *Third Programme*. On June 6, 1958, Wynter participated in a forum on the West Indian novel, along with Carew, Errol John, Lamming, Naipaul, Edgar Mittleholzer, and Fernando Henriques, that discussed Stuart Hall's claim that "the West Indian novel has two functions to perform: to dramatise and evaluate. It must give us an eye with which to see our society, and an eye with which to measure ourselves in our search for our identity."[68] While Wynter's role at the BBC was smaller than Marson's, she nevertheless strived to articulate Caribbean aesthetics through her creative work and on-air commentary, and her radio plays served as a laboratory for collaboration between Caribbean actors and musicians. In a quite literal sense, Wynter had been honing her voice as a cultural critic for over a decade before she published the essays that are now cited as her earliest critical works.

Wynter's commentary as guest editor for *Caribbean Voices* is a useful place to begin the discussion. On June 8, 1958, she selected material for the program and offered her appraisals, establishing criteria for West Indian writing that also informed her own work. The broadcast begins with its customary opening: "This is London Calling the Caribbean." The announcer, Billy Pilgrim, continues: "Good evening. Tonight and for the next four weeks 'Caribbean Voices' will be edited by West Indians, each of whom has made a mark in the field of writing in recent years, and each of whom has appeared as both reader and author at some time in these programmes." Wynter then offers this overview:

> Writing as a West Indian one starts off with a great advantage. That of exceedingly rich and varied cultural heritage. But the very wealth and abundance of the material at our disposal brings in the problem of evolving a new and adequate form. The question of technique, selection of material, discrimination in our use of words, of rhythms, becomes our most urgent problem. The story that you will hear now is a story that I chose because I think technically it succeeds altogether.[69]

The piece in question was the Trinidadian author Michael Anthony's short story "Pita and the Deep Sea," an allegorical tale about a fish attempting (and ultimately failing) to avoid capture. But Wynter's commentary on the work is not thematic, but rather technical. Conveying an interest in literary craft, she further elaborates that it is "poetic in concept, his style is terse and simple, he uses the rhythms of speeches as selective as he uses his words, and it is obvious that he has pared down his story to its barest essentials." Her choice of the words "selection," "discrimination," and "pared down" suggests a process of creative discernment that was not commonly attributed to early West Indian writing.[70]

Wynter's emphasis on "the problem of evolving a new and adequate form" might be taken quite directly in terms of a quest for the artistic forms best suited to the articulation of Caribbean experience. Wynter engages in ongoing debates about the literary merits of "dialect forms of English":

> I have commented at length on this story because it displays all of the qualities I consider to be the best assets of a West Indian writer. A French critic said that when reading Jan Carew's prose he could feel, he could touch, he could smell. . . . We have at our disposal dialect forms of English which spoken by a peasant people retained strength, freshness, directness, precision, the simplicity of a spoken language used to communicate and not to evade. This simplicity and directness is I think our greatest asset. . . . Not that I am advocating a false folksy quaintness. . . . But I think that over generations of use, the written language has to be re-examined in the light of the spoken, and purged of its accretions.[71]

The use of dialect in radio programs for West Indian audiences was by no means new, with precedent in the work of the Jamaican poet Louise Bennett. Describing Bennett's "frequent and popular presence" on *Caribbean Voices* and other BBC programs, Alejandra Bronfman explains how Bennett first built an audience through local theater. Her poems were published in the widely read *Daily Gleaner*, making them available for local circulation and community recitations in which Bennett herself often participated. "By the time her poems and theater sketches arrived on the radio," Bronfman explains, "Jamaican listeners were attuned to her particular use of nation language." But the space that Bennett opens up for dialect was yet "fragile and contested." Her work both delighted the public and "irritated prominent gatekeepers," who were afraid that children would refuse to speak in anything but dialect after hearing Bennett's poems.[72]

Wynter inserted herself into this debate by extolling dialect as "our greatest asset." Yet her aim is not to argue that literature could lend legitimacy to dialect, but rather that Black vernacular speech might elevate literature. She does not insist that West Indian writing ought to emulate spoken vernacular, but rather that it needs to be "re-examined in the light of the spoken." This reexamination hinged on an emphasis on embodiment: language's ability to allow the reader to "feel, touch and smell," and to suggest, as she notes later in the same broadcast, a "more graphic and more physical sense."

Wynter also reminds listeners that "simplicity" should not be confused with a "false folksy quaintness," a sentiment that she reinforces in her 1970 play *Maskarade*:

> Now some people might think, say
> That the tale I going to tell
> Just a nice little piece of "ethnic" business!
> So let me warn you from the beginning
> I'm no folklore Uncle Remus
> With a fake lore masquerade
> For some of you to come and get
> Your doctorate on![73]

Directly addressing the audience "in the style of the calypsonian," the play's central storyteller, Lovey, warns against reductive, condescending appropriations of folk culture, particularly by academics. Folk culture should not be dismissed as a "little piece of ethnic business," Lovey insists. Instead, he extols on the modernity of these forms, their immediacy, their relevance for the now, and their ongoing capacity to "To carry on / that first / invent that man invent," the creation of the self.[74]

Anticipating *Maskarade*, Wynter adopted the medium of radio to theorize as well as enact this relationship among aurality, embodiment, and invention across various genres and forms. In using Anthony's short story as a case study, Wynter's *Caribbean Voices* commentary further develops a framework for her own short fiction, which she had debuted on the program in the years prior. Indeed, though Wynter was on the brink of debuting her plays and would soon embark on an elaborate narrative that she pointedly calls "an anticolonial, not a nationalist novel," it is in these "pared down" stories that she introduces the themes and techniques that would come to fruition in later works. Short stories were the most featured form on *Caribbean Voices*. Their prevalence was in part, practical—they were short enough to be read over the air all at once, while also providing enough material to fill that segment. As Hyacinth M. Simpson observes, short story readings on *Caribbean Voices* became integral to the program's process of "discovering and fine-tuning an oral aesthetic."[75] This oral aesthetic was also an *aural* aesthetic, given the ways that "the written and spoken word were conjoined by radio technology."[76]

I now turn to "Paramour" and "Bat and Ball," which were transmitted on *Caribbean Voices* on November 25, 1956, and August 11, 1957, respectively.[77] Wynter read the stories herself. Narrated in the first person, both tales explore the poetics of landscape through the lens of Black girlhood. Wynter's stories take stock of the stifling constraints faced by girls and women bound to the home and to expectations of marriage. Each story explores the tension between the freedom and danger of the outdoors, as well as the confinement of women and girls to domestic spaces, which are often oppressive but sometimes suggestive of sensuous possibility. As I argued in chapter 1 of this book, short forms often do a specific kind of work in depicting experience—tending to focus on brief yet transformative episodes in characters' lives rather than monumental narratives of community and nation. They were an ideal mode for working through, in miniature, the rich interpersonal themes that would inhabit Wynter's later work.

In "Bat and Ball," the narrator describes the cricket games that take place on a "rough clearing" of land backing her family's vegetable garden: "Paradise was a long, narrow strip of land which prolonged our backyard and vegetable garden into an estate. Thickly covered with 'single-bible' cacti and divi-divi trees, this strip had long resisted my mother's pioneering attempts and remained stubbornly jungle." What obstinately resists cultivation is nevertheless a site of possibility, albeit one to which the female narrator holds limited access. The cricket patch—whimsically dubbed "Paradise"— is a boy's domain. For the narrator's older brother, Rance, "progress to Paradise was simple" given his status as the "eldest, a manchild, and as such, born to freedom." Rance's "escape meant no more than a lordly stepping out of the breakfast room, down the stone steps, into the backyard, down through the vegetable garden, and under a tanglefull of bushes unto the rough clearing originally intended by my mother for lettuces but now serving as our cricket patch."[78] It is the roughness of the cricket patch, its indeterminate condition between "ruinate and cultivate," that enables its transformative potential.

While Rance and his male companions enjoy access to Paradise as a matter of course, "escape was a different matter" for the narrator. Normally confined to the house doing "girl-work" with her mother, the narrator's escapes require more calculation. This planning usually comes in the form of deliberate ineptitude with household chores, such as spilling water on freshly polished floors. When her mother's anger flares out, "it was quite in order for me to run." While the narrator's flight from the house supplies the pretext to steal away to Paradise, it also allows sensuous communion with the cultivated landscape: "the beaten earth of the backyard hot with sun under my feet, the sweet stinging smell of limes as I flew past, the hens squawking and fluttering under the breadfruit tree, the ducks in ordered line alongside the mud trench."[79]

Upon the narrator's arrival at Paradise, the boys reluctantly agree to let her serve as a fielder. The position involves crawling through barbed wire and thornbushes to retrieve the ball. Happy to be included, the narrator performs such tasks "zealously," cherishing her scars. After all, the bat and the ball "fused themselves together into a summer's day dance," replete with ritualistic splendor."[80] But one day after a particularly tiresome game, she finally demands to bat. "I tired of fielding! I want to bat too!" In the hush that follows, "the wind was still yet the trees leaned to listen. The hush of the others was like that of an old-faded photograph."[81] The landscape is animated and receptive compared to the stillness and silence of her peers. "If is bat you must bat, bowl me out first!" replies Rance, the batsman, annoyed to have his showboating interrupted. Stepping up to bowl, anxiously aware of the heightened stakes of the task, the narrator readies herself:

The ball fitted itself into the curve of my hand. The bat in Rance's hand poised itself, a thing of elegance and surety waiting to wing the ball away into the oblivion of a six. I didn't throw the ball over with the fanfare of flourishes which I had seen Timothy use. Instead my arm whipped under, my wrist twisting itself in some preknown rhythm, and the ball hurtled away in an inverted arc which trailed in its wake the whittled sticks of the wicket.[82]

Finally, the narrator throws the ball and smashes the wicket. But the would-be triumph is reduced to a nonevent. Her victory is met with no resounding praise, or even acknowledgment: "Timothy and the two boys, without turning their backs or closing their eyes, managed not to see me."[83]

Later, Wynter alludes to the autobiographical nature of the story, noting that "my 'Bat and Ball' story shows that because of the division of labor, I had to be at home helping my mother to wash and clean and the boys could go out on the bottom of the yard and play cricket."[84] In the story, as in Wynter's own youth, the cricket patch offered momentary escape from the domestic sphere and the interminable mandate to "catch a husband." Her participation in cricket enables a "rough clearing" for other forms of sociality to which the narrator otherwise would lack access: "like showering together, seeing who could hold one's breath longest underwater . . . happily unending arguments as to whose hen had been foolish enough to lay its eggs from the heights of a breadfruit tree, cooking together over open wood-fires, ackee and saltfish, rice and dumplings . . . money making ventures like the time we had given picture shows and charged a penny for admission."[85] In effect, cricket opens the door to a world of belonging to which the narrator would otherwise have little access. By the end of the story, however, she comes to the ironic realization that her success at the sport—and therefore her disruption of the myth of male mastery— disqualifies her from further participation.

Listeners who heard Wynter read "Bat and Ball" may have been struck by Mittelholzer's incongruous introduction: "There are few of us who do not like being reminded of the carefree escapades of childhood, and I'm sure quite a number of our listeners in the Caribbean will be thrown into a nostalgic mood by the story which we are presenting this week."[86] If "carefree escapades" seems hardly the right phrase to encapsulate the social themes of "Bat and Ball," his introductory remarks for "Paramour" sounded quite a different note: "This time, we hear the grim note of social realism."[87]

This story begins as the protagonist Victoria's walk home from school is interrupted by an unexpected storm. After a voice beckons her to take shelter in a nearby home, Victoria meets the beautiful Miss Edna. Having noticed Victoria's love of books, Miss Edna begs the girl to teach her to read and write. They begin with a love letter from a suitor who vows to love Miss Edna "even in death," a phrase that foreshadows the story's grim ending. Beyond the love letters, Miss Edna is an eager pupil who takes special pleasure in learning how to write her own name. But when Victoria's mother learns of this visit, she angrily forbids her daughter from returning to the house of that "paramour," the mother's word for a "kept woman." Victoria returns anyway, and she soon learns that though Edna is indeed the mistress of the powerful Dr. Edward, the letters come from another suitor and her true love, a humble student who wants to marry her. This rosy future is cut short when on the third visit, Victoria finds two dead bodies: Miss Edna, shot through the chest, and Dr. Edward, with a hole in his temple.

Mittelholzer's label of "social realism" notwithstanding, "Paramour" reads more like a gothic tale in which mysterious forces lead inexorably to tragic ends, akin to those in Eric Walrond's *Tropic Death*. The comparison might also extend to the story's description of scorched surroundings reminiscent of Walrond's "Drought":

> The road was long and dusty and the tall slender coconut palms offered no shade from the sun which burnt down, weaving the air into a shimmering curtain of heat. The pebbles kicked loosely under my feet as with my eyes glued to the pages of a novel I moved on my accustomed route walking with the sure instinct that belongs only to wild things. . . . On this particular day, as I walked home from school, my mind seemed to have taken on an added quality of awareness, stretching out beyond the printed page to note the grass on the side of the road hanging lifelessly dry, and the buttercups quite withered away, and I was reminded that this was the drought season.[88]

While in "Bat and Ball," the landscape offers sumptuous retreat and the promise of collectivity, in "Paramour," it offers no such respite. The drought-ravaged setting makes the sudden downpour all the more surprising and fateful, driving the story's action toward the interior in both a literal and metaphorical sense. When Miss Edna's voice calls out, inviting Victoria to take shelter, she is led into an old rambling house "crammed with heavy mahogany furniture menacing like shrouded ghosts in the storm-darkened room, whilst across the further wall crimson velvet curtains and a matching crimson divan blazed out into the somberness."[89]

Despite the heaviness of the room, it seemed to the narrator "like a palace." The hostess appears, a woman of transfixing beauty who introduces herself as Miss Edna:

> —Ah see you pass here every day an ah say to meself what a strange child she is reading an walking along like that, an never looking to right nor left, and always alone, never with other children. An ah wanted to talk to you but ah didn't know how. You ever seen me before?
> —No mam, ah never see you before, mam.
> —Don't call me mam. Call me Edna. That's what ah name. An you?
> —Ah name Victoria, Miss Edna.[90]

Although the exchange culminates in Miss Edna's request for the bookish protagonist to teach her to read and write, here the woman and girl mirror each other's subtle vernacular. Even in the absence of a recording, the radio script reveals the understated form of Wynter's dialect, as Brent Hayes Edwards puts it, the "orthographic technique by which written language represents oral language."[91] The elongated "ah," in place of "I," the clipped consonant where "and" becomes "an," and so forth. Although Edna and Victoria's interactions will center on acts of reading and writing, this rendering of spoken vernacular remains just as important to the main themes of language and literacy on which the story centers. Theirs is not a unilateral exchange of knowledge, as Victoria learns new vocabulary from Edna as well. After Victoria reads aloud a love letter from Miss Edna's suitor, Johnny, Miss Edna declares: "Him must be really love me then and as a good woman, not as a paramour." Victoria muses, "The word 'paramour' was new to me and beautiful. I couldn't understand why she should pronounce it with such contempt. 'Paramour' sounded as she was, soft and sibilant and sweet, and from that moment in my mind her name was miss Edna Paramour." For Victoria, the word "paramour" provides an opening, not merely in its promise of romance, but in its suggestion of a yet-imagined alternative to the constraints of respectability.[92]

If language provides an opening, so does music. Miss Edna places a record on the gramophone and invites Victoria to "listen." The tune is the jazz standard "I'm in the Mood for Love." Providing another counterpoint to the story's focus on literacy, this scene of listening emphasizes forms of knowledge that are transmitted aurally. Here, not only does the gramophone signal transgressive desire, but it is also the mode through which a transnational aesthetics, in the form of Depression-era American music, enters the story. The music suggests the tantalizing, if melancholic, promise of an elsewhere. But for Miss Edna, it is ultimately an escape into the interior. Victoria notices that this music has taken Miss Edna "far away": "Her tone was kind, but I knew that she far away from me, lost in herself, and so I did not linger."[93]

Ultimately, Miss Edna's romance of escape not only proves to be unattainable, but also provokes the scorn of those around her. Upon learning of her daughter's visit to Miss Edna, Victoria's mother exclaims: "[Y]ou with your color and education can get anywhere but now you want to be a slut, a paramour like dat woman!" Miss Edna invites scorn not only because she is a "paramour," but also because she is the child of a Chinese grocer and his common-law wife, or as Victoria's mother sneers, a "half-chiney wretch." Victoria's mother fears a similar fate for her daughter, who is also "bastard born," the daughter of a "white backra." She explains that "he was me boss and I had to do what he say." However, despite the circumstances of her daughter's birth, she sets her heart on Victoria becoming "a worthwhile woman that I could be proud of."[94] Miss Edna's demise seems as much a manifestation of her social alienation as a result of possessive masculinity. Women who indulge in the romance of escape are not only subject to exclusion and violence, but also to the erasure of that violence from public record. The local newspaper reports Miss Edna's death as a part of a "suicide pact" rather than a murder.

Rather than a cautionary tale, "Paramour" exposes the problematic absence of a social framework in which a "paramour," especially one of mixed heritage, can exist as a part of the community. If the story is rather heavy-handed in its depiction of the punishment of transgressive women, its young protagonist offers a glimpse of what it might mean to admire and guard their dreams. After stumbling upon the violent scene, Victoria honors Miss Edna with a private, yet poignant gesture: "A little way off, also on the floor, the letter that I had read two days before, lay crumpled. Without knowing why I did this, only knowing that Miss Edna would have wanted it, I picked up the letter and placed it in my school-bag. On the side-board was the plate with 'grater cakes,' white with pink on top which I knew that Miss Edna would have bought for me. I took these also and put them in my bag."[95] Through her association with Miss Edna (and the subtle acts of care and solidarity she enacts after her death), the narrator absorbs an alternative conception of what it means to be a "good woman"—one that departs from the standard conceptions of pure birth, sexual propriety, and enclosure within the framework of marriage.

Alongside her plays and novel, these stories cast further light on Wynter's complicated and often controversial gender politics. Critics commonly allude to Wynter's afterword to the feminist anthology *Out of the Kumbla*, edited by Carole Boyce Davies and Elaine Savery Fido. In "Beyond Miranda's Meanings: Un/Silencing the Demonic Ground of Caliban's Woman," Wynter turns to William Shakespeare's *The Tempest* to expound that "patriarchal discourse" falls short in explaining the power relation between Caliban, an "incarnation of . . . the subordinated 'irrational' and 'savage' native," and the white Miranda, "a co-participant . . . in the power and privileges generated by the empirical supremacy of her own population."[96] In such a schema (which furthermore relies on the absenting or silence of "Caliban's Woman"), Miranda holds power over Caliban, not vice versa. Wynter not only aims to disrupt the understanding of "woman" as a universal category on which theories of feminism are to be based, but also questions that idea that patriarchal relations describe structures of dominance in colonial societies. As Xhercis Méndez and Yomaira C. Figueroa-Vásquez observe, "[N]otably this is one example where women of color and some decolonial feminists might part ways with Wynter, because while it is the case that Caliban's relationship to Miranda, specifically, is not one characterized by Patriarchy with a capital P, it is also true that this literary example does not help us better understand the relationship between Caliban and any racialized women. Women of color are precisely the bodies absented from the play."[97]

Méndez and Figueroa-Vásquez cogently assert that decolonial feminists have "substantively contributed to Wynter's political goal of moving beyond the genre of 'Man,'" while also pointing out that men of color have not been denied access to patriarchy simply by virtue of their colonization.[98] But a similar counternarrative can also be found in Wynter's own creative work. As Natasha Barnes observes, "If Wynter comes to the conclusion in her 1990 afterword in *Out of the Kumbla* that gender has no ontological status in Caribbean teleology, a considerably more hesitant, nuanced position appears to be worked out in the political geography of her 1962 'nation novel' *The Hills of Hebron*."[99] She outlines the novel's exposure of the subjugation of women as being integral to the revivalist Hebron sect (which was modeled after the Bedwardism movement). Citing Wynter's critique of charismatic male leadership, Barnes highlights the novel's depiction of "performative and liturgical realm dominated by women celebrants whose capacity for spirit possession made pocomania a uniquely female-gendered mode of religiosity."[100]

While Barnes concludes that "the feminist energies of the text . . . were recognized neither by the author nor its conservative critics," I argue that a consideration of Wynter's stories and dramatic work shows that such energies were consistent and intentional.[101] Indeed, racialized women's bodies are not "absented from the play" in her own creative work, which consistently centers on the experiences of women and girls. This is not to make the facile claim that stories featuring women have inherently progressive gender politics. Rather, Wynter's works display a critique of nationalist discourses of home and family that hinge upon the subordination of women. As Shirley Toland-Dix conveys, "feminist critics have observed that nationalist discourses have consistently cast women as guardians of culture whose primary responsibility to the nation is the bearing and raising of children," and often, "women are invested in the very gender dichotomies that often contain them."[102] Instead of depicting feminist heroines, Wynter's stories and plays emphasize the structures that constrain their creativity, bodily autonomy, and intellect. At the same time, Wynter re-enchants folk culture to provide glimpses, however subtle, of "otherwise possibilities."[103]

THE CEREMONY FOUND:
THE BARREN ONE'S SONIC DISRUPTIONS

A few months after editing *Caribbean Voices*, Wynter began rehearsals for *The Barren One*, her adaptation of Garcia Lorca's 1934 play *Yerma*. In encountering *The Barren One* as a script rather than a recording, one loses a sure sense of how the play sounded. At the same time, through stage directions, musical cues, and handwritten adjustments—lines crossed out, additions, asterisks—one gains details about how those effects were produced. Furthermore, the script brings us to the "event" of the recording as it took shape in the face-to-face rehearsals and the recording prior to broadcast—a reminder that the radio play was not only an acoustic form, but a space of embodied encounters and an immersive, collaborative enterprise.

The script for *The Barren One* shows a rehearsal schedule for the week of December 1, 1958, from 10:30 A.M. to 5 P.M. at the Langham Hotel, with a recording on December 5 and a broadcast of January 7, 1959 from 8 to 9:25 P.M. Among the people in the room were the Jamaican actress Cleo Laine and the Trinidadian playwright Errol John in the lead roles of John and Irma (Juan and Yerma in the original). Sheila Clarke, the wife of Boscoe Holder and a dancer in his company, played "Devil Woman" in a carnival scene near the play's climax. (An alternative version of the cast list names Wynter in this role.) Music was provided by the guitarist Fitzroy Coleman and the drummer Emmanuel Myers, who had also performed with the Holder troupe. Even without a live audience, the rehearsal and the recording represented a transnational Caribbean mode of gathering in the metropole, a gathering that built on Wynter's previous experience as a dancer and student.

Beyond the scene of the recording, archival materials also illuminate the BBC's appraisal process for radio drama. Although Wynter eventually received a fee of 70 guineas for the script, an early memo expresses reservations about the project. In an internal memo dated May 14, 1958, the producer Robin Midgely praised Wynter's "lively" translation, but admitted:

> I am not too sure about the play. It seems to me unfortunate that the leading character should have just this one fixation, natural though it may be, and because the whole scene is shot through with this one lens, several of the characters seem to lack the necessary dramatic dimensions. More than most plays, it would depend on how it was done. The repetition could make it very powerful, or very boring, though its classical form and rich language would, I think, make it particularly suitable for radio.

Responding to a revised version of the script, Midgely remarked, "This seems a great improvement of the previous version. Although perhaps a little too long, it must rely for its effect largely on the cumulative nature of the dialogue, though the stylised scene with the washerwomen could be simplified a little."[104]

Midgely's claim that the play was "shot through this one lens" referred to the original plot of *Yerma*, in which a woman in a rural Spanish village prays obsessively and in vain for children. Yerma's longing is only heightened by the apparent indifference of her husband, Juan. Over the course of the play, and despite the counsel of other women both young and old, Yerma becomes increasingly desperate, turning to superstition (conjure work) and religious methods. Along with other childless women, Yerma makes a pilgrimage (called a *romería*) to a sacred site where she hopes to be granted the blessing of children. When her husband finally reveals that he never wanted children and tries to convince her to abandon her desire, she strangles him in a rage. "I have killed my child!" she exclaims as the final curtain falls.

The question of the play's success depending on "how it was done" had occupied radio dramatists ever since the birth of the form, spawning a number of guidebooks that commonly emphasized "clarity over obscurity" in adapting material for radio.[105] Arguably, such aims were in tension with modernist dramas like Lorca's, which relied on the very "stylised scenes" and ritualistic fixations that Midgely wanted simplified. Of course, Wynter formed her own ideas about how it should be done. As she explained in a publicity statement for *Radio Times*:

> I once read an English translation of *Yerma* and was impressed by its incongruity. England has no peasant society to correspond with Spain's, and the whole thing had an air of falseness. In Jamaica we still have a small-holding society. I began to translate *Yerma* again, setting it among these people. In almost any small village or town, and the transposition worked naturally, even to the evocative expressions of speech and the old Spanish-style songs of the Maroons.[106]

In implying that Jamaica served as a more congruous setting than England for transposing a Spanish play, Wynter also displaces England as the obvious point of comparison with its soon-to-be-former colony. Her transposition of Lorca's "peasant society" enables her to link the play's imagery of Spanish agricultural labor, earth, and landscape to the legacy of the Caribbean plantation and plot. In the "old Spanish style songs of the Maroons," one discerns the legacy of Spanish colonialism in Jamaica and the patterns of the *palenques*, settlements in which, as Wynter explains elsewhere, "maroons humanized their mountainous interior with adaptations of their own culture."[107] These transformative entanglements of land, folk culture, and embodied resistance also drive Wynter's approach to translation: the words and phrases that she emphasizes most relate to the natural world. The titles of her two adaptations foreground this emphasis. She retitles *Yerma* as *The Barren One*, alluding not only to the presumed infertility of the central character, but also to the importance of cultivation broadly. Likewise, *La Casa de Bernarda Alba* (The House of Bernarda Alba) becomes *The House and Land of Mrs. Alba*.

On the one hand, Wynter's adaptations bring out the themes of earth that already exist in Lorca's work. Describing his rural trilogy, Wynter observes:

> the sun, the rain, the drought, the flood, are understood by the people of a traditional unindustrialized society, as economic forces. Their living depends on these forces. Natural forces, in the imagery of the people and of Lorca, play something of the part of an all-powerful Fate. The people to whom such

imagery is meaningful tend to accept the nature of their society as something decreed and comparable to the irrational inevitability of drought or flood.[108]

On the other hand, Wynter's claim that the transposition "worked naturally" seems an overstatement, given the considerable labor that went into her adaptation. She takes considerable liberties with the source material, as her use of the word "transposition" indicates. If the basic definition of "transpose" (to transfer from one place or context to another) signals the shift in setting, the word's musical definition (to transfer or perform in a different key) provides insight into Wynter's more elusive aim of adapting Lorca's "evocative expressions" to a Caribbean context.

Building on the sonic elements of Lorca's play, Wynter crafts a Caribbean soundscape, including Jamaican folk songs, work songs, and vernacular expressions. Some changes correspond directly to elements of *Yerma*: a conjurer (*conjudora*) becomes an Obeah woman; a work scene in the olive groves becomes "machetes cutting the cane and the men singing a worksong in unison."[109] *Yerma*'s depiction of the *romería*, a Spanish spiritual pilgrimage (traveled, in this case, by women wishing for children) that culminates in feast and dancing, is transformed in *The Barren One* to a carnival scene that features the song of the "Devil Woman," a traditional mas (masque) character. In addition to these transpositions, Wynter introduces new elements, such as the "wild rhythms" of Shango drumming, which interrupt the play at moments where no music is present in the original.

Wynter's approach might contrast with that of another translator of Lorca, Langston Hughes. During the Spanish Civil War, Hughes began translating *Bodas de sangre* (*Blood Wedding*). He completed the first draft in 1938 but never published or produced the play, turning his energies instead to a translated collection of Lorca's poems, *Gypsy Ballads*. Melia Bensussen, who located the manuscript among Hughes's papers in the Beinecke Collection at Yale University, notes that "Hughes was obviously concerned with staying as close as possible to the original, but also with making changes necessary to capture in English the essence of Lorca's poetry." With such changes as replacing "*señora*" with "darling" rather than the more literal "Mrs.," Bensussen contends, Hughes translated the play "culturally, to his African American idioms."[110] However, I would argue that such linguistic adaptations are far subtler than the vernaculars of Hughes's own work, as well as his translations of Guillén's poems (as discussed in chapter 3), in which Hughes made choices about how to render dialect orthographically. More than with his other translations, he took a high-fidelity approach to translation when it came to *Blood Wedding*.

In contrast, Wynter takes a radical approach to adaptation, in which Caribbean vernacular and music do not merely serve as folk material analogous to Lorca's Andalusia, but rather as forms of sonic disruption that alert us to new historical connections and possibilities for self-invention. One such instance of sonic disruption occurs in *The Barren One* during the following exchange between Irma and her husband, John:

IRMA: I want to drink water but I have no glass, I have no water. I want to climb up into the hills, I have no feet to climb with . . . I want to embroider my chemise with flowers, I have no thread to embroider flowers.

JOHN: The trouble with you is that you not a real woman at all, and you seeking the downfall of a weak man like me . . .

(OFF IN THE DISTANCE DRUMMING STARTS. SHANGO DRUM-MING . . . BEGIN TO BRING UP UNDER THE FOLLOWING.)

IRMA: I don't know what I am, but leave me be to wander up and down the streets and ease my suffering. I don't do anything wrong 'gainst you. . . .

JOHN: I don't want nobody to point their finger at me. That's why I want to see this door closed and everybody inside their house.

(THE DRUMMING IS LOUD NOW. THE DOOR OPENS AND ONE OF THE SISTERS ENTERS.)

What you want?

ELDER SIS: To close the window and shut out the drumming.[111]

The choice to add music to this scene is Wynter's own, as no music is indicated during this exchange in Lorca's script. Further, the sister comes in to "close the window and shut out the drumming," acknowledging the music as occurring within the world of the play rather than as a score. It is significant that the line comes from one of John's two extremely pious sisters, who have come to live with the couple to keep a watchful eye on the wayward Irma. The drumming must be "shut out" because it obtrusively suggests a life outside the strictures of Christian domesticity and hints, perhaps, at alternative definitions of womanhood and sexuality.

While the drums build dramatic tension in this moment of conflict between Irma and her husband, the specificity of Shango—an African-derived spiritual practice of Trinidad—orients the play to broader horizons of Caribbean culture and spirituality. The idea that Wynter draws upon Trinidadian ritual in a play set in Jamaica should not surprise us. Aside from suggesting flows of cultural exchange in the West Indies, the music and dance of Shango had become part of the Caribbean performance vocabulary by midcentury. It is present in the choreography of Beryl McBurnie, who performed *Spirit of Shango* in 1947, as well as in the repertoires of Dunham, Rex Nettleford, and Boscoe Holder. Wynter also engaged in the performative juxtaposition of Caribbean cultural elements culled from various traditions—in *Maskarade*, for example, Jamaican dub and Jonkonnu mingle with Trinidadian calypso and carnival rituals.

It is impossible to know exactly how the drums sounded without a recording, but the script provides some clues. Rather than a traditional Shango ensemble of three drums, Wynter's drumming was supplied by a single musician, Emmanuel Myers, who had performed with the Holder dance troupe, as well as in Wynter's production of *Under the Sun*, which aired on October 28, 1958. The script's various changes in tempo and intensity suggest the traditional ebbs and flows of a Shango feast, ranging from "soft and very slow" to an "irruption of violence," suggesting a moment of spirit possession. Later, during the pilgrimage scene, the script directs the musicians to "bring up a slow drum which matches the marching feet of the pilgrim women,"[112] which may suggest the "military march" tempo of the Shango hand, a "distinctive and prominent rhythm in Shango drumming."[113]

Rather than simply providing a "local color" score, Wynter follows in the footsteps of Marson in bringing an "alternative cultural acoustics to the theatre."[114] Marson's 1934 play *Pocomania*, which was staged in 1938 at the Ward Theatre in Kingston, begins with a sonic disruption. The young protagonist, Stella, is awakened by the sound of revivalist drumming in the distance. While her siblings are frightened by the sound of these late-night pocomania ceremonies, the young girl is delighted and intrigued: "I could lie awake all night just listening to them . . . don't you think they are wonderful?"[115] Prohibited from attending the meetings by her religious parents, Stella vows to learn more on her own. In *Pocomania*, drums represent another way of being and knowing outside conventional Christian spirituality.

Like Marson's representation of pocomania, Wynter introduces Shango not merely to elevate or legitimize it, but rather to highlight its subversive function.[116] Immediately after the confrontation with her husband, Irma goes out onto the verandah, where the drumming is heard again:

Irma walks out, opens door. Immediately bring up, but keep remote, the sound of
shango drumming and the singing of a shango chant, ago, ago, ago go yon etc.
Irma talks to herself as if in time to the sudden wild rhythms of the drum which
alternates between a formal pattern and an eruption of violence.
IRMA: Oh my god what a broad park of pain this is,
   What a gate shut fast 'gainst beauty . . .
   I beg to bear a child, a pickney-child, the wind
   Blows me orchids from the sleeping moon . . .[117]

While Irma's poetic speech expresses a melancholic contrast between the bounty of nature and her own perceived barrenness, the drums signal a frantic, perhaps rebellious interiority. The drums continue to sound on and off through the end of the play, culminating in a carnival scene at the site of the pilgrimage in which two figures, a Devil Man and Devil Woman, sing a song imagining the erotic transformation of the "sad wife" into a "flameheart flower."[118] The drums are now accompanied by guitar, maracas, "stamping of feet, hand clapping," and shouts of "Caiso!" a West African exclamation encouraging collective participation. Critics of Lorca's original play commonly interpret this scene as the surfacing of a "substratum of pagan tradition" presenting a more natural, wholistic alternative to "the veneer of the Christian ethos."[119] But by transposing this scene to a Caribbean carnival tradition, Wynter expands its meaning by suggesting the "overturning of an order"—the potential to elude the hold of colonial ways of knowing and being.

Along with other works and practices that I have discussed in this chapter, *The Barren One* enacts forms of ceremony, which Wynter theorizes about in her 1984 essay "The Ceremony Must Be Found." It begins with an epigraph from John Paul Bishop's "Speaking of Poetry," which begins: "the ceremony must be found that will wed Desdemona to the huge Moor," Shakespeare's Othello.[120] Such a ceremony cannot be found because, as Tiffany Lethabo King explains, "the wedding, as it is imagined within humanism and as a function of instituting the human, has no protocol or performative act that can yet announce Othello as a man."[121] As Wynter elaborates in "Unsettling the Coloniality of Being," the ceremony is in fact unthinkable due to the ways in which the Western bourgeois conception of Man "overrepresents itself as if it were the human itself."[122]

Yet this is not the end of the story. A subsequent essay, "The Ceremony Found," answers and revises the possibilities envisioned in "The Ceremony Must Be Found" by taking "as its point of departure Franz Fanon's 'gaze from below' perspective of otherness."[123] Such an orientation also emerges in the essay's subtitle, "Towards the Autopoetic Turn/Overturn," which borrows from the Rastafari movement's "underlying counter-cosmogony in whose logic words are semantically turned upside-down."[124] As a poetics and an episteme, this inverted perspective allows Wynter to perceive the "underside reality" of W. E. B. Du Bois's sorrow songs, for example, or the Martinican poet Aimé Césaire's new "science of the word."[125] Such frameworks inspire Wynter to formulate an "entirely new answer to the question of who-we-are over and against our present globally hegemonic, (neo)Liberal-humanist cum monohumanist answer," redressing the ways in which her "heresy remained incomplete" in the original essay.[126]

Such heresy changes the terms of ceremony altogether. On the one hand, one might be less concerned with the marriage of Desdemona and Othello than with the "marriage of Shango and Durga," for example, as the Guyanese novelist Roy A. K. Heath envisions the cultural exchange between Black and Indo-Caribbeans.[127] Or, moving beyond the metaphor of marriage as the quintessential form of ceremony, we might, as King suggests, engage "with Wynter's concept of ceremony at the level of embodied, quotidian, and transformative practice." King elaborates, "Ceremony unsettles the body, Western epistemologies, and notions of time and space. The labor of ceremony requires a simultaneous reclamation and surrender of the body to a collective agreement to enter into chaos."[128] Following King's insight, I regard ceremony as an everyday practice of invention taking shape across various forms and media. Indeed, the resonance of ceremony as metaphor is made viable through its life as a material practice, which exists in various representations and enactments of Black culture.

Having laid the groundwork for a practice of ceremony in London, Wynter returned to Jamaica in 1962 with the intention of setting up a folk theater that would help to "project new Jamaican images."[129] Out of this venture came *1865: Ballad for a Rebellion*, written for the centennial of the Morant Bay Rebellion in 1965. In 1968, Wynter published another Lorca adaptation, the one-act play *The House and Land of Mrs. Alba*, in *Jamaica*

Journal. With Alex Gradussov, the founding editor of *Jamaica Journal,* she wrote a pantomime called *Rockstone Anancy,* which starred Louise Bennett as "Mother Balm" in a 1970 Little Theatre Movement production. Her best-known play, *Maskarade* appeared in 1970, and was later produced as a teleplay for the Jamaica Broadcasting Company, and then for a theatrical production at the 1979 Carifesta Festival in Cuba. That same year, Wynter also published a translation of Francisco Cueva's play *Jamaica Is the Eye of Bolivar.* Contextualizing this work in her first essay for *Jamaica Journal,* Wynter posed the question, "What is a Jamaican? We are Jamaicans but who are 'we'?" She later remarked, "I wanted us to assume our past: slaves, slave masters and all. And then, *reconceptualize* that past."[130] With its focus on intimacy, embodiment, and ever-changing performances of social life, theater provides a fertile ground for this reconceptualization. When Wynter writes of the need to "performatively enact" ourselves as humans, and further asserts that being human is "always a doing," she emerges as a consummate theorist and practitioner of performance and culture who helps to reveal, in ways both astonishing and familiar, the transformative aesthetics and politics of folk culture.[131]

CODA

Toward an Ontological Sovereignty

To move elsewhere and practice otherwise, I retrace my breath, loop back, and move with the opaque air. In the unseen, unknown expanse of blackness, I move inside the palimpsest of what exists prior, or beside us.

—FAHIMA IFE, *MAROON CHOREOGRAPHY*, IX

This book tells a story about how a distinctive group of writers and artists—Jean Toomer, Eric Walrond, Zora Neale Hurston, Jean Price-Mars, Eusebia Cosme, Nicolás Guillén, Langston Hughes, and Sylvia Wynter—reinvented folk culture to craft new epistemologies of blackness. They offer visions of Black modernity that are no longer tethered to authenticity, but rather concerned with the unruly: that which cannot be easily contained, disciplined, or managed. I have also sought to tell a parallel story about form. While chapters 1 and 2 discuss innovative uses of literary forms (the short story and ethnography), in chapters 3 and 4, the literary breaks open into the Black performance archive, culminating in formal and epistemic upheavals of Wynter's work across criticism, dance, and radio. Thus, the book's emphasis on radical interplays of form, genre, and media serves to model how Black experimental practices amass new ways of imagining Black social life.

I conclude this book by extending my consideration of Wynter's concept of "ontological sovereignty" and its relationship to ceremony. Her use of that term brings into focus the limits of political and economic sovereignty, which, she attests, are inadequate frameworks for engaging the condition of Black being. Her engagement with anticolonial thought does not end with national liberation; rather, it is an ongoing project "*to grasp the revolutionary significance of the counter-invention of the self*—which I see as the *central and universally applicable strategy of the 'politics of black culture.'*"[1] Across her many works, Wynter embarks on the dual project of rhetorically dismantling Western liberal humanism's foundational myths, while also documenting the ways that Black cultural practices theorize alternative genres of existence, even when encircled by the violence of coloniality. A robust body of scholarship is invested in thinking with Wynter along these lines. Zakiyyah Iman Jackson argues that while African diasporic literature has often been read as a "plea for human recognition," key texts "move beyond a critique of bestialization to generate new possibilities of rethinking ontology: our being, fleshy materiality, and the nature of what exists and what we can claim to know about existence." Jackson charts the various ways that Black thinkers have crafted "alternative conceptions of being and the nonhuman," turning for example to sex, genre, and "insect poetics" in Octavia Butler's short story collection *Bloodchild*.[2] Moving into speculative fiction and the world-making power of Black music, Jayna Brown asks, "[W]hat if the answer to the entire question of being were not ontological sovereignty at all but a different ontology altogether, other forms of awareness beyond the self, beyond individuated autonomous will?"[3]

Both Brown and Jackson engage with a Black feminist framework that is "distrustful of the ability for 'posthumanism' to be accountable to Black and Indigenous peoples."[4] At the same time, they offer compelling and profoundly necessary readings of how Black subjects imagine the condition of being beyond Western conceptions of "Man," and indeed beyond the boundaries of the human altogether. When Brown declares, "my provocation is that utopia may not include humans at all," she is drawing on different ontologies and complex life worlds that Black and brown people have long envisioned.[5]

Still, I want to dwell, with Wynter, on the alternative "genres of the human" that reside within "secretive histories" of folk culture. It is my sense that we have only begun to account for the multifarious theories of being and knowing humanity that are forged through Black experimental practices often labeled, and sometimes dismissed, as "folk." As Alexis Pauline Gumbs observes in *Dub: Finding Ceremony*, such reinvention alters the stories that we tell: "Wynter says we are not *Homo sapiens*, we are *Homo narrans*, not those who know, but the ones who tell ourselves what we know. She says we therefore have the capacity to know differently. We are word made flesh. But we make words."[6] With new words, new stories emerge. In Wynter's work, and in the various examples I have explored in this book, such stories function not as traditional linear narratives, but as poetics, as the reinvention of language, as folklore, as possession, as recursive embodied practices, as renegade writing, as an accumulation of unwieldy—and unruly—details. As such, they have the power to move, as Fahima Ife suggests in the epigraph that starts this chapter, in the "unseen, unknown, expanse of blackness," between the ground and air, in a maroon choreography that is both recursive and sequential.

Ceremony bears implications for Wynter's claim that being human is a praxis.[7] While I have proposed a return to discourses of folk culture that emerged in the first half of the twentieth century, I am interested in thinking more broadly about the ongoing relationship, and often tension, between ceremony—as a set of ritual observances and procedures that require structure—and the unruly: that which disrupts order. But perhaps this relation is not such a contradiction. Black feminist scholars have held ceremony, in the words of King, to be a "space-making practice" and "a geography."[8] Or, as Gumbs declares, "ceremony is form."[9] As a set of formal practices, ceremony helps us realize a theory of Black creativity that is both unruly and structured, in which imagining alternative ways of being requires attention to processes of doing, making, and moving. More specifically, I have sought to address Wynter's question: "[W]hat are the mechanisms, what are the technologies, what are strategies by which we prescribe our own roles?"[10] Speaking of one such example in the spiritual excess of possession, Wynter writes, "This self, through the ritual observance, now 'knew where it was from,' and knew that it had a destiny other than that of being a mere producer of surplus value; since *its* destiny, the where it was going, was quite other than the destiny allowed it in the plantation slave labor archipelago's master plan." For the self to know "where it was from," is one aspect of ontological sovereignty; to know where it is going is another.[11]

While I am suggesting that the key figures in my study perform ceremony through their reinvention of Black folk culture, to what extent do these practices constitute Black freedom? Rinaldo Walcott emphasizes a distinction between freedom (autonomy, bodily sovereignty, and ways of being in the world) and emancipation (the time after the formal end of slavery: a legal juridical process). Citing Black studies' ongoing engagement with fugitivity and marronage,[12] Walcott cautions against the recuperation of maroon practices as a form of freedom: "Flight is not freedom, and neither is subterfuge. Marronage is a temporal self-emancipation that must collude with its other captivity. Making the claim that I am making is not to undo what Maroon communities have meant historically; rather, I want to draw our attention to the limits of recuperating such strategies for our now."[13] I read Walcott's distinction between "temporal self-emancipation" and "freedom" as a caution against romanticizing marronage and fugitivity as grand narratives of Black freedom. Yet Wynter's thinking moves dexterously between the grand and the small. On the one hand, as Greg Thomas notes, Wynter allows us to understand marronage as "an epic political project of African/diasporic resistance anchored all across the Americas."[14] But the often understated, everyday "struggle to name our lives as sovereign, on our own terms," as Ife phrases it, is also part of the ritual practice of marronage that Wynter urges us to name.[15]

Like marronage, the strategies that I identify in this book—opacity, compelling insinuation, translation, interruption, reinterpretation—cannot be equated with "freedom" per se if freedom is understood as disentanglement from the violence of empire. Rather, as Walcott phrases it, they enable "*glimpses of Black freedom*, those moments of the something more that exist inside of the dire conditions of our present Black unfreedom."[16] In Wynter's view, that something more is nothing less than a "cultural counter world to the pervasive dominant world of Western rationality." If only in glimpses and snatches, they alter the temporality of Black freedom.[17] As she shows in "We Know Where We're From: The Politics of Black Culture," through the rituals of Vodou and possession, of death and funerals, "spirituals, blues, the culture of exile," and through the practice of writing, Black subjects "transmuted the Beyond into the *now* of the ritual itself." Refusing linear narratives of progress, such rituals establish recursive temporalities of Black liberation.[18]

As formal practice, ceremony affects not only a symbolic overturning of the order, but also periodic ruptures in the fabric of empire. King notes that over time, Wynter has worked through "her own ceremonial acts of heresy—rupture, overturning, and emancipatory openings."[19] In her interviews and writings, Wynter often refers to one such historical rupture that played a definitive role in her intellectual formation:

A profound transformation had been effected in what had been, up until then, the stable order of the colonial world of a British imperial Jamaica. This rupture had occurred as the direct result of a sustained series of "native labour" strikes. . . . In the global context of the aftermath of the 1929 Economic Crash and subsequent Great Depression, a large-scale uprising in May 1938 shut down the capital city, Kingston. If only for a brief interregnum, these disturbances overturned an imperial order which hitherto had seemed, to us, its "native" subjects, to be impregnable to any such challenge.[20]

Wynter explains that this "order-overturning (i.e. *an-archical*) 'movement from below' . . . set in motion an unstoppable dynamic of an increasingly generalised form of the anti-colonial / anti-imperial movement." She deems this "brief interregnum" as significant, but not because it permanently "shut down" the imperial order. As she acknowledges, the uprising was "brutally repressed by the joint military and police forces of the colonial authorities (by the very logic of them having to act as such authorities)."[21] Nor does she recognize 1938 simply for its role in the march toward Jamaican independence. Indeed, in her ongoing critique of Jamaican nationalism, Wynter is careful to distinguish independence from the fundamental question of ontological sovereignty. Rather, the moment was transformative because it constituted an epistemic rupture—a disordering of imperial knowledge. As evidence that a new world could be imagined and actively sought, 1938 was one moment in a recursive process of unsettling the coloniality of being.

As I have sought to show in this book, Black cultural practices make space for such ruptures. Later, in "We Know Where We're From," Wynter turns to Bob Marley's anthem "Exodus," observing that it is "the world outside the song, the so-called objective reality is delegitimated as that of Babylon, the non-real world, the world of Babylon's capitalistic illusions that must be burnt."[22] To turn the world upside down, to refuse and reinterpret the reality that we have been given (and to which we have been given over) constitute the resounding quest of Black experimental culture.

NOTES

PROLOGUE

1. From "Regional Conference on Ecology, Archaeology, and Folkdance," hosted by Jamaica in 1970. Cited in Helmut K. Anheier and Yudhishthir Raj Isar, eds., *Cultures and Globalization: The Cultural Economy* (London: Sage, 2008), 119.

2. Sylvia Wynter, "Jonkonnu in Jamaica: Towards the Interpretation of Folk Dance as a Cultural Process," *Jamaica Journal* 4, no. 2 (June 1970): 47.

3. Wynter, "Jonkonnu in Jamaica," 36. Emphasis as per the original text.

4. Wynter, "Jonkonnu in Jamaica," 36.

5. Saidiya Hartman, "Preface: The Hold of Slavery," in *Scenes of Subjection: Terror, Slavery and Self-Making in Nineteenth-Century America* (revised and updated) (New York: Norton, 2022), xxxi.

6. Wynter elaborates: "The dominant conception of Jamaican folk dance was being put forward by Rex Nettleford and his NTDC (National Theatre Dance Company). Now I think Rex is one of the most brilliant dancers I have ever seen, but I did not agree with the conceptualization of Jamaica's folk dances which he based his choreography on. So I set out to write my paper with the idea that I was going to put forward an alternative conceptualization." Sylvia Wynter, "The Re-Enchantment of Humanism: An Interview with Sylvia Wynter," interview by David Scott, *Small Axe* 8 (September 2000): 161.

7. As Deborah Thomas observes, "Jamaica's independence from Britain was marked, therefore, with the establishment of a cultural policy that sought to promote a new idea of cultural citizenship by bestowing new public prominence upon Jamaica's 'folk' culture, now understood as part of the country's 'African heritage.'" Ultimately, she argues, "the actual process of privileging certain elements of Jamaica's African heritage also marginalized alternative visions." Deborah A. Thomas,

Modern Blackness: Nationalism, Globalization, and the Politics of Culture in Jamaica (Durham, NC: Duke University Press, 2004), 5.

8. Sylvia Wynter, "Review of *One Love—Rhetoric or Reality? Aspects of Afro-Jamaicanism*, by Audvil King, Althea Helps, Pam Wint, and Frank Hasfal," *Caribbean Studies* 12, no. 3 (1972): 85.

9. Wynter, "The Re-Enchantment of Humanism," 170.

10. Mimi Sheller, *Citizenship from Below: Erotic Agency and Caribbean Freedom* (Durham, NC: Duke University Press, 2012), 7.

11. Wynter, "The Re-Enchantment of Humanism," 137.

12. Jean Price-Mars, *So Spoke the Uncle*, trans. Magdaline W. Shannon (Washington, DC: Three Continents, 1983), 7. Quoted in Wynter, "Jonkonnu in Jamaica," 34.

13. Sylvia Wynter, *Black Metamorphosis: New Natives in a New World*, unpublished manuscript (Institute of the Black World Papers, Schomburg Center for Research in Black Culture, New York), 14.

14. Erica R. Edwards, *The Other Side of Terror: Black Women and the Culture of U.S. Empire* (New York: New York University Press, 2021), 2.

15. Katherine McKittrick, "Plantation Futures," *Small Axe* 17, no. 3 (2013): 12.

16. Trouillot states that "*modernity* is a murky term that belongs to a family or words we may label 'North Atlantic universals.' By that, I mean words inherited from what we now call the West—which I prefer to call the North Atlantic, not only for the sake of geographical precision—that project the North Atlantic experience on a universal scale that they have helped to create." Michel-Rolph Trouillot, "The Otherwise Modern: Caribbean Lessons from the Savage Slot," in *Trouillot Remixed*, ed. Yarimar Bonilla, Greg Beckett, and Mayanthi L. Fernando (Durham, NC: Duke University Press, 2021), 142.

17. Norval Edwards, "'Talking about a Little Culture': Sylvia Wynter's Early Essays," *Journal of West Indian Literature* 10, nos. 1/2 (2001): 12.

18. Zora Neale Hurston, "Characteristics of Negro Expression," in *The Jazz Cadence of American Culture*, ed. Robert G. O'Meally (New York: Columbia University Press, 1998), 304.

19. Sylvia Wynter, "Sylvia Wynter: An Oral History," interview by Natalie Marine-Street, November 22, 2017, Stanford Historical Society, Stanford, CA, 20.

20. Ifeoma Kiddoe Nwankwo, "Living the West Indian Dream: Archipelagic Cosmopolitanism and Triangulated Economies of Desire in Jamaican Popular Culture," in *Archipelagic American Studies*, ed. Brian Russell Roberts and Michelle Ann Stephens (Durham, NC: Duke University Press, 2017), 390.

21. Paul Gilroy, *The Black Atlantic: Modernity and Double-Consciousness* (London: Verso, 1993), 19; Brent Hayes Edwards, *The Practice of Diaspora: Literature, Translation, and the Rise of Black Internationalism* (Cambridge, MA: Harvard University Press, 2003), 7.

22. Deborah A. Thomas, "Public Secrets, Militarization, and the Cultivation of Doubt: Kingston 2010," in *Caribbean Military Encounters*, ed. Shalini Puri and Laura Putnam (New York: Palgrave Macmillan, 2017), 290.

23. Édouard Glissant, *Caribbean Discourse*, trans. J. Michael Dash (Charlottesville: University Press of Virginia, 1989), 26.

24. Barbara Christian, "The Race for Theory," *Cultural Critique*, no. 6 (1987): 56.

25. Charles W. Chesnutt, "The Future American: What the Race Is Likely to Become in the Process of Time," in *Essays and Speeches*, ed. Joseph R. McElrath Jr., Robert C. Leitz III, and Jesse S. Crisler (Stanford, CA: Stanford University Press, 1999), 49.
26. Shalini Puri and Lara Putnam, eds., "Introduction: Subjections of Militarization," in *Caribbean Military Encounters* (New York: Palgrave Macmillan, 2017), 1.
27. Glissant, *Caribbean Discourse*, 112.
28. Erich Nunn, "Folk," in *Keywords for Southern Studies*, ed. Scott Romine and Jennifer Rae Greeson (Athens: University of Georgia Press, 2016), 189.
29. Henry Louis Gates Jr. and Gene Andrew Jarrett, eds., *The New Negro: Readings on Race, Representation, and African American Culture, 1892–1938* (Princeton, NJ: Princeton University Press, 2007), 9.
30. Hazel Carby, "The Politics of Fiction, Anthropology, and the Folk: Zora Neale Hurston," in *Zora Neale Hurston's* Their Eyes Were Watching God: *A Casebook*, ed. Cheryl A. Wall (New York: Oxford University Press, 2000), 121.
31. David Nicholls, *Conjuring the Folk: Forms of Modernity in African America* (Ann Arbor: University of Michigan Press, 2000), 12.
32. Eric Walrond, "The Negro Literati," from *Brentano's Book Chat*, March/April 1925, in *"Winds Can Wake Up the Dead": An Eric Walrond Reader*, ed. Louis J. Parascandola (Detroit: Wayne State University Press, 1998), 130.
33. Gates and Jarrett, *The New Negro*, 9.
34. Hurston, "Characteristics of Negro Expression," 302.
35. Anthea Kraut, *Choreographing the Folk: The Dance Stagings of Zora Neale Hurston* (Minneapolis: University of Minnesota Press, 2008), 17.
36. Carby, "The Politics of Fiction, Anthropology, and the Folk," 121.
37. Sonnet Retman, *Real Folks: Race and Genre in the Great Depression* (Durham, NC: Duke University Press, 2011), 4.
38. Daphne Lamothe, *Inventing the New Negro: Narrative, Culture, and Ethnography* (Philadelphia: University of Pennsylvania Press, 2008), 12.
39. Michel-Rolph Trouillot, "Anthropology and the Savage Slot: The Poetics and Politics of Otherness," in *Global Transformations: Anthropology and the Modern World* (New York: Palgrave Macmillan, 2003). As Kevin Quashie argues in *Black Aliveness*, aliveness "is a process, not an answer: not a recipe for how to be, certainly not a chastisement to any of us, but a study, a determination to try to think about the being of one's being." Kevin Quashie, *Black Aliveness, or a Poetics of Being* (Durham, NC: Duke University Press, 2021), 141.
40. Lindsay V. Reckson, *Realist Ecstasy: Religion, Race, and Performance in American Literature* (New York: New York University Press, 2020), 111.
41. Jean Toomer, *Cane*, originally published by Boni and Liveright in 1923 (New York: Norton, 1988), 25.
42. Zora Neale Hurston, "Spirituals and Neo-Spirituals," in *Zora Neale Hurston: Folklore, Memoirs, and Other Writings*, ed. Cheryl A. Wall (New York: Library of America, 1995), 870.
43. Daphne Brooks, *Liner Notes for the Revolution: The Intellectual Life of Black Feminist Sound* (Cambridge, MA: Harvard University Press, 2021), 279.
44. Benjamin Filene, *Romancing the Folk: Public Memory and American Roots Music* (Chapel Hill: University of North Carolina Press, 2000), 58.

45. Discussing literary forms that she dubs "signifying ethnography" and "modernist burlesque," Retman shows how Depression-era writers contested the seductions of the "real" by inventing forms that "inhabit that which they mean to critique, using exaggeration, irony, and reversal to reveal the performative dimensions of their object of scrutiny." She traces the self-reflexive critiques that emerge within the works themselves. My work expands Retman's quest for unruly forms by interpreting the folk comparatively, delving more deeply into its subversive and disorienting potential. Retman, *Real Folks.*

46. As Anthea Kraut explains in her recovery of Hurston's concert productions, authenticity "carried distinct liabilities for Hurston. In commending her revues' naturalness and unaffectedness, critics concomitantly cast the productions as effortless, unpremeditated, and unmediated, thereby jeopardizing recognition of her artistry." Kraut, *Choreographing the Folk,* 52.

47. Glissant, *Caribbean Discourse,* 107. Emphasis as per the original text.

48. Édouard Glissant, *Poetics of Relation* (Ann Arbor: University of Michigan Press, 1997), 192, 190.

49. La Marr Jurelle Bruce, *How to Go Mad Without Losing Your Mind: Madness and Black Radical Creativity* (Durham, NC: Duke University Press, 2021), 37.

50. Samantha Pinto, *Difficult Diasporas: The Transnational Feminist Aesthetic of the Black Atlantic* (New York: New York University Press, 2013), 4.

51. Pinto, *Difficult Diasporas,* 5.

52. Eric Hayot and Rebecca L. Walkowitz, eds., *A New Vocabulary for Global Modernism* (New York: Columbia University Press, 2016), 1.

53. Alexandra T. Vazquez, *Listening in Detail: Performances of Cuban Music* (Durham, NC: Duke University Press, 2013), 19, 12.

54. Vazquez, *Listening in Detail,* 17.

55. Jason M. Colby, *The Business of Empire: United Fruit, Race, and U.S. Expansion in Central America* (Ithaca, NY: Cornell University Press, 2011), 87.

56. As Jean-Christophe Cloutier observes in *Shadow Archives,* such "investigative deep dives . . . call for radical reassessment of an author's overall oeuvre while at the same time serving as practical scenarios for negotiating literary archives in contemporary scholarly practice." Jean-Christophe Cloutier, *Shadow Archives: The Lifecycles of African American Literature* (New York: Columbia University Press, 2019), 13.

57. In my approach to the archive as a site of Black speculation and experimentation, I am indebted to the recent work of Jean-Christophe Cloutier, Daphne Brooks, Saidiya Hartman, and Jenny Sharpe, among others.

58. Jill Kuhnheim, *Beyond the Page: Poetry and Performance in Spanish America* (Tucson: University of Arizona Press, 2014), 18.

59. See Carole Boyce Davies, "From Masquerade to Maskarade: Caribbean Cultural Resistance and the Rehumanizing Project," in *Sylvia Wynter: On Being Human as Praxis,* ed. Katherine McKittrick (Durham, NC: Duke University Press, 2015), 203–225.

60. Sylvia Wynter, "The Ceremony Found: Towards the Autopoetic Turn/Overturn, Its Autonomy of Human Agency, and Extraterritoriality of (Self-)Cognition," in *Black Knowledges/Black Struggles: Essays in Critical Epistemology,* ed. Jason R. Ambroise and Sabine Broeck (Liverpool: Liverpool University Press, 2015), 196.

61. Wynter, "Jonkonnu in Jamaica," 47.
62. Davies, "From Masquerade to Maskarade," 222.
63. Wynter, "The Re-Enchantment of Humanism," 136.
64. Sylvia Wynter, "Novel and History: Plot and Plantation," *Savacou* 5 (1971): 100.
65. Alexander G. Weheliye, *Habeas Viscus: Racializing Assemblages, Biopolitics, and Black Feminist Theories of the Human* (Durham, NC: Duke University Press, 2014), 4.

1. GEORGIA DUSK AND PANAMA GOLD: JEAN TOOMER, ERIC WALROND, AND THE "DEATH" OF FOLK CULTURE

1. Francis Davis, *The History of the Blues: The Roots, the Music, the People* (Boston: Da Capo, 2003), 129.
2. Yusef Komunyakaa, *Condition Red: Essays, Interviews, and Commentaries*, ed. Radiclani Clytus (Ann Arbor: University of Michigan Press, 2017), 32.
3. Natalie Melas, *All the Difference in the World: Postcoloniality and the Ends of Comparison* (Stanford, CA: Stanford University Press, 2006), xiii.
4. M. Jacqui Alexander, *Pedagogies of Crossing: Meditations on Feminism, Sexual Politics, Memory, and the Sacred* (Durham, NC: Duke University Press, 2005), 8.
5. Jean Toomer, quoted in Darwin T. Turner, *The Wayward and the Seeking: A Collection of Writings by Jean Toomer* (Washington, DC: Howard University Press, 1980), 123.
6. Grace Kyungwon Hong, *Death beyond Disavowal: The Impossible Politics of Difference* (Minneapolis: University of Minnesota Press, 2015), 30.
7. Jean Toomer, *Cane*, orig. 1926 (New York: Liveright, 2011), 25.
8. Quashie writes, "Black living is compassed by being alive, where aliveness sets the parameters for understanding loss, pain, belonging, for countenancing love, grace, healing." Kevin Quashie, *Black Aliveness, or a Poetics of Being* (Durham, NC: Duke University Press, 2021), 10.
9. Vincent Brown, *The Reaper's Garden: Death and Power in the World of Atlantic Slavery* (Cambridge, MA: Harvard University Press, 2008), 4.
10. Sterling Brown called *Cane* and *Tropic Death* "two striking books of the movement," noting that "these authors were alike in being masters of their craft and, unfortunately, in falling silent after the publication of one book each." Sterling Brown, "A Century of Negro Portraiture in American Literature," *Massachusetts Review* 17, no. 1 (1966): 85. Brown is echoed by Kenneth Ramchand, who asserted that "the two stylists of the movement were Jean Toomer, strange author of a single work, a neglected masterpiece *Cane*, and Eric Walrond." Kenneth Ramchand, "The Writer Who Ran Away: Eric Walrond and *Tropic Death*," *Savacou* 2 (1970): 68. In fact, neither writer actually fell silent, as evidenced by subsequent collections of their later writings. Although neither writer produced another masterwork on the scale of his original debut, they both continued to publish throughout their lives. See Jean Toomer, *A Jean Toomer Reader: Selected Unpublished Writings*, ed. Frederick Rusch (New York: Oxford University Press, 1993); and Louis J. Parascandola and Carl A. Wade, eds., *In Search of Asylum: The Later Writings of Eric Walrond* (Gainesville: University Press of Florida, 2011).
11. Michelle Ann Stephens, "Eric Walrond's *Tropic Death* and the Discontents of American Modernity," in *Prospero's Isles: The Presence of the Caribbean in the*

American Imaginary, ed. Diane Accaria-Zavala and Rodolfo Popelnik (Oxford, UK: Macmillan Caribbean, 2004), 173.

12. James C. Davis, *Commerce in Color: Race, Consumer Culture, and American Literature, 1893–1933* (Ann Arbor: University of Michigan Press, 2007), 171.

13. Seth Moglen, *Mourning Modernity: Literary Modernism and the Injuries of American Capitalism* (Stanford, CA: Stanford University Press, 2007), 45, 46.

14. That phrase is taken from the title of Jamaica Kincaid's *A Small Place*, orig. 1988 (New York: Farrar, Straus, and Giroux, 2000).

15. Eric Walrond, "The Negro Literati," from *Brentano's Book Chat*, March/April 1925, in *"Winds Can Wake Up the Dead": An Eric Walrond Reader*, ed. Louis J. Parascandola (Detroit: Wayne State University Press, 1998), 130–131.

16. Langston Hughes, "The Negro Artist and the Racial Mountain," in *The Collected Works of Langston Hughes*, ed. Christopher C. De Santis (Columbia: University of Missouri Press, 2002), 31–36.

17. Eric Walrond to Alain Locke, July 25, 1925, Box 164-91, Folder 38, Alain Locke Papers, Moorland Spingarn Research Center, quoted in James C. Davis, *Eric Walrond: A Life in the Harlem Renaissance and the Transatlantic Caribbean* (New York: Columbia University Press), 154.

18. Shane Vogel, *The Scene of Harlem Cabaret: Race, Sexuality, Performance* (Chicago: University of Chicago Press, 2009), 12.

19. Arna Bontemps, "Commentary on Jean Toomer and *Cane*," in *Cane: A Norton Critical Edition*, ed. Darwin T. Turner (New York: Norton, 1988), 187.

20. W. E. B. Du Bois and Alain Locke, "The Younger Literary Movement," *Crisis* 27 (February 1924): 161–163, reprinted in Henry Louis Gates Jr. and Gene Andrew Jarrett, *The New Negro: Readings on Race, Representation, and African American Culture, 1892–1938* (Princeton, NJ: Princeton University Press, 2007), 220.

21. Alfred Kreymborg, quoted in Bontemps, "Commentary on Jean Toomer and *Cane*," 189.

22. Mary White Ovington, "Book Chat: 'Tropic Death,'" *Amsterdam News*, November 24, 1926, 15.

23. W. E. B. Du Bois, "Five Books," *Crisis*, January 1927, 152.

24. Waldo Frank, "Our American Language: Review of *Tropic Death* by Eric Walrond," *Opportunity* 4 (1926): 352.

25. Samantha Pinto, *Difficult Diasporas: The Transnational Feminist Aesthetic of the Black Atlantic* (New York: New York University Press, 2013), 4.

26. Alain Locke, "The New Negro," in *The New Negro: Readings on Race, Representation, and African American Culture, 1892–1938*, ed. Henry Louis Gates Jr. and Gene Andrew Jarrett (Princeton, NJ: Princeton University Press, 2007), 114.

27. Sonnet Retman, *Real Folks: Race and Genre in the Great Depression* (Durham, NC: Duke University Press, 2011), 2.

28. Andreas Huyssen, "High/Low in an Expanded Field," *Modernism/Modernity* 9, no. 3 (2002): 363.

29. Eric Walrond, *Tropic Death*, orig. 1926 (New York: Liveright, 2013), 22. Subsequent citations refer to this edition.

30. The imaginary "Sepia, Georgia" plays on the sonic resonances between Sparta, the site of Toomer's Georgia pilgrimage, and Sempter, *Cane*'s fictionalized version.

31. Walrond, *Tropic Death*, 25.

32. Jean Toomer, quoted in Turner, *The Wayward and the Seeking*, 123.

33. Toomer, *Cane*, 38.

34. Jean Toomer, "Letter to Gorham Munson," October 31, 1922, in *The Letters of Jean Toomer, 1919–1924*, ed. Mark Whalan (Knoxville: University of Tennessee Press, 2006), 92.

35. Among the poems of *Cane*, "Portrait in Georgia" is especially notable for its use of metonymy, not metaphor, to draw connections between the portrait of a Southern belle and a lynched Black body. This distinction is significant: Toomer does not merely wish to draw similarities between white women and lynched Black bodies (as metaphor would suggest), but rather to insist that they are both entangled in the same web of social meaning. Indeed, the function of metonymy that Jacqueline Goldsby locates in the earlier work of James Weldon Johnson might also be applied to this poem: "where metaphors encourage us to suspend judgment, metonyms urge us to discern relations and draw conclusions, an activity that puts us in close touch with history's concatenation of time, persons and events, the significance of which we can never know in advance." Jacqueline Goldsby, *A Spectacular Secret: Lynching in American Life and Literature* (Chicago: Chicago University Press, 2006), 184. We preserve the sanctity of this image at our peril, the poem suggests. The poem, which immediately precedes "Blood Burning Moon," sets the stage for that story's treatment of lynching.

36. Toomer, *Cane*, 16.

37. Vera Kutzinski, "Unseasonal Flowers: Nature and History in Placido and Jean Toomer," *Yale Journal of Criticism* 3, no. 2 (Spring 1990): 171.

38. Brown, "A Century of Negro Portraiture," 85.

39. Brown, "A Century of Negro Portraiture," 86.

40. Brown, "A Century of Negro Portraiture," 86.

41. Judith Musser, "African American Women's Short Stories in the Harlem Renaissance: Bridging a Tradition," *MELUS* 23, no. 2 (June 1998): 27.

42. Davis, *Eric Walrond: A Life*, 102.

43. Both Toomer and Walrond played key and sometimes controversial roles in shaping this terrain. In February 1924, Charles S. Johnson wrote Locke about "a matter which is being planned by Walrond, Cullen, Gwendolyn Bennet, myself and others, which hopes to interest and include you." Davis, *Eric Walrond: A Life*, 112. The matter in question was the planning of the Civic Club Dinner, an event that would serve as "the dress rehearsal of what was soon to be known as the 'Harlem Renaissance.'" David Levering Lewis, *When Harlem Was in Vogue* (New York: Penguin, 1979), 90. The official occasion was a celebration of Jessie Fauset's novel *There Is Confusion*. But with a guest list of 125 writers, luminaries, patrons, and publishers, the dinner served as a launching pad for the new movement. As Cheryl Wall notes, "[W]hat started out to be an informal gathering honoring Fauset turned into the well-orchestrated 'debut of the younger school of Negro writers.'" Cheryl A. Wall, *Women of the Harlem Renaissance* (Bloomington: Indiana University Press, 1995), 69.

   Although Toomer was not present at the Civic Club dinner, the publication of *Cane* by Boni and Liveright had caused a stir the year before, and Johnson considered Toomer a key member of the "newer school" of writers whom he wanted to promote. When the publisher Horace Liveright rose to speak, he highlighted *Cane* rather than *There Is Confusion*, which he had published just seven months earlier.

This omission was only one part of what Fauset, who was then the literary editor of *Crisis*, would remember as the evening's colossal snub. Years later, she would recall the way that Locke and the various speakers (most of them male) "strove to keep speech and comment away from the person for whom the occasion was meant." Quoted in Wall, *Women of the Harlem Renaissance*, 70.

On the one hand, such a snub was emblematic of a misogynist literary sphere that failed to acknowledge the innovations of work, usually authored by women, which addressed the domestic sphere and the marriage plot. On the other hand, as Walrond later elaborated on in his essay "The Negro Literati" (*Brentano's Book Chat*, March/April 1925, 31–33), the matter also concerned a generational debate about the form and politics of Black writing. The contrast between *Cane* and *There Is Confusion* highlighted not only starkly different content, but also divergent approaches to literary form. Such a contrast is evident in the early correspondence between Fauset and Toomer. Fauset had known Toomer for several years and had facilitated the publication of his work, including the poem "Song of the Son," which appeared in the April 1922 issue of *Crisis*. Although Fauset praised Toomer's work she also warned him to avoid opaque experimentalism. In a letter dated February 17, 1922, Fauset critiques his inclination to "achieve style at the expense of clearness." She continues: "I think the modern tendency is toward an involving of ideas—a sort of inmeshing [sic] of the kernel of thought in envelopes of words. I don't like it and hope that you will not fall too deeply into it." Jesse Fauset, "Fauset to Jean Toomer," February 17, 1922, Box 1, Folder 37, Jean Toomer Papers, James Weldon Johnson, Beinecke Rare Book and Manuscript Library, Yale University, New Haven, CT.

In fact, Toomer did fall deeply into it. *Cane*, which was already under contract at Boni and Liveright, was full of such "modern" tendencies. Though intended as a critique, Fauset's warning is nevertheless usefully descriptive. The "inmeshing of the kernel of thought in envelopes of words" aptly describes the strategies of works such as the metonymic poem "Portrait in Georgia." Further, as a "collection of vignettes," *Cane* departed from the conventional forms of storytelling and plot upon which Fauset's novel relied. Despite the book's poor sales, it was clear that *Cane* would lead the way. The promotion of *Cane* at the Civic Club dinner was also a statement about the direction of publishing. Along with Knopf and Harcourt, Boni and Liveright played an especially important role in the first years of the movement.

Having published Eliot's *The Waste Land*, as well as works by Sherwood Anderson, Waldo Frank, and Ezra Pound—the very work Toomer had been reading in the early 1920s—the press published *Cane* in 1923 and *There Is Confusion* in 1924. In keeping with a growing preference for formally experimental texts, the press would subsequently reject Fauset's second novel, instead turning its energies to *Tropic Death* in 1926.

44. Darwin T. Turner, "Contrasts and Limitations in *Cane*," in *Cane: A Norton Critical Edition*, ed. Darwin T. Turner (New York: Norton, 1988), 207–208.

45. As Frederik L. Rusch remarks, "[W]hile Bone discusses *Cane* in his critique of the Negro novel, the individual pieces seem in both genre and narrative too disparate to make up a unified novel in any traditional sense. Rather, the unity of the work springs from its stylistic experimentation and thematic consistency." Frederik L. Rusch, "Form, Function, and Creative Tension in *Cane*: Jean Toomer and the Need for the Avant-Garde," *MELUS* 17, no. 4 (1991): 15.

46. Waldo Frank to Jean Toomer, 1922, in Kathleen Pfeiffer, ed., *Brother Mine: The Correspondence of Jean Toomer and Waldo Frank* (Champaign: University of Illinois Press, 2010), 36.

47. Jean Toomer to Waldo Frank, April 26, 1922, in Pfeiffer, *Brother Mine*, 38.

48. Jean Toomer to John McClure, July 22, 1922, in Toomer, *A Jean Toomer Reader*, 12.

49. Jean Toomer to Waldo Frank, December 12, 1922, in Pfeiffer, *Brother Mine*, 86.

50. Rachel Farebrother, *The Collage Aesthetic in the Harlem Renaissance* (New York: Routledge, 2009), 81.

51. Jean Toomer, *Cane*, dust jacket, JWJ 26, Box 611, Digital Collections, Beinecke Rare Book and Manuscript Library, Yale University, New Haven, CT. For further discussion of the dust jacket, see Nellie Y. McKay, *Jean Toomer, Artist: A Study of His Literary Life and Work, 1894–1936* (Chapel Hill: University of North Carolina Press, 1984), 83, 238, and Barbara Foley, *Jean Toomer: Race, Repression, and Revolution* (Champaign: University of Illinois Press, 2014), 103.

52. See Michael Soto, "Jean Toomer and Horace Liveright; or, A New Negro Gets 'Into the Swing of It,'" in *Jean Toomer and the Harlem Renaissance*, ed. Geneviève Fabre and Michel Feith (New Brunswick, NJ: Rutgers University Press, 2001), 162–187.

53. Foley, *Race, Repression, and Revolution*, 104.

54. Jayna Brown, *Babylon Girls: Black Women Performers and the Shaping of the Modern* (Durham, NC: Duke University Press, 2008), 4.

55. T. Austin Graham, *The Great American Songbooks: Musical Texts, Modernism, and the Value of Popular Culture* (New York: Oxford University Press, 2012), 117.

56. Parker Fishel, "Alan Lomax's Southern Journey and the Sound of Authenticity," *Sounding Out!* (blog), April 16, 2015, https://soundstudiesblog.com/2015/04/16/alan-lomaxs-southern-journey-and-the-sound-of-authenticity/.

57. Farebrother, *Collage Aesthetic*, 90.

58. Jean Toomer, "Letter to Lola Ridge," January 1923, in *The Letters of Jean Toomer, 1919–1924*, ed. Mark Whalan (Knoxville: University of Tennessee Press, 2006), 123.

59. Darwin T. Turner, "Introduction to the 1975 Edition of *Cane*," in *Cane: A Norton Critical Edition*, ed. Darwin T. Turner (New York: Norton, 1988), 122.

60. Natalie J. Ring, "Tropics," in *Keywords for Southern Studies*, ed. Scott Romine and Jennifer Rae Greeson (Athens: University of Georgia Press, 2016), 95.

61. Depicting a single palm tree silhouetted against a backdrop of mountains and sea, the image may seem an odd point of entry for a text so firmly rooted in the American South. Precisely where do we place this "dark, Africanized, raced nightscape"? In the context of the ongoing vogue for all things primitive, such marketing decisions were not uncommon. Toomer's publisher, Boni and Liveright, may have tried to appeal to readers' tastes for the exotic, whetted in part by a publishing market increasingly saturated by sensational travel narratives written by U.S. marines. Jennifer Sorenson, *Modernist Experiments in Genre, Media, and Transatlantic Print Culture* (New York: Routledge, 2017), 114.

62. Vogel, *The Scene of Harlem Cabaret*, 36.

63. Mark Whalan, "Jean Toomer and the Avant-Garde," in *Cambridge Companion to the Harlem Renaissance*, ed. George Hutchinson (Cambridge: Cambridge University Press, 2007), 71.

64. Toomer, *Cane*, 17.

65. For an alternative reading, see Charles Scruggs and Lee VanDemarr, *Jean Toomer and the Terrors of American History* (Philadelphia: University of Pennsylvania Press, 1998), 164.

66. Daphne Lamothe, *Inventing the New Negro: Narrative, Culture, and Ethnography* (Philadelphia: University of Pennsylvania Press, 2008), 1.

67. Lamothe, *Inventing the New Negro*, 1.

68. Toomer, *Cane*, 114.

69. Jean Toomer to Waldo Frank, January 1923, in Pfeiffer, *Brother Mine*, 102.

70. Karen Jackson Ford, *Split Gut Song: Jean Toomer and the Poetics of Modernity* (Tuscaloosa: University of Alabama Press, 2005), 3.

71. Toomer, *Cane*, 22, 23.

72. Toomer, *Cane*, 25–26.

73. Susan L. Blake, "The Spectatorial Artist in Part One of *Cane*," in *Cane: A Norton Critical Edition*, ed. Darwin T. Turner (New York: Norton, 1988), 218.

74. Nathaniel Mackey, *Discrepant Engagement: Dissonance, Cross-Culturality, and Experimental Writing* (Cambridge: Cambridge University Press, 1993), 252–253.

75. Daphne Brooks, *Bodies in Dissent: Spectacular Performances of Race and Freedom, 1850–1910* (Durham, NC: Duke University Press, 2006), 8.

76. Jean Toomer to Waldo Frank, undated, Jean Toomer Papers, Box 3, Folder 83, Beinecke Rare Book and Manuscript Library, Yale University, New Haven, CT.

77. Although critics frequently emphasize *Cane*'s lyricism, the book's poetic voice vacillates between "lyric essence" and "internal tightness, conflict, and chaos," revealing the "terrible strain" of its composition.

78. Jean Toomer, quoted in Turner, *The Wayward and the Seeking*, 123.

79. Toomer, *Cane*, 122.

80. Toomer, *Cane*, 123.

81. Toomer, *Cane*, 115.

82. Roland Barthes, "The Grain of the Voice," in *Image, Music, Text*, ed. Stephen Heath (New York: Hill and Wang, 1977), 188.

83. Toomer, *Cane*, 124.

84. Historical Marker, Mary Turner Site, "Mary Turner and the Lynching Rampage of 1918," erected 2010, Lowndes County, Georgia.

85. Toomer, *Cane*, 124.

86. Fred Moten, *Black and Blur* (Durham, NC: Duke University Press, 2017), ix.

87. Ashon Crawley, *Blackpentacostal Breath: The Aesthetics of Possibility* (New York: Fordham University Press, 2017), 157.

88. Toomer, *Cane*, 37.

89. Ford, *Split Gut Song*, 54.

90. Barbara Foley, " 'In the Land of Cotton': Economics and Violence in Jean Toomer's *Cane*," *African American Review* 50, no. 4 (2017): 992.

91. Ford, *Split Gut Song*, 54.

92. Mackey, *Discrepant Engagement*, 253.

93. Farah Jasmine Griffin, *Who Set You Flowin'? The African-American Migration Narrative* (New York: Oxford University Press, 1995), 25.

94. Margo Natalie Crawford, *Black Post-Blackness: The Black Arts Movement and Twenty-First-Century Aesthetics* (Chicago: University of Illinois Press, 2017), 24.

95. Du Bois, "Five Books," 152.
96. See Parascandola and Wade, *In Search of Asylum: The Later Writings of Eric Walrond.*
97. Imani D. Owens, "'Hard Reading': US Empire and Black Modernist Aesthetics in Eric Walrond's *Tropic Death,*" *MELUS* 41, no. 4 (December 2016): 96–115.
98. Davis, *Eric Walrond: A Life,* 5.
99. See Louis J. Parascandola, ed., *"Winds Can Wake Up the Dead": An Eric Walrond Reader* (Detroit: Wayne State University Press, 1998), 11–12, 13.
100. Luis Pulido Ritter, "Notas sobre Eric Walrond: La inmigración caribeña y la transnacionalidad literaria en Panamá: Una excursión por las calles de la memoria, la reflexión y los espacios en movimiento," *Intercambio* 5, no. 6 (2008): 179. Ritter calls Walrond a "escritor guyanés-barbadiense-panameño [Guyanese-Barbadian-Panamanian writer]," simultaneously restoring him to the literature of Panama and reviving the narrative of transnationality that the Panamanian national literature has suppressed.
101. Davis, *Eric Walrond: A Life,* 5.
102. Ovington, "Book Chat," 15.
103. Irma Watkins-Owens, *Blood Relations: Caribbean Immigrants and the Harlem Community, 1900–1930* (Bloomington: Indiana University Press, 1996), 14.
104. Albert Peters, entry in "Competition for the Best True Stories of Life and Work on the Isthmus during Construction Days for Non-United States Citizens who Worked on the Isthmus Prior to 1915," Isthmian Historical Society, Canal Zone Library, 1963, 2–3.
105. Robert Bone, *Down Home: A History of Afro-American Short Fiction from Its Beginnings to the End of the Harlem Renaissance* (New York: G. P. Putnam's Sons, 1975), 194.
106. "The 'son' soon learns that terror and beauty in the South are intertwined; the 'singing tree' and the lynching tree are the same tree." Scruggs and VanDemarr, *Terrors,* 164.
107. Maryse Condé, "What Is a Caribbean Writer?," in *The Journey of a Caribbean Writer,* trans. Richard Philcox (London: Seagull, 2014), 1.
108. Walrond, *Tropic Death,* 67.
109. Louis Chude-Sokei, "Foreign Negro Flash Agents: Eric Walrond and the Discrepancies of Diaspora," in *Eric Walrond: The Critical Heritage,* ed. Louis J. Parascandola and Carl A. Wade (Kingston, Jamaica: University Press of the West Indies, 2012), 76.
110. Walrond, *Tropic Death,* 57–58.
111. Benjamin Brawley may have borne such passages in mind when he observed that "certainly a writer of Mr. Walrond's ability can now dispense altogether with hectic writing in gaining his effects." Benjamin Brawley, "The Negro Literary Renaissance," in *The New Negro: Readings on Race, Representation, and African American Culture, 1892–1938,* ed. Henry Louis Gates Jr. and Gene Andrew Jarrett (Princeton, NJ: Princeton University Press, 2007), 234.
112. Édouard Glissant, *Poetics of Relation* (Ann Arbor: University of Michigan Press, 1997), 194.
113. Paul Gilroy, *The Black Atlantic: Modernity and Double-Consciousness* (London: Verso, 1993), xi.

114. Eric Walrond, "From Cotton, Cane, and Rice Fields," in *Winds Can Wake Up the Dead": An Eric Walrond Reader*, ed. Louis J. Parascandola (Detroit: Wayne State University Press, 1998), 131–141.
115. Lara Putnam, "Provincializing Harlem: The 'Negro Metropolis' as Northern Frontier of a Connected Caribbean," *Modernism/Modernity* 20, no. 3 (2013): 471.
116. Rhonda Frederick, *Colón Man a Come: Mythographies of Panamá Canal Migration* (New York: Lexington Books, 2005), 127.
117. Langston Hughes, "Marl Dust and West Indian Sun," *New York Herald Tribune*, December 5, 1926, 9.
118. Walrond, *Tropic Death*, 101.
119. Kaysha Corinealdi, *Panama in Black: Afro-Caribbean World Making in the Twentieth Century* (Durham, NC: Duke University Press, 2022), 14.
120. Walrond, *Tropic Death*, 99–100.
121. Whalan observes that Toomer made a distinction "between the wish to return to nature, and the desire to touch the soil. Nature . . . is a virginal tract of land. The soil is tilled land, saturate with the life of those who have worked it." As Whalan notes, "the subtext of *Cane* [1923] is the brutal and enslaved nature of that 'saturation.'" Whalan, "Jean Toomer and the Avant-Garde," 74.
122. The song "Strange Fruit" was written by Abel Meeropol (under the pseudonym Lewis Allan) in 1937.
123. Jesse Matz, *Literary Impressionism and Modernist Aesthetics* (Cambridge: Cambridge University Press, 2001), 1. Emphasis as per the original text.
124. Walrond, *Tropic Death*, 99.
125. Walrond, *Tropic Death*, 101.
126. Walrond, *Tropic Death*, 101, 100, 101.
127. Walrond, *Tropic Death*, 107.
128. Walrond, *Tropic Death*, 110.
129. Walrond, *Tropic Death*, 111.
130. Walrond, *Tropic Death*, 103.
131. Walrond, *Tropic Death*, 111. Emphasis added by the author.
132. Frederick, *Colón Man a Come*, 161.
133. Walrond, *Tropic Death*, 34, 21, 22.
134. Walrond, *Tropic Death*, 26, 28.
135. Walrond, *Tropic Death*, 27, 28.
136. Walrond, *Tropic Death*, 32.
137. Walrond, *Tropic Death*, 34.
138. Walrond, *Tropic Death*, 40.
139. Eric Walrond, "The Godless City," in *Winds Can Wake Up the Dead": An Eric Walrond Reader*, ed. Louis J. Parascandola (Detroit: Wayne State University Press, 1998), 161.
140. Jason M. Colby, *The Business of Empire: United Fruit, Race, and U.S. Expansion in Central America* (Ithaca, NY: Cornell University Press, 2011), 87.
141. Walrond, "The Godless City," 165.
142. Walrond, "The Godless City," 164.
143. Walrond, "The Godless City," 172.
144. Leigh Anne Duck, *The Nation's Region: Southern Modernism, Segregation, and U.S. Nationalism* (Athens: University of Georgia Press, 2006), 24.

2. COMPELLING INSINUATION AND THE USES OF ETHNOGRAPHY: ZORA NEALE HURSTON, JEAN PRICE-MARS, AND THE U.S. OCCUPATION OF HAITI

1. Ellen Harold, ed., "Introduction," in *Haitian Diary: Papers and Correspondence from Alan Lomax's Haitian Journey* (San Francisco: Harte Recordings, 2009), 7.
2. Harold, "Introduction," 3.
3. Katherine Dunham, *Island Possessed* (New York: Doubleday, 1969), 23.
4. Mary Renda, *Taking Haiti: Military Occupation and the Culture of U.S. Imperialism, 1915–1940* (Chapel Hill: University of North Carolina Press, 2001), 185.
5. Michael Largey, *Vodou Nation: Haitian Art Music and Cultural Nationalism* (Chicago: University of Chicago Press, 2006), 24.
6. M. Jacqui Alexander, *Pedagogies of Crossing: Meditations on Feminism, Sexual Politics, Memory, and the Sacred* (Durham, NC: Duke University Press, 2005), 12.
7. Deborah A. Thomas, "Haiti, Politics, and Sovereign (Mis)recognitions," in *The Haiti Exception: Anthropology and the Predicament of Narrative*, ed. Alessandra Benedicty-Kokken, Kaiama L. Glover, Mark Schuller, and Jhon Picard Byron (Liverpool: Liverpool University Press, 2016), 138.
8. Sylvia Wynter, "The Re-Enchantment of Humanism: An Interview with Sylvia Wynter," interview by David Scott, *Small Axe* 8 (September 2000): 136.
9. Jean Price-Mars, *So Spoke the Uncle*, trans. Magdaline W. Shannon (Washington, DC: Three Continents, 1983), 12.
10. Price-Mars, *So Spoke the Uncle*, 43.
11. Price-Mars, *So Spoke the Uncle*, 25.
12. Price-Mars, *So Spoke the Uncle*, 8.
13. Jean Price-Mars, "Lemba Pétro: Un culte secret," *Revue de la société d'histoire et de géographie d'Haiti* 9, no. 28 (1938): 21. It also was quoted in Largey, *Vodou Nation*, 25.
14. Largey, *Vodou Nation*, 21.
15. Kate Ramsey, *The Spirits and the Law: Vodou and Power in Haiti* (Chicago: University of Chicago Press, 2011), 242.
16. Sylvia Wynter, *Black Metamorphosis: New Natives in a New World*, unpublished manuscript, Institute of the Black World Papers, Schomburg Center for Research in Black Culture, New York, 14.
17. Zora Neale Hurston, *Tell My Horse: Voodoo and Life in Haiti and Jamaica*, orig. 1938 (New York: Harper Perennial, 2009), 72.
18. Brandon Byrd, *The Black Republic: African Americans and the Fate of Haiti* (Philadelphia: University of Pennsylvania Press, 2020), 197.
19. Ramsey, *The Spirits and the Law*, 177.
20. Leigh Anne Duck, "'Rebirth of a Nation': Hurston in Haiti," *Journal of American Folklore* 117, no. 464 (2004): 132.
21. Sylvia Wynter, "The Pope Must Have Been Drunk, the King of Castile a Madman: Culture as Actuality, and the Caribbean Rethinking Modernity," in *Reordering of Culture: Latin America, the Caribbean, and Canada in the 'Hood*, ed. Alvina Ruprecht and Cecila Taiana (Ottawa, Canada: Carleton University Press, 1995), 22.
22. James Clifford, "On Ethnographic Authority," *Representations*, no. 2 (1983): 120.

23. Colin Dayan, *Haiti, History, and the Gods* (Berkeley: University of California Press, 1998), xvii.

24. Wynter, "The Pope Must Have Been Drunk," 22.

25. Zora Neale Hurston, "Characteristics of Negro Expression," in *The Jazz Cadence of American Culture*, ed. Robert G. O'Meally (New York: Columbia University Press, 1998), 302.

26. Samantha Pinto, *Difficult Diasporas: The Transnational Feminist Aesthetic of the Black Atlantic* (New York: New York University Press, 2013), 107.

27. Hurston, *Tell My Horse*, 219.

28. Hurston, *Tell My Horse*, 220.

29. Celia Weiss Bambara, "Did You Say Banda? Geoffrey Holder and How Stories Circulate," *Journal of Haitian Studies* 17, no. 1 (Spring 2011): 183.

30. Daphne A. Brooks and/for José Muñoz, "Open Channels: Some Thoughts on Blackness, the Body, and Sound(ing) Women in the (Summer) Time of Trayvon," *Performance Research: A Journal of the Performing Arts* 19, no. 3 (2014): 67.

31. Emily A. Maguire, *Racial Experiments in Cuban Literature and Ethnography* (Gainesville: University Press of Florida, 2011), 151.

32. Hurston, "Characteristics of Negro Expression," 302.

33. Michel-Rolph Trouillot, "The Caribbean Region: An Open Frontier in Anthropological Theory," in *Trouillot Remixed*, ed. Yarimar Bonilla, Greg Beckett, and Mayanthi L. Fernando (Durham, NC: Duke University Press, 2021), 173.

34. Jean Price-Mars, *Le bilan des études ethnologiques en Haïti et le cycle du Nègre* (Port-au-Prince, Haiti: Imprimerie de l'État, 1954), 15, 16. Translation by the author.

35. Michel-Rolph Trouillot, *Global Transformations: Anthropology and the Modern World* (New York: Palgrave Macmillan, 2003), 124–125.

36. Trouillot, *Global Transformations*, 133.

37. Gérarde Magloire and Kevin A. Yelvington, "Haiti and the Anthropological Imagination," *Gradhiva* 1 (2005): 3.

38. Jhon Picard Byron, "Transforming Ethnology: Understanding the Stakes and Challenges of Price-Mars in the Development of Anthropology in Haiti," in *The Haiti Experiment: Anthropology and the Predicaments of Narrative*, ed. Alessandra Benedicty-Kokken, Kaiama L. Glover, Mark Schuller, and Jhon Picard Byron (Liverpool: Liverpool University Press, 2016), 40.

39. J. Michael Dash, "Review of *So Spoke the Uncle* by Jean Price-Mars," trans. Magdaline W. Shannon, *Social and Economic Studies* 34, no. 3 (June 1985): 317.

40. Magdaline Shannon, *Jean Price-Mars and the American Occupation, 1915–35* (London: Macmillan, 1996), 7.

41. James Weldon Johnson, "Self-Determining Haiti," in *James Weldon Johnson: Writings*, ed. William L. Andrews (New York: Library of America, 2004), 662.

42. James Weldon Johnson, *Along This Way*, in *James Weldon Johnson: Writings*, ed. William L. Andrews (New York: Library of America, 2004), 517.

43. Jean Price-Mars, "Letter to James Weldon Johnson," April 17, 1920, JWJ MSS 49, Box 8, Folder 183.

44. Jean Price-Mars, "Calling Card to Herbert Seligmann," April 1920, JWJ MSS 49, Box 8, Folder 183.

45. Jean Price-Mars, *La vocation de l'Élite*, orig. 1919 (Port-au-Prince, Haiti: Editions des presses nationales d'Haiti, 2001), ix.

46. Hurston, "Characteristics of Negro Expression," 302.

47. Magloire and Yelvington, "Haiti and the Anthropological Imagination," 6.

48. Charlemagne Péralte, quoted in Robert Debs Heinl Jr. and Nancy Gordon, *Written in Blood: The Story of the Haitian People, 1492–1971* (Boston: Houghton Mifflin, 1978), 452.

49. Ramsey, *The Spirits and the Law*, 132.

50. Grace Sanders-Johnson, "Occupied Thoroughfares: Haitian Women, Public Space, and the United States Occupation," in *Caribbean Military Encounters*, ed. Shalini Puri and Lara Putnam (New York: Palgrave McMillan, 2017), 71–83.

51. Matthew K. Smith, *Red and Black in Haiti: Radicalism, Conflict, and Political Change, 1934–1957* (Chapel Hill: University of North Carolina Press, 2009), 8–9.

52. Price-Mars, *La vocation de l'Élite*, 91.

53. Price-Mars, *La vocation de l'Élite*, 8.

54. Price-Mars, *La vocation de l'Élite*, 179.

55. Booker T. Washington, "Dr. Booker T. Washington on American Occupation of Haiti: Tuskegee Educator Sounds Note of Warning Urging U.S. to Be Patient with Black Republic," *New York Age*, October 21, 1915, 1. Washington's perspective on U.S. intervention echoes the uplift ideology that he promoted in the United States: "I feel that we should embrace the opportunity for constructive policy that will remake Haiti, that will make the Haitians a new people, and from an economic point of view and every other point of view will make Haiti of increasing value not alone to the Haitians but to our own country and civilization as well," he reflected. Washington, "Tuskegee Educator Sounds Note of Warning," 5.

56. Washington writes: "A ship lost at sea for many days suddenly sighted a friendly vessel. From the mast of the unfortunate vessel was seen a signal, 'Water, water; we die of thirst!' The answer from the friendly vessel at once came back, 'Cast down your bucket where you are.' A second time the signal, 'Water, water; send us water!' ran up from the distressed vessel, and was answered, 'Cast down your bucket where you are.' And a third and fourth signal for water was answered, 'Cast down your bucket where you are.' The captain of the distressed vessel, at last heeding the injunction, cast down his bucket, and it came up full of fresh, sparkling water from the mouth of the Amazon River." Booker T. Washington, "The Atlanta Exposition Address," in *Three Negro Classics* (New York: Avon, 1965), 145.

57. As Largey contends, Price-Mars's formulation is a "metaphor for U.S.-Haitian relations," in which "the vast ocean of salt water was like the rapacious imperialism of the United States." Largey, *Vodou Nation*, 3. Given the context of the ongoing occupation (at that point seventeen years in), the parable of the ships invokes the arrival of the U.S.S. *Washington* in the harbor at Port-au-Prince in July 1915, marking the beginning of the occupation and the continuation of the U.S. policy of gunboat diplomacy. Price-Mars's parable acknowledges the imperial symbolism of seafaring vessels, invoking an ongoing New World history of conquest and exploitation.

58. Jean Price-Mars, "A propos de la Renaissance nègre aux États-Unis," *La Relève* 1, nos. 1–3 (1932): 14.

59. Price-Mars, "A propos de la Renaissance nègre," 14.

60. Washington, "Tuskegee Educator Sounds Note of Warning."

61. Kevin Gaines, "Black Americans' Uplift Ideology as Civilizing Mission: Pauline E. Hopkins," in *Cultures of United States Imperialism*, ed. Amy Kaplan and Donald E. Pease (Durham, NC: Duke University Press, 1993), 437.

62. Mayanthi L. Fernando, "Ethnography and the Politics of Silence," *Cultural Dynamics* 26, no. 2 (July 2014): 236.
63. Price-Mars, *So Spoke the Uncle*, 7.
64. Here, I follow Trouillot's claim that "[c]ommunities need to be studied in reference to a 'larger context' that includes networks of local institutions but also the development of colonies and empires. . . . In short, heterogeneity cannot be grasped without serious reference to history." Trouillot, "The Caribbean Region," 172.
65. Price-Mars, *So Spoke the Uncle*, 7.
66. Price-Mars, *So Spoke the Uncle*, 9.
67. Sylvia Wynter, "Review of *One Love—Rhetoric or Reality? Aspects of Afro-Jamaican-ism*, by Audvil King, Althea Helps, Pam Wint, and Frank Hasfal," *Caribbean Studies* 12, no. 3 (1972): 65.
68. Wynter, "Review of *One Love*," 65.
69. Price-Mars, *So Spoke the Uncle*, 139.
70. Michel-Rolph Trouillot, "Review of *So Spoke the Uncle* by Jean Price-Mars," trans. Magdaline W. Shannon, *Research in African Literatures* 17, no. 4 (1986): 596.
71. Trouillot, "The Caribbean Region," 178–179.
72. Price-Mars, *So Spoke the Uncle*, 120.
73. Price-Mars, *So Spoke the Uncle*, 18–19.
74. Yarimar Bonilla, *Non-Sovereign Futures: French Caribbean Politics in the Wake of Disenchantment* (Chicago: University of Chicago Press, 2015), xvi.
75. Price-Mars, *So Spoke the Uncle*, 24–25.
76. Price-Mars, *So Spoke the Uncle*, 25.
77. Alejandra Bronfman, *Isles of Noise: Sonic Media in the Caribbean* (Chapel Hill: University of North Carolina Press, 2016), 93.
78. Price-Mars, *So Spoke the Uncle*, 26–27.
79. Price-Mars, *So Spoke the Uncle*, 26.
80. Price-Mars, *So Spoke the Uncle*, 27.
81. Price-Mars, *So Spoke the Uncle*, 26. The English translation misses the rhyme in "*où l'on conte et où l'on chante.*"
82. Price-Mars, *So Spoke the Uncle*, 25.
83. Price-Mars, *So Spoke the Uncle*, 27.
84. Price-Mars, *So Spoke the Uncle*, 28.
85. Price-Mars, *So Spoke the Uncle*, 13.
86. Largey, *Vodou Nation*, 4.
87. Price-Mars, *So Spoke the Uncle*, 34.
88. Brent Hayes Edwards, "The Seemingly Eclipsed Window of Form: James Weldon Johnson's Prefaces," in *The Jazz Cadence of American Culture*, ed. Robert G. O'Meally (New York: Columbia University Press, 1998), 596.
89. J. C. Dorsainvil, quoted in Price-Mars, *So Spoke the Uncle*, 117.
90. Alexander, *Pedagogies of Crossing*, 328.
91. Price-Mars, *So Spoke the Uncle*, 174.
92. Jenny Sharpe, *Immaterial Archives: An African Diaspora Poetics of Loss* (Evanston, IL: Northwestern University Press, 2020), 61.
93. Price-Mars, *So Spoke the Uncle*, 122–123.
94. Price-Mars, *So Spoke the Uncle*, 123.
95. Price-Mars, *So Spoke the Uncle*, 125.

96. Price-Mars, *So Spoke the Uncle*, 126.
97. Karen McCarthy Brown, "Afro-Caribbean Spirituality: A Haitian Case Study," in *Vodou in Haitian Life and Culture: Invisible Powers*, ed. Claudine Michel and Patrick Bellegarde-Smith (New York: Palgrave Macmillan, 2006), 13.
98. Claudine Michel and Patrick Bellegarde-Smith, "Invisible Powers: An Introduction," in *Vodou in Haitian Life and Culture: Invisible Powers*, ed. Claudine Michel and Patrick Bellegarde-Smith (New York: Palgrave Macmillan, 2006), xi.
99. Price-Mars, *So Spoke the Uncle*, 130–131.
100. Price-Mars, *So Spoke the Uncle*, 130–131.
101. Price-Mars also adopts a comparative approach to reinforce a key premise of his discussion of Vodou possession: "to reject the opinion that makes this phenomenon an attribute of race." On the contrary, he contends, "any individual of any race" could be "susceptible to having a voodooistic crisis." Much to the probable chagrin of some of his readers, he closes with an anecdote of whites being overcome by spirit possession: "the historiographer of the colony, Moreau de Saint-Méry, informs us [that the] magnetism exercised by the dance of Voodoo is such that Whites found watching the mysteries of this sect and touched by one of its members who had discovered them began to dance themselves." Thus Price-Mars creates a framework for comparison that subverts race, even as he sought to vindicate Black culture. Price-Mars, *So Spoke the Uncle*, 134.
102. Zora Neale Hurston, "The Sanctified Church," in *Zora Neale Hurston: Folklore, Memoirs, and Other Writings*, ed. Cheryl A. Wall (New York: Library of America, 1995), 902.
103. Zora Neale Hurston, "Shouting," in *Zora Neale Hurston: Folklore, Memoirs, and Other Writings*, ed. Cheryl A. Wall (New York: Library of America, 1995), 852.
104. Hurston, "The Sanctified Church," 902.
105. Zora Neale Hurston, "Folklore and Music," in *Zora Neale Hurston: Folklore, Memoirs, and Other Writings*, ed. Cheryl A. Wall (New York: Library of America, 1995), 890.
106. Zora Neale Hurston, "Letter to Alan Lomax," November 25, 1936, in *Haitian Diary: Papers and Correspondence from Alan Lomax's Haitian Journey*, ed. Ellen Harold (San Francisco: Harte Recordings, 2009), 19–20.
107. Hurston, *Tell My Horse*, 204.
108. Zora Neale Hurston, quoted in Robert E. Hemenway, *Zora Neale Hurston: A Literary Biography* (Urbana: University of Illinois Press, 1977), 227.
109. Hurston, "Folklore and Music," 890.
110. Hazel Carby, "The Politics of Fiction, Anthropology, and the Folk: Zora Neale Hurston," in *Zora Neale Hurston's Their Eyes Were Watching God: A Casebook*, ed. Cheryl A. Wall (New York: Oxford University Press, 2000), 127.
111. Zora Neale Hurston, "Letter to Henry Allen Moe," January 3, 1937, in *Zora Neale Hurston: A Life in Letters*, ed. Carla Kaplan (New York: Knopf, 2007), 392.
112. Cited in M. Genevieve West, *Zora Neale Hurston and American Literary Culture* (Gainesville: University Press of Florida, 2005), 136–138.
113. William Seabrook, quoted in West, *Zora Neale Hurston and American Literary Culture*, 138.
114. The chapter title is a startling allusion to D. W. Griffith's white supremacist film, *The Birth of a Nation* (1915). As Leigh Ann Duck observes, "[G]iven the strangeness of

Hurston's narrative, it seems certain that she was signifying on this tremendously successful film," which was released the same year that American marines landed in Port-au-Prince. Duck argues that Hurston's allusion to *The Birth of a Nation* paradoxically "serves to express what Hurston's narrative vigorously suppresses— the effect of the occupation on Haitian racial and political ideologies." The film's premise that African American involvement in the Reconstruction government constituted "the beginnings of a 'Black Empire'" which had to be suppressed at any cost would seem to bear special implications for Haiti, the Black Republic of the Western Hemisphere. Duck concludes that Hurston's invocation of the film "suggests her awareness that the occupation disrupted the relationship between the state and the public in a particularly destructive way." Duck, "'Rebirth of a Nation,'" 138, 139.

While I agree that Hurston's use of this title exposes the seams of her own narrative, the idea that Hurston was being deliberately ironic is unsatisfying. Even though irony was always an important weapon in her arsenal, Hurston's analysis in the subsequent chapters of *Tell My Horse* seems to support the ideas that she sets forth in "Rebirth of a Nation." To be clear, Hurston never sanctioned the violent policing inherent in the rise of the Ku Klux Klan that Griffith's film celebrates. Still, Hurston unnervingly links rebirth to the paternalistic effort of a "foreign white power" to restore order to a hopelessly dysfunctional (Black) state. If Haiti's birth had been a "savage lunge for freedom," its rebirth would be a civilized march toward democracy. Hurston then, seems to support the civilizing mission of the United States, even as she concedes that it is a last resort. As I have suggested, however, the phrase "rebirth of a nation" also encompasses Hurston's effort to re-create Haiti in her own image. To pave the way for her own entry into this milieu, she creates a fictional Haiti in which the agency of the Haitian people has been displaced—not just by occupation forces, but by her own prophetic voice. It is only after she has established this authoritative voice that Hurston, the folklorist, is able to re-enter the scene, and the first person "I" reappears to take ownership of the ideas being set forth in the book. Hurston, *Tell My Horse*, 74, 73.

115. Hurston, *Tell My Horse*, 71.

116. Hurston, *Tell My Horse*, 72.

117. Hurston, *Tell My Horse*, 66.

118. Hurston, *Tell My Horse*, 72.

119. Autumn Womack, *The Matter of Black Living: The Aesthetic Experiment of Racial Data, 1880–1930* (Chicago: University of Chicago Press, 2021), 188.

120. Zora Neale Hurston, *Mules and Men*, orig. 1935, in *Zora Neale Hurston: Folklore, Memoirs, and Other Writings*, ed. Cheryl A. Wall (New York: Library of America, 1995), 9.

121. Karen Jacobs, *The Eye's Mind: Literary Modernism and Visual Culture* (Ithaca, NY: Cornell University Press, 2001), 112.

122. Ifeoma Kiddoe Nwankwo, "Insider and Outsider, Black and American: Rethinking Zora Neale Hurston's Caribbean Ethnography," *Radical History Review* 87 (2003): 51.

123. Nwankwo, "Insider and Outsider," 52.

124. Nwankwo, "Insider and Outsider," 64.

125. Zora Neale Hurston, *Their Eyes Were Watching God*, orig. 1937 (New York: Perennial Classics, 1998), 32.

126. Hurston, *Tell My Horse*, 74.
127. Hurston, *Tell My Horse*, 75–77.
128. Erica R. Edwards, *Charisma and the Fictions of Black Leadership* (Minneapolis: University of Minnesota Press, 2012), 81.
129. Hurston, *Tell My Horse*, 74.
130. Carby, "The Politics of Fiction," 131.
131. Nwankwo, "Insider and Outsider," 49.
132. Hurston, *Tell My Horse*, 74.
133. Hurston is likely referring to Frédéric Duvigneau, Minister of the Interior from 1937–1941.
134. Hurston, *Tell My Horse*, 74.
135. Hurston, *Tell My Horse*, 92.
136. Hurston, *Tell My Horse*, 81.
137. Duck, " 'Rebirth of a Nation,' " 132.
138. Hurston, *Tell My Horse*, 85.
139. Hurston, *Tell My Horse*, 86.
140. Trouillot, *Global Transformations*, 25.
141. Duck, " 'Rebirth of a Nation,' " 137.
142. Hurston, *Tell My Horse*, 204.
143. Amy Fass Emery, "The Zombie in/as the Text: Zora Neale Hurston's *Tell My Horse*," *African American Review* 39, no. 3 (2005): 329.
144. Hurston, *Tell My Horse*, 82, 84, 86.
145. Hurston, *Tell My Horse*, 204.
146. Hurston, *Tell My Horse*, 92.
147. Hurston, *Tell My Horse*, 113.
148. Hurston, *Tell My Horse*, 121.
149. Price-Mars, *So Spoke the Uncle*, 126.
150. Pinto, *Difficult Diasporas*, 116.
151. Hurston, *Tell My Horse*, 219–220.
152. Hurston, *Tell My Horse*, 221.
153. Hurston, *Tell My Horse*, 220.
154. Hurston, *Tell My Horse*, 219.
155. Anthea Kraut, *Choreographing the Folk: The Dance Stagings of Zora Neale Hurston* (Minneapolis: University of Minnesota Press, 2008), 3.
156. Dasha A. Chapman, Erin L. Durban-Albrecht, and Mario LaMothe, "*Nou Mache Ansanm* (We Walk Together): Queer Haitian Performance and Affiliation," *Women & Performance: A Journal of Feminist Theory* 27, no. 2 (2017): 150.
157. Joanna Dee Das, "Choreographing a New World: Katherine Dunham and the Politics of Dance" (Ann Arbor, Michigan: ProQuest Dissertations Publishing, 2014), 271.
158. Dunham, *Island Possessed*, 99. Papa Guedé later appears in Dunham's Black Power program in 1968. See Das, "Choreographing a New World," 271.
159. Hurston, *Tell My Horse*, 183. Emphasis added by the author.
160. Hurston, *Tell My Horse*, 181.
161. Tavia Nyong'o, "The Scene of Occupation," *TDR: The Drama Review* 56, no. 4 (2012): 142.
162. Annette Trefzer, "Possessing the Self: Caribbean Identities in Zora Neale Hurston's *Tell My Horse*," *African American Review* 34, no. 2 (2000): 305.

163. Hurston, *Tell My Horse*, 223, 222.
164. Renda, *Taking Haiti*, 290.
165. Hurston, *Tell My Horse*, 75.
166. Hurston, *Tell My Horse*, 223.
167. Trefzer, "Possessing the Self," 307.
168. Hurston, *Tell My Horse*, 222.
169. Omise'eke Natasha Tinsley, *Ezili's Mirrors: Imagining Queer Black Genders* (Durham, NC: Duke University Press, 2018), 9, 11.
170. Jill H. Casid, *Scenes of Projection: Recasting the Enlightenment Subject* (Minneapolis: University of Minnesota Press, 2015), 154.
171. Renda, *Taking Haiti*, 290.
172. Paul Christopher Johnson, "Secretism and the Apotheosis of Duvalier," *Journal of the American Academy of Religion* 74, no. 2 (June 2006): 422.
173. Dany Laferrière, "Jean Price-Mars: Un intellectuel en otage," in *Jean Price-Mars Ainsi Parla l'Oncle suivi de Revister l'Oncle* (Montreal, Canada: Memoire D'Encrier, 2009), 263. Translation by the author.
174. Aimé Césaire, "Cahier d'un retour au pays natal," in *The Original 1939 Notebook of a Return to the Native Land*, ed. Clayton Eshleman and A. James Arnold (Middletown, CT: Wesleyan University Press, 2013), 18.
175. Laferrière, "Jean Price-Mars: Un intellectuel en otage," 270. Translation by the author.
176. Gina Athena Ulysse, "Why Rasanblaj, Why Now? New Salutations to the Four Cardinal Points in Haitian Studies," *Journal of Haitian Studies* 23, no. 2 (2017): 69, 70.
177. Here, I follow Diana Taylor's argument that the archive and the repertoire "exist in a constant state of interaction." Diana Taylor, *The Archive and the Repertoire: Performing Cultural Memory in the Americas* (Durham, NC: Duke University Press, 2003), 22.

3. "CUBAN EVENING": EMBODIED POETICS OF TRANSLATION IN THE WORK OF EUSEBIA COSME, NICOLÁS GUILLÉN, AND LANGSTON HUGHES

1. Katherine Dunham, "Letter to Langston Hughes," February 2, 1946, Langston Hughes Papers (hereafter LHP), JWJ MSS 26, Box 57, Folder 1085, Beinecke Rare Book and Manuscript Library, Yale University, New Haven, CT.
2. "Harlem's Spanish Section Raves about Cuba's Premier Dramatic Artist, Eusebia Cosme," *Pittsburgh Courier*, September 10, 1938, 13.
3. Joaquín Pelayo, "Cubans, Our Neighbors," *Chicago Defender*, February 3, 1940, 13.
4. Fernando Ortiz, "La poesía mulata: Presentación de Eusebia Cosme, la recitadora," in *Eusebia Cosme: La rosa canela*, ed. Nydia Sarabia (Santiago de Cuba: Ediciones Caserón, 2013), 49.
5. See Keith Ellis, "Nicolás Guillén and Langston Hughes: Convergences and Divergences," in *Between Race and Empire: African Americans and Cubans before the Cuban Revolution*, ed. Lisa Brock and Digna Castaneda Fuertes (Philadelphia: Temple University Press, 1998), 159–167; Frank Guridy, *Forging Diaspora: Afro-Cubans and African Americans in a World of Empire and Jim Crow* (Chapel Hill:

University of North Carolina Press, 2010); Monica Kaup, "'Our America' That Is Not One: Transnational Black Atlantic Disclosures in Nicolás Guillén and Langston Hughes," *Discourse* 22, no. 3 (2000): 87–114; Ryan Kernan, *New World Maker: Radical Poetics, Black Internationalism, and the Translations of Langston Hughes* (Evanston, IL: Northwestern University Press, 2022); Vera Kutzinski, "Fearful Asymmetries: Langston Hughes, Nicolás Guillén, and *Cuba Libre*," *Diacritics* 34, no. 3 (2004): 112–142; Vera Kutzinski, *The Worlds of Langston Hughes: Modernism and Translation in the Americas* (Ithaca, NY: Cornell University Press, 2012); John Patrick Leary, "Havana Reads the Harlem Renaissance: Langston Hughes, Nicolás Guillén, and the Dialectics of Transnational American Literature," *Comparative Literature Studies* 47, no. 2 (2010): 133–158; Arnold Rampersad, *The Life of Langston Hughes, Volume I: 1902–1941* (New York: Oxford University Press, 1986); William Scott, "Motivos of Translation," *New Centennial Review* 5, no. 2 (2005): 35–71; Ian Smart, *Nicolás Guillén: Popular Poet of the Caribbean* (Columbia: University of Missouri Press, 1990).

6. Langston Hughes, quoted in Arnold Rampersad, *The Life of Langston Hughes, Volume II: 1941–1967* (New York: Oxford University Press, 1988), 163.

7. Kutzinski, "Fearful Asymmetries," 115; Kutzinski, *Worlds of Langston Hughes*, 132.

8. Kernan, *New World Maker*, 80, 77.

9. The full quote (in Spanish) reads: "*Siempre me preguntaban qué cuáles eran mis antecedentes literarios. Yo respondía sin titubear: Nicolás Guillén; porque realmente lo es, en muchas líneas. Pero no había una mujer. Busqué sobre el tema incesantemente a lo largo de toda la literatura cubana, sobre todo en la poesía cubana de los años treinta, periodo durante el cual afloró el movimiento llamado negrista, afrocubano, como quiera llamársele. No había una mujer, a excepción de la recitadora y actriz Eusebia Cosme.*" Nancy Morejón and Juanamaría Cordones-Cook, "Tertuliando con Nancy Morejón," *Afro-Hispanic Review* 31, no. 2 (2012): 213.

10. Licia Fiol-Matta, *The Great Woman Singer: Gender and Voice in Puerto Rican Music* (Durham, NC: Duke University Press, 2017), 83.

11. Nicolás Guillén, "Letter to Langston Hughes," April 21, 1930, LHP, Box 70, Folder 1366, Beinecke Rare Book and Manuscript Library, Yale University, New Haven, CT.

12. See Rampersad, *Life of Langston Hughes, Volume I*, 181 and Smart, *Nicolás Guillén*, respectively.

13. Gustavo E. Urrutia, "Letter to Langston Hughes," April 20, 1930, LHP, Box 158, Folder 2926, Beinecke Rare Book and Manuscript Library, Yale University, New Haven, CT.

14. Jill Kuhnheim, *Beyond the Page: Poetry and Performance in Spanish America* (Tucson: University of Arizona Press, 2014), 18.

15. Emilio De Torre, "Hablando con Eusebia Cosme," *Ecos de Nueva York: Semanario del Mundo Hispano*, December 12, 1946, Eusebia Cosme Papers, Schomburg Center for Research in Black Culture, New York, 18.

16. Glenn A. Chambers, "The Rise of *Son* and the Legitimization of African-Derived Culture in Cuba, 1908–1940," *Callaloo* 30, no. 2 (2007): 499–504; "Cuba Bans Beating of African Bongo Drum; Used as Jungle Wireless and in Voodoo Rites," *New York Times*, February 17, 1929.

17. Magali Roy-Féquière, *Women, Creole Identity, and Intellectual Life in Early-Twentieth-Century Puerto Rico* (Philadelphia: Temple University Press, 2004), 226.

18. De Torre, "Hablando con Eusebia Cosme," 17. Translation by the author.
19. Meta DuEwa Jones, *The Muse Is Music: Jazz Poetry from the Harlem Renaissance to Spoken Word* (Urbana: University of Illinois Press, 2011), 34.
20. Antonio López, *Unbecoming Blackness: The Diaspora Cultures of Afro-Cuban America* (New York: New York University Press, 2012), 63.
21. Nicolás Guillén, "West Indies, Ltd," in *Sóngoro cosongo, Motivos de son, West Indies, Ltd., España* (Cuarta Edición), Biblioteca clásica y contemporánea (Buenos Aires: Editorial Losada, 1952).
22. Ralph Ellison, *Invisible Man* (New York: Random House, 1952), 13.
23. Kandice Chuh, *The Difference Aesthetics Makes: On the Humanities After Man* (Durham, NC: Duke University Press, 2019), 54.
24. Andrew Brooks, "A Poetics of Interruption: Fugitive Speech Acts and the Politics of Noise," (PhD dissertation, UNSW Art and Design, Sydney, 2017), 1.
25. Nicolás Guillén, "Prólogo," in *Obra poética, 1922–1958*, ed. Angel Augier (Havana, Cuba: Editorial Letras Cubanas, 1980), 102.
26. Brent Hayes Edwards, *The Practice of Diaspora: Literature, Translation, and the Rise of Black Internationalism* (Cambridge, MA: Harvard University Press, 2003), 7. Emphasis as per the original text.
27. Brent Hayes Edwards, "The Taste of the Archive," *Callaloo* 35, no. 4 (2012): 952. Emphasis as per the original text.
28. Nicolás Guillén, "Conversación con Langston Hughes," in *Langston Hughes in the Hispanic World and Haiti*, ed. Edward J. Mullen (Hamden, CT: Archon, 1977), 174.
29. Guillén, "Conversación con Langston Hughes," 175. Translation by the author.
30. William Scott, "Motivos of Translation," *New Centennial Review* 5, no. 2 (2005): 59–60.
31. Hazel Carby, "The Politics of Fiction, Anthropology, and the Folk: Zora Neale Hurston," in *Zora Neale Hurston's Their Eyes Were Watching God: A Casebook*, ed. Cheryl A. Wall (New York: Oxford University Press, 2000), 117–136.
32. Langston Hughes, "Cuba Libre, Selection of Poems Used for Katherine Dunham 'Cuban Evening Performance,'" 1946, LHP, JWJ MSS 26, Box 425, Folder 9447, Beinecke Rare Book and Manuscript Library, Yale University, New Haven, CT.
33. Katherine Dunham, "Katherine Dunham School of Arts and Research: Brochure, 1946–1947," in *Kaiso! Writings by and about Katherine Dunham*, ed. VéVé A. Clark and Margaret B. Wilkerson (Madison: University of Wisconsin Press, 2005), 472–478.
34. Katherine Dunham, "Letter to Nicolás Guillén," June 18, 1946, Katherine Dunham Papers, Box 8, Folder 6. Southern Illinois University Library, Carbondale, IL.
35. Joanna Dee Das, *Katherine Dunham: Dance and the African Diaspora* (Oxford: Oxford University Press, 2017), 112.
36. Joyce Aschenbrenner, *Katherine Dunham: Dancing a Life* (Champaign: University of Illinois Press, 2002), 205.
37. Langston Hughes, "Letter to Carl Van Vechten," November 8, 1941, in *Remember Me to Harlem: Letters of Langston Hughes and Carl Van Vechten, 1923–1964*, ed. Emily Bernard (New York: Knopf, 2001), 199.
38. Shane Vogel, "*Jamaica* on Broadway: The Popular Caribbean and Mock Transnational Performance," *Theatre Journal* 62, no. 1 (2010): 9.
39. Vogel, "*Jamaica* on Broadway," 7–8.

40. Vèvè Clark, "Performing the Memory of Difference in Afro-Caribbean Dance: Katherine Dunham's Choreography, 1938–1987," in *Kaiso! Writings by and about Katherine Dunham* (Madison: University of Wisconsin Press, 2005), 326.

41. Das, *Katherine Dunham*, 84.

42. John Pratt, "Letter to Langston Hughes," February 2, 1946, LHP, JWJ MSS 26, Box 57, Folder 1085, Beinecke Rare Book and Manuscript Library, Yale University, New Haven, CT.

43. Benjamin F. Carruthers, "Eusebia Cosme and Nicolás Guillén," *Theatre Arts* 29, no. 11 (1945): 662. Eusebia Cosme Papers, Reel 1, Schomburg Center for Research in Black Culture, New York.

44. "Cuban Artist Gives Recital: Program in Spanish," *New York Amsterdam News*, June 10, 1939, 4.

45. Nicolás Guillén, "Balada de los dos abuelos," in *Sóngoro cosongo, Motivos de son, West Indies, Ltd., España* (Buenos Aires: Editorial Losada, S.A., 1952), 55–56.

46. Nicolás Guillén, "Maracas," in *Sóngoro cosongo, Motivos de son, West Indies, Ltd., España* (Cuarta Edición), (Buenos Aires: Editorial Losada, 1952). Translation by Ben Frederic Carruthers, LHP, JWJ MSS 26, Box 425, Folder 9447. Carruthers initials the poem "B.C."

47. As Jerome Branche notes, the central metaphor of *West Indies, Ltd.* is the region's "historical and contemporaneous subjection to international capital" (*sometimiento regional histórico y contemporáneo al capital internacional*). Jerome Branche, "Para hablar en caribeño de verdad: Sobre martirio y mitopoiesis en la literatura caribeña," in *Lo que teníamos que tener: Raza y revolución en Nicolás Guillén*, ed. Jerome Branche (Pittsburgh: Instituto Internacional de Literatura Iberoamericana, 2003), 201.

48. Guillén was born in 1902, at the end of a four-year U.S. military occupation following the Spanish Civil War. By the late 1920s, North American businesses controlled 80 percent of sugar production on the island.

49. Nicolás Guillén, "Canción del bongó," in *Sóngoro cosongo, Motivos de son, West Indies, Ltd., España* (Buenos Aires: Editorial Losada, S.A., 1952), 12.

50. Kutzinski, *Worlds of Langston Hughes*, 150.

51. Ned Sublette, *Cuba and Its Music: From the First Drums to the Mambo* (Chicago: Chicago Review, 2004), 258.

52. Jones, *The Muse Is Music*, 51.

53. One might note the sudden interjection of maracas (the instrument) in his long poem *Ask Your Mama*, a work well known for the musical stage directions printed in italics in the margins of each page. Alongside one poetic stanza describing a scene in the American South, a marginal note calls for the band to play "When the Saints Go Marching In joyously two for choruses with maracas." Langston Hughes, *Ask Your Mama: 12 Moods for Jazz* (New York: Knopf, 1961), reprinted in *The Collected Poems of Langston Hughes*, ed. Arnold Rampersad and David Roessel (New York: Vintage, 1995), 481.

54. Hughes, *Ask Your Mama*, 483.

55. Guillén, "Conversación con Langston Hughes," 173.

56. Carruthers, "Eusebia Cosme and Nicolás Guillén," 663.

57. Andrés Ituarte, "Eusebia Cosme," *Revista Hispánica Moderna: Boletin del Instituto de las Españas* 5 (1939): 86.

58. Tom McEnaney, *Acoustic Properties: Radio, Narrative, and the New Neighborhood of the Americas* (Evanston, IL: Northwestern University Press, 2017), 131.

59. Langston Hughes, *The Big Sea*, orig. 1940 (New York: Hill and Wang, 2015), 11.

60. Nicolás Guillén, "Regreso de Eusebia Cosme," in *Eusebia Cosme: La rosa canela*, ed. Nydia Sarabia (Santiago de Cuba: Ediciones Caserón, 2013), 74. Translation by the author.

61. Guillén, "Regreso de Eusebia Cosme," 75.

62. Robin L. Moore, *Nationalizing Blackness: Afrocubanismo and Artistic Revolution in Havana, 1920–1940* (Pittsburgh: University of Pittsburgh Press, 1997), 145.

63. Guillén, "Regreso de Eusebia Cosme," 74.

64. Guillén, "Prólogo," 102.

65. Vera Kutzinski, *Sugar's Secrets: Race and the Erotics of Cuban Nationalism* (Charlottesville: University Press of Virginia, 1993), 5.

66. Kutzinski, *Sugar's Secrets*, 154.

67. Emily A. Maguire, *Racial Experiments in Cuban Literature and Ethnography* (Gainesville: University Press of Florida, 2011), 176.

68. Guillén, "Regreso de Eusebia Cosme," 76.

69. Emily A. Maguire, "The Eusebia Cosme Show: Translating an Afro-Antillian Identity," in *Writing the Afro-Hispanic: Essays on Africa and Africans in the Spanish Caribbean*, ed. C. James (Birmingham, UK: Centre for West African Studies, 2012), 92.

70. López, *Unbecoming Blackness*, 74.

71. Shane Vogel, *Stolen Time: Black Fad Performance and the Calypso Craze* (Chicago: University of Chicago Press, 2018), 12. Emphasis as per the original text.

72. Guillén, "Regreso de Eusebia Cosme," 73.

73. López, *Unbecoming Blackness*, 91.

74. Julia de Burgos, "Con Eusebia Cosme: Gran recitadora cubana," in *Julia de Burgos: Periodista en Nueva York*, ed. Juan Antonio Rodríguez Pagán (San Juan, Puerto Rico: Ateneo Puertorriqueño, 1992), 48.

75. Félix B. Caignet, "Letter to Eusebia Cosme," February 12, 1936, Eusebia Cosme Papers, Reel 1, Schomburg Center for Research in Black Culture, New York.

76. Ortiz, "La poesía mulata," 42.

77. Ortiz, "La poesía mulata," 43.

78. Ortiz, "La poesía mulata," 50.

79. Ortiz, "La poesía mulata," 47.

80. Maguire, "The Eusebia Cosme Show," 91.

81. Maguire, "The Eusebia Cosme Show," 83.

82. Guillén, "Regreso de Eusebia Cosme," 72.

83. Daphne A. Brooks and/for José Muñoz, "Open Channels: Some Thoughts on Blackness, the Body, and Sound(ing) Women in the (Summer) Time of Trayvon," *Performance Research: A Journal of the Performing Arts* 19, no. 3 (2014): 67.

84. Daphne Brooks, *Bodies in Dissent: Spectacular Performances of Race and Freedom, 1850–1910* (Durham, NC: Duke University Press, 2006), 9.

85. Juan Bonich, "Charlando con Eusebia Cosme," in *Eusebia Cosme: La rosa canela*, ed. Nydia Sarabia (Santiago de Cuba: Ediciones Caserón, 2013), 51.

86. Bonich, "Charlando con Eusebia Cosme," 53.

87. López, *Unbecoming Blackness*, 98.

88. Eusebia Cosme, "Eusebia Cosme Radio Show," August 25, 1944, Columbia Broadcasting System, Eusebia Cosme Papers, Scripts, Box 3, Folder 8, Page I, Schomburg Center for Research in Black Culture, New York.

89. Langston Hughes, "I, Too," in *The Collected Poems of Langston Hughes*, ed. Arnold Rampersad and David Roessel (New York: Vintage, 1995), 46.

90. Kutzinski, *Worlds of Langston Hughes*, 77.

91. Cosme, "Eusebia Cosme Radio Show."

92. Edwards, *The Practice of Diaspora*, 38.

93. Langston Hughes, "1927 Trip South: Memphis, New Orleans, Havana, Mobile, Tuskegee, Zora, New York," Memo Pad, LHP, Box 492, Folder 12433, Beinecke Rare Book and Manuscript Library, Yale University, New Haven, CT.

94. Hughes, *The Big Sea*, 325.

95. Hughes, quoted in Rampersad, *Life of Langston Hughes, Volume I*, 176.

96. Hughes, *The Big Sea*, 324.

97. Hughes, "1927 Trip South."

98. Guillén, "Conversación con Langston Hughes," 175.

99. Langston Hughes, *I Wonder as I Wander*, orig. 1956, ed. Joseph McLaren (Columbia: University of Missouri Press, 2003), 43.

100. Guillén, "Conversación con Langston Hughes," 175.

101. Nicolás Guillén, "Pequeña oda a un negro boxeador," translation by Langston Hughes, "Little Ode to a Cuban Boxer," LHP, Box 425, Folder 9447.

102. Guillén, "Pequeña oda a un negro boxeador," translation by Hughes, "Little Ode to a Cuban Boxer."

103. Nicolás Guillén, "Small Ode to a Black Cuban Boxer," in *Man-Making Words: Selected Poems of Nicolás Guillén*, ed. Roberto Márquez and David Arthur McMurray (Amherst: University of Massachusetts Press, 1972), 54.

104. John Patrick Leary, "Havana Reads the Harlem Renaissance: Langston Hughes, Nicolás Guillén, and the Dialectics of Transnational American Literature," *Comparative Literature Studies* 47, no. 2 (2010): 144.

105. Leary, "Havana Reads the Harlem Renaissance," 147.

106. Nicolás Guillén, *Obra poética, 1920–1972*, vol. 1, ed. Angel Augier (Havana, Cuba: Editorial de Arte y Literatura, 1974), 101.

4. REINTERPRETING FOLK CULTURE AT THE "END OF THE WORLD": SYLVIA WYNTER'S DANCE AND RADIO DRAMA

1. Sylvia Wynter, "Letter to Laurence Gilliam," November 12, 1958, BBC Written Archives Center, Caversham, UK.

2. Sylvia Wynter, "The Re-Enchantment of Humanism: An Interview with Sylvia Wynter," interview by David Scott. *Small Axe* 8 (September 2000): 127.

3. Hugh Chignell, "British Radio Drama and the Avant-Garde in the 1950s," *Historical Journal of Film, Radio, and Television* 37, no. 4 (October 2017): 650.

4. Sylvia Wynter, "We Must Learn to Sit Down Together and Talk about a Little Culture," *Jamaica Journal* 2, no. 4 (1968): 24.

5. Sylvia Wynter, "Novel and History: Plot and Plantation," *Savacou* 5 (1971): 100.

6. Cedric Robinson, *Black Marxism: The Making of the Black Radical Tradition* (Chapel Hill: University of North Carolina Press, 1983).

7. Quoted in Derrick White, "Black Metamorphosis: A Prelude to Sylvia Wynter's Theory of the Human," *CLR James Journal* 16, no. 1 (2010): 127–148. www.jstor.org /stable/26758878. Accessed December 1, 2020.

8. Wynter continues with audible excitement: "I never did get to meet her, but I could have fallen out. I didn't know that rhythm could be so powerful. It was like taking the roof off, you know. She made me begin to understand that I am lucky because I belong to this powerful tradition and the fact that it had come in the slave ships. Nevertheless, it was there, alive and powerful. It would give me a tremendous pride because usually we were ashamed of our African heritage. We are taught to be ashamed of it. That was part of the anti-colonial struggle." Sylvia Wynter, "Sylvia Wynter: An Oral History," interview by Natalie Marine-Street, November 22, 2017, Stanford Historical Society, Stanford, CA, 21.

9. Wynter, "An Oral History," 20–21.

10. Wynter, "An Oral History," 20.

11. Aaron Kamugisha, *Beyond Coloniality: Citizenship and Freedom in the Caribbean Intellectual Tradition* (Bloomington: Indiana University Press, 2019), 187.

12. See Natasha Barnes, "Reluctant Matriarch: Sylvia Wynter and the Woman Question," in *Cultural Conundrums: Gender, Race, Nation, and the Making of Caribbean Cultural Politics* (Ann Arbor: University of Michigan Press, 2006), 135–173.

13. Carole Boyce Davies, "The Caribbean Creative/Theoretical," in *The Caribbean Woman Writer as Scholar: Creating, Imagining, Theorizing*, ed. Keisha N. Abraham (Coconut Grove, FL: Caribbean Studies Press, 2009), xi–xiv.

14. Carole Boyce Davies, "From Masquerade to Maskarade: Caribbean Cultural Resistance and the Rehumanizing Project," in *Sylvia Wynter: On Being Human as Praxis*, ed. Katherine McKittrick (Durham, NC: Duke University Press, 2015), 203–225.

15. Katherine McKittrick, "Rebellion/Invention/Groove," *Small Axe* 20, no. 49 (2016): 85. Emphasis as per the original text.

16. Wynter, "Novel and History," 97.

17. Wynter, "Novel and History," 18.

18. Sonya Posmentier, *Cultivation and Catastrophe: The Lyric Ecology of Modern Black Literature* (Baltimore, MD: Johns Hopkins University Press, 2017), 18.

19. Nathaniel Mackey, *Discrepant Engagement: Dissonance, Cross-Culturality, and Experimental Writing* (Cambridge: Cambridge University Press, 1993), 240.

20. Posmentier, *Cultivation and Catastrophe*, 18.

21. Wynter, "Re-Enchantment of Humanism," 161.

22. Sylvia Wynter, "Jonkonnu in Jamaica: Towards the Interpretation of Folk Dance as a Cultural Process," *Jamaica Journal* 4, no. 2 (June 1970): 35.

23. Wynter, "Jonkonnu in Jamaica," 47.

24. Elizabeth Maddock Dillon, *New World Drama: The Performative Commons in the Atlantic World, 1649–1849* (Durham, NC: Duke University Press, 2012), 205.

25. Wynter reflects that "the continuity here is that it had also been on these islands and specifically on the island shared today between Haiti and the Dominican Republic that the initial culturally legitimized divisions of labour, based on the West's 16th century 'invention of man' . . . had established the hierarchical structures that were to be founding both to the Caribbean and to what is today's world system." Sylvia

Wynter, "The Pope Must Have Been Drunk, the King of Castile a Madman: Culture as Actuality, and the Caribbean Rethinking Modernity," in *Reordering of Culture: Latin America, the Caribbean, and Canada in the 'Hood*, ed. Alvina Ruprecht and Cecila Taiana (Ottawa, Canada: Carleton University Press, 1995), 24.
26. Yomaira C. Figueroa-Vásquez, *Decolonizing Diasporas: Radical Mappings of Afro-Atlantic Literature* (Evanston, IL: Northwestern University Press, 2020), 147.
27. Wynter, "Re-Enchantment of Humanism," 101.
28. See Wynter's works such as "Jonkonnu in Jamaica," "The Pope Must Have Been Drunk," "Review of *One Love—Rhetoric or Reality? Aspects of Afro-Jamaicanism*, by Audvil King, Althea Helps, Pam Wint, and Frank Hasfal," *Caribbean Studies* 12, no. 3 (1972): 64–97, and *Black Metamorphosis: New Natives in a New World*, unpublished manuscript, Institute of the Black World Papers, Schomburg Center for Research in Black Culture, New York.
29. Wynter, *Black Metamorphosis*, 18.
30. Wynter, "Re-Enchantment of Humanism."
31. Wynter, "Re-Enchantment of Humanism," 128.
32. J. Dillon Brown and Leah Reade Rosenberg, "Introduction: Looking Beyond Windrush," in *Beyond Windrush: Rethinking Postwar Anglophone Caribbean Literature*, ed. J. Dillon Brown and Leah Reade Rosenberg (Jackson: University of Mississippi Press, 2015), 4.
33. Wynter, "Re-Enchantment of Humanism," 131.
34. Wynter, "Re-Enchantment of Humanism," 129, 130.
35. Christian Holder, "Boscoe Holder," http://www.christianholder.com/boscoe-holder.
36. Boscoe Holder, "Boscoe Holder Interview," directed by Bruce Paddington, Banyan Archive, Alexander Street, 2000. https://video-alexanderstreet-com.proxy.libraries.rutgers.edu/watch/boscoe-holder-interview; John Cowley, "Obituary: Boscoe Holder," *The Guardian*, May 1, 2007. For more on the Nardal sisters, see T. Denean Sharpley-Whiting, *Negritude Women* (Minneapolis: University of Minnesota Press, 2002).
37. Earl Leaf, *Isles of Rhythm* (New York: A. S. Barnes, 1948), 183. Holder claims that his appearance in this photograph garnered him an invitation to the Dunham School in 1947. Katherine Dunham also wrote the foreword to *Isles of Rhythm*.
38. Holder, "Boscoe Holder Interview."
39. Shane Vogel, *Stolen Time: Black Fad Performance and the Calypso Craze* (Chicago: University of Chicago Press, 2018), 186.
40. Boscoe Holder, "Drum Dance," Boscoe Holder's troupe perform Caribbean dancing and drumming at the Cote d'Azure Club in London, British Pathé, 1956. https://www.britishpathe.com/video/drum-dance.
41. Anthea Kraut, *Choreographing the Folk: The Dance Stagings of Zora Neale Hurston* (Minneapolis: University of Minnesota Press, 2008), 150.
42. Wynter, "An Oral History," 20.
43. Stefano Harney and Fred Moten, *The Undercommons: Fugitive Practice and Black Study* (New York: Minor Compositions, 2013), 26.
44. Wynter, "Review of *One Love*," 65.
45. Alexandra T. Vazquez, *Listening in Detail: Performances of Cuban Music* (Durham, NC: Duke University Press, 2013), 96.
46. Wynter, "Re-Enchantment of Humanism," 129. Also mentioned in Wynter, "An Oral History," 22.

47. Vogel, *Stolen Time*, 173–174.

48. Wynter continues: "I came to the conclusion that the question of 'consciousness' cannot be solved within the terms of the Western system of knowledge, which is the system of knowledge in which the modern world is brought into existence. In a sense, then, to be 'modern,' to be 'academics,' we are all Westerners. I read where LeRoi Jones/Amiri Baraka in his wonderful *Blues People* (1963) said that we need to look at the West from a landscape outside the West." Sylvia Wynter, "ProudFlesh Inter/Views Sylvia Wynter," interview by Greg Thomas, *ProudFlesh: New Afrikan Journal of Culture, Politics, and Consciousness* 4 (2006): 4.

49. Brent Hayes Edwards, "The Shadow of Shadows," *Positions: East Asia Cultures Critique* 11, no. 1 (2003): 12.

50. Wynter, "Jonkonnu in Jamaica," 37.

51. Katherine McKittrick, *Demonic Grounds: Black Women and the Cartographies of Struggle* (Minneapolis: University of Minnesota Press, 2006), xxii.

52. Édouard Glissant, *Caribbean Discourse*, trans. J. Michael Dash (Charlottesville: University Press of Virginia, 1989), 105.

53. McKittrick, *Demonic Grounds*, xxiii.

54. "Bound," *Merriam-Webster.com Dictionary*. https://www.merriam-webster.com /dictionary/bound. Accessed June 24, 2021.

55. Mimi Sheller, *Citizenship from Below: Erotic Agency and Caribbean Freedom* (Durham, NC: Duke University Press, 2012), 9.

56. Sylvia Wynter, "Essay and Play Extract: The House and Land of Mrs. Alba," *Jamaica Journal* 2, no. 3 (September 1968): 53.

57. Mayra Rivera, "Embodied Counterpoetics: Sylvia Wynter on Religion and Race," in *Beyond Man: Race, Coloniality, and Philosophy of Religion*, ed. An Yountae and Eleanor Craig (Durham, NC: Duke University Press, 2021), 80.

58. Koritha Mitchell, *Living with Lynching: African American Lynching Plays, Performance, and Citizenship, 1890–1930* (Champaign: University of Illinois Press, 2011), 5.

59. Wynter, "Novel and History," 99.

60. Wynter, "Re-Enchantment of Humanism," 129–130.

61. James Procter, "The Empire Scripts Back," *BBC History Research Blog*, October 26, 2018. https://www.bbc.co.uk/blogs/bbchistoryresearch/entries/75ecb85c-7c40-4eca -b9bb-8e5f5195ce70.

62. One recording does exist of Wynter performing in Errol John's radio play *Small Island Moon*, in which Wynter plays Rosa, the girlfriend of Ephraim, a trolley bus driver who longs to leave Trinidad and travel to Europe. "This country has nothing for me," he proclaims. When he goes, he leaves behind a pregnant Rosa, who pines for him with audible desperation. Perhaps Rosa, rather than Ephraim, could have benefited most from the change of scene, although understanding the difficulties that await Caribbean migrants in the metropole, there is no certainty that Ephraim's quest for fulfillment will be successful. Errol John, *Small Island Moon* on *Third Programme*, May 27, 1958, BBC Sound Archive, The British Library, London, UK.

63. Wynter, "An Oral History," 24.

64. Peter J. Kalliney, *Commonwealth of Letters: British Literary Culture and the Emergence of Postcolonial Aesthetics* (Oxford: Oxford University Press, 2013), 120.

65. Kalliney, *Commonwealth of Letters*, 119.

66. Kalliney, *Commonwealth of Letters*, 4.
67. James Procter, "Una Marson at the BBC," *Small Axe* 19, no. 3 (November 2015): 6.
68. Stuart Hall, "Lamming, Selvon and Some Trends in the West Indian Novel," *BIM* (December 1955): 172.
69. Sylvia Wynter, "Commentary," *Caribbean Voices*, June 8, 1958, Program Scripts, BBC Written Archives Center, Caversham, UK.
70. Wynter, "Commentary," 7.
71. Wynter, "Commentary," 8.
72. Alejandra Bronfman, *Isles of Noise: Sonic Media in the Caribbean* (Chapel Hill: University of North Carolina Press, 2016), 100, 115, 114.
73. Sylvia Wynter, *Maskarade*, orig. 1970, in *Mixed Company: Three Early Jamaican Plays*, ed. Yvonne Brewster (London: Oberon, 2012), 28.
74. Wynter, *Maskarade*, 29.
75. Hyacinth M. Simpson, "The BBC's Caribbean Voices and the Making of an Oral Aesthetic in the West Indian Short Story," *Journal of the Short Story in English* 57 (Autumn 2011): 81.
76. Glyne Griffith, *The BBC and the Development of Anglophone Caribbean Literature, 1943–1958* (New York: Palgrave Macmillan, 2016), 3.
77. Sylvia Wynter, "Paramour," *Caribbean Voices*, November 25, 1956, Radio Script, BBC Written Archives Centre, Caversham, UK; Sylvia Wynter, "Bat and Ball," *Caribbean Voices*, August 11, 1957, Radio Script, BBC Written Archives Centre, Caversham, UK.
78. Wynter, "Bat and Ball," 1.
79. Wynter, "Bat and Ball," 1, 2.
80. Wynter, "Bat and Ball," 4.
81. Wynter, "Bat and Ball," 5.
82. Wynter, "Bat and Ball," 7.
83. Wynter, "Bat and Ball," 7.
84. Wynter, "An Oral History," 28.
85. Wynter, "Bat and Ball," 6.
86. Wynter, "Bat and Ball," cover page.
87. Wynter, "Paramour," 6.
88. Wynter, "Paramour," 7.
89. Wynter, "Paramour," 7.
90. Wynter, "Paramour," 8.
91. Brent Hayes Edwards, *Epistrophies: Jazz and the Literary Imagination* (Cambridge, MA: Harvard University Press, 2017), 60.
92. Wynter, "Paramour," 9.
93. Wynter, "Paramour," 10.
94. Wynter, "Paramour," 11.
95. Wynter, "Paramour," 12.
96. Sylvia Wynter, "Beyond Miranda's Meanings: Un/Silencing the Demonic Ground of Caliban's Woman," in *Out of the Kumbla: Caribbean Woman and Literature*, ed. Carole Boyce Davies and Elaine Savory Fido (Trenton, NJ: Africa World Press, 1990), 355–372.
97. Xhercis Méndez and Yomaira C. Figueroa-Vásquez, "Not Your Papa's Wynter: Women of Color Contributions Toward Decolonial Futures," in *Beyond the Doctrine*

of Man: Decolonial Visions of the Human, ed. Joseph Drexler-Dreis and Kristien Justaert (New York: Fordham University Press, 2020), 65.

98. Méndez and Figueroa-Vásquez, "Not Your Papa's Wynter," 76.

99. Natasha Barnes, *Cultural Conundrums: Gender, Race, Nation, and the Making of Caribbean Cultural Politics* (Ann Arbor: University of Michigan Press, 2006), 144.

100. Barnes, *Cultural Conundrums*, 159.

101. Barnes, *Cultural Conundrums*, 144.

102. Shirley Toland-Dix, "The Hills of Hebron: Sylvia Wynter's Disruption of the Narrative of the Nation," *Small Axe* 12, no. 1 (2008): 68–69.

103. As Ashon Crawley writes, "Otherwise, as a word, otherwise possibilities, as a phrase, announces the fact of infinite alternatives to what *is*. And what *is* is about being, about existence, about ontology." Ashon Crawley, *Blackpentacostal Breath: The Aesthetics of Possibility* (New York: Fordham University Press, 2017), 2.

104. Robin Midgely, "Memo," September 19, 1958, BBC Written Archives Center, Caversham, UK.

105. As Jacob Stulberg explains, with the publication of Gordon Lea's book *Radio Drama and How to Write It* in 1926, radio drama guidebooks emerged as a new genre of nonfiction. Many such guidebooks were in circulation by the 1950s. While they offered a range of advice, they more or less shared Lea's goal of "fostering a playwriting style suited to the conditions of radio. Central to this style was an emphasis on clarity and coherence. Well into the 1950s, even the BBC's more experimental radio plays tended to maintain strong and audible distinctions among characters, plotlines, and sound effects." Jacob Stulburg, "How (Not) to Write Broadcast Plays: Pinter and the BBC," *Modern Drama* 58, no. 4 (Winter 2015): 509.

106. Sylvia Wynter, "Cleo Laine and Errol John in *The Barren One* [Publicity Statement]," *Radio Times*, Issue 1834, London, January 2, 1959, 55.

107. Wynter, "Jonkonnu in Jamaica," 36.

108. Wynter, "Essay and Play Extract," 50.

109. Sylvia Wynter, *The Barren One* on BBC Third Programme, January 7, 1959, Radio Script, BBC Written Archives Centre, Caversham, UK.

110. Melia Bensussen, "Introduction," in *Blood Wedding and Yerma*, Federico García Lorca, trans. Langston Hughes and W. S. Merwin (New York: Theatre Communications Group, 1994), xi.

111. Wynter, *The Barren One*, 24.

112. Wynter, *The Barren One*, 35.

113. Ryan J. Bazinet, "Two Sides to a Drum: Duality in Trinidad Orisha Music and Culture," (PhD dissertation, The City University of New York, 2013), 305.

114. Alison Donnell, "Introduction," in *Pocomania and London Calling* (Kingston, Jamaica: Blue Banyan, 2017), xix.

115. Una Marson, *Pocomania and London Calling* (Kingston, Jamaica: Blue Banyan, 2017), 5.

116. This drumming may constitute another example of Wynter's engagement with Bertolt Brecht's "alienation effects," salient reminders of theatre's artificiality that are designed to prompt reflection on the larger social context of which the play is part. See Bertolt Brecht, *Brecht on Theatre: The Development of an Aesthetic*, ed. and trans. John Willett (New York: Hill and Wang, 1964), 92. Wynter engages Brecht explicitly in her introductory essay to "The House and Land of Mrs. Alba": "The

alienation effects which Brecht advises then, tend to this purpose. To go behind the apparent surface of windmills to see what lies behind." Wynter, "Essay and Play Extract," 51.

117. Wynter, *The Barren One*, 24–25.
118. Wynter, *The Barren One*, 38.
119. Robert Lima, "Toward the Dionysiac: Pagan Elements and Rites in *Yerma*," *Journal of Dramatic Theory and Criticism* 4, no. 2 (Spring 1990): 65.
120. Sylvia Wynter, "The Ceremony Must Be Found: After Humanism," *Boundary 2* 12/13, no. 3/1 (1984): 19. Accessed June 16, 2021, www.jstor.org/stable/302808.
121. Tiffany Lethabo King, *The Black Shoals: Offshore Formations of Black and Native Studies* (Durham, NC: Duke University Press, 2019), 199.
122. Sylvia Wynter, "Unsettling the Coloniality of Being/Power/Truth/Freedom: Towards the Human, After Man, Its Overrepresentation—An Argument," *CR: The New Centennial Review* 3, no. 3 (2003): 260.
123. Sylvia Wynter, "The Ceremony Found: Towards the Autopoetic Turn/Overturn, Its Autonomy of Human Agency, and Extraterritoriality of (Self-)Cognition," in *Black Knowledges/Black Struggles: Essays in Critical Epistemology*, ed. Jason R. Ambroise and Sabine Broeck (Liverpool: Liverpool University Press, 2015), 194.
124. Wynter, "The Ceremony Found," 207.
125. Wynter, "The Ceremony Found," 209–210. Wynter is referencing Aimé Césaire, "Poetry and Knowledge," in *Lyric and Dramatic Poetry, 1946–82*, trans. Clayton Eshleman and Annette Smith (Charlottesville: University of Virginia Press, 1990), xlii–lvi.
126. Wynter, "The Ceremony Found," 191, 190.
127. Roy A. K. Heath, *The Ministry of Hope* (London: Marion Boyars, 2000), quoted in Chiji Akoma, *Folklore in New World Black Fiction: Writing and the Oral Traditional Aesthetics* (Columbus: Ohio State University Press, 2007), 21.
128. King, *The Black Shoals*, 198, 204.
129. "First Novel Wins Acclaim," *Kingston Gleaner*, August 11, 1962, 24.
130. Sylvia Wynter, "Lady Nugent's Journal," *Jamaica Journal* 1, no. 1 (1969): 24.
131. Wynter, "The Ceremony Found," 210.

CODA: TOWARD AN ONTOLOGICAL SOVEREIGNTY

1. Sylvia Wynter, "We Know Where We're From: The Politics of Black Culture from Myal to Marley," in *We Must Learn to Sit Down Together and Talk about a Little Culture: Decolonising Essays, 1967–1984*, ed. Demetrius L. Eudell (Leeds, UK: Peepal Tree, 2022), 484. Emphasis as per the original text.
2. Zakiyyah Iman Jackson, *Becoming Human: Matter and Meaning in an Antiblack World* (New York: New York University Press, 2020), 1, 3.
3. Jayna Brown, *Black Utopias: Speculative Life and the Music of Other Worlds* (Durham, NC: Duke University Press, 2021), 9.
4. Tiffany Lethabo King, "Humans Involved: Lurking in the Lines of Posthumanist Flight," *Critical Ethnic Studies* 3, no. 1 (Spring 2017): 166.
5. Brown, *Black Utopias*, 112.
6. Alexis Pauline Gumbs, *Dub: Finding Ceremony* (Durham, NC: Duke University Press, 2020), xi.

7. Sylvia Wynter, "Unparalleled Catastrophe for Our Species? Or, to Give Humanness a Different Future: Conversations," interview by Katherine McKittrick, in *Sylvia Wynter: On Being Human as Praxis*, ed. Katherine McKittrick (Durham, NC: Duke University Press, 2016), 23.

8. Tiffany Lethabo King, *The Black Shoals: Offshore Formations of Black and Native Studies* (Durham, NC: Duke University Press, 2019), 205.

9. Alexis Pauline Gumbs, "Keynote: Creative Dialogue with Crystal Wilkinson and Alexis Pauline Gumbs," Then You Don't Want Me: Canonizing Gayl Jones, May 14, 2022, Virtual Symposium.

10. Wynter, "Unparalleled Catastrophe," 34.

11. Wynter, "We Know Where We're From," 485.

12. Neil Roberts, *Freedom as Marronage* (Chicago: University of Chicago Press, 2015).

13. Rinaldo Walcott, *The Long Emancipation: Toward Black Freedom* (Durham, NC: Duke University Press, 2021), 107.

14. Greg Thomas, "*Marronnons* Let's Maroon: Sylvia Wynter's 'Black Metamorphosis' as a Species of Maroonage," *Small Axe* 20, no. 1 (March 2016): abstract.

15. Fahima Ife, *Maroon Choreography* (Durham, NC: Duke University Press, 2021), 81.

16. Walcott, *The Long Emancipation*, 2.

17. Wynter, "We Know Where We're From," 456. Zimitri Erasmus observes, Wynter's "counter-cartography maps a history of human life onto specific African and African-diasporic modes of praxis that suture natural and symbolic birth, life, and death through ritual. These modes of life are concerned *not* with evolutionary time, but with the co-constitution of genres of time: womb- and body-time; memory- and dream-time; plantation- and plot-time; freedom- and symbolic-time." Zimitri Erasmus, "Sylvia Wynter's Theory of the Human: Counter-, Not Post-Humanist," *Theory, Culture, and Society* 37, no. 6 (2020): 53.

18. Wynter, "We Know Where We're From," 486.

19. King, *Black Shoals*, 200.

20. Sylvia Wynter, "Preface," in *We Must Learn to Sit Down Together and Talk about a Little Culture: Decolonising Essays, 1967–1984*, ed. Demetrius L. Eudell (Leeds, UK: Peepal Tree, 2022), 8.

21. Wynter, "Preface," 8.

22. Wynter, "We Know Where We're From," 487.

BIBLIOGRAPHY

Akọma, Chiji. *Folklore in New World Black Fiction: Writing and the Oral Traditional Aesthetics*. Columbus: Ohio State University Press, 2007.

Alexander, M. Jacqui. *Pedagogies of Crossing: Meditations on Feminism, Sexual Politics, Memory, and the Sacred*. Durham, NC: Duke University Press, 2005.

Anheier, Helmut K., and Yudhishthir Raj Isar, eds. *Cultures and Globalization: The Cultural Economy*. London: Sage, 2008.

Aschenbrenner, Joyce. *Katherine Dunham: Dancing a Life*. Champaign: University of Illinois Press, 2002.

Bambara, Celia Weiss. "Did You Say Banda? Geoffrey Holder and How Stories Circulate." *Journal of Haitian Studies* 17, no. 1 (Spring 2011): 180–192.

Barnes, Natasha. *Cultural Conundrums: Gender, Race, Nation, and the Making of Caribbean Cultural Politics*. Ann Arbor: University of Michigan Press, 2006.

——. "Reluctant Matriarch: Sylvia Wynter and the Woman Question." In *Cultural Conundrums: Gender, Race, Nation, and the Making of Caribbean Cultural Politics*, 135–173. Ann Arbor: University of Michigan Press, 2006.

Barthes, Roland. "The Grain of the Voice." In *Image, Music, Text*, ed. Stephen Heath, 179–189. New York: Hill and Wang, 1977.

Bazinet, Ryan J. "Two Sides to a Drum: Duality in Trinidad Orisha Music and Culture." PhD dissertation, City University of New York, 2013.

——. "When Field Recordings Meet Field Research: Examining Change in the Shango Drumming of Postwar Trinidad." *Ethnomusicology* 61, no. 2 (2017): 287–311.

Benítez-Rojo, Antonio. *The Repeating Island: The Caribbean and the Postmodern Perspective*. Durham, NC: Duke University Press, 1996.

Bensussen, Melia. "Introduction." In *Blood Wedding and Yerma*, Federico García Lorca, trans. Langston Hughes and W. S. Merwin, vii–xiii. New York: Theatre Communications Group, 1994.

Bernard, Emily, ed. *Remember Me to Harlem: Letters of Langston Hughes and Carl Van Vechten, 1923–1964*. New York: Knopf, 2001.

Blackwell, Louise. "Jean Toomer's *Cane* and Biblical Myth." *CLA Journal* 17, no. 4 (1974): 535–542.

Blake, Susan L. "The Spectatorial Artist in Part One of *Cane*." In *Cane: A Norton Critical Edition*, ed. Darwin T. Turner, 217–223. New York: Norton, 1988.

Bogues, Anthony. "Rex Nettleford: The Canepiece, Labour, Education, and the Caribbean Intellectual." *Caribbean Quarterly* 57, nos. 3–4 (2011): 20–32.

Bone, Robert. *Down Home: A History of Afro-American Short Fiction from Its Beginnings to the End of the Harlem Renaissance*. New York: G. P. Putnam's Sons, 1975.

Bonich, Juan. "Charlando con Eusebia Cosme." In *Eusebia Cosme: La rosa canela*, ed. Nydia Sarabia, 51–53. Santiago de Cuba: Ediciones Caserón, 2013.

Bonilla, Yarimar. *Non-Sovereign Futures: French Caribbean Politics in the Wake of Disenchantment*. Chicago: University of Chicago Press, 2015.

Bontemps, Arna. "Commentary on Jean Toomer and *Cane*." In *Cane: A Norton Critical Edition*, ed. Darwin T. Turner, 186–192. New York: Norton, 1988.

Bornstein, George. *Material Modernism: The Politics of the Page*. Cambridge: Cambridge University Press, 2001.

Branche, Jerome. "Para hablar en caribeño de verdad: Sobre martirio y mitopoiesis en la literatura caribeña." In *Lo que teníamos que tener: Raza y revolución en Nicolás Guillén*, ed. Jerome Branche, 199–228. Pittsburgh: Instituto Internacional de Literatura Iberoamericana, 2003.

Brawley, Benjamin. "The Negro Literary Renaissance." In *The New Negro: Readings on Race, Representation, and African American Culture, 1892–1938*, ed. Henry Louis Gates Jr. and Gene Andrew Jarrett, 233–236. Princeton, NJ: Princeton University Press, 2007.

Brecht, Bertolt. *Brecht on Theatre: The Development of an Aesthetic*, ed. and trans. John Willett. New York: Hill and Wang, 1964.

Bronfman, Alejandra. *Isles of Noise: Sonic Media in the Caribbean*. Chapel Hill: University of North Carolina Press, 2016.

——. *Measures of Equality: Social Science, Citizenship, and Race in Cuba, 1902–1940*. Chapel Hill: University of North Carolina Press, 2004.

Brooks, Andrew. "A Poetics of Interruption: Fugitive Speech Acts and the Politics of Noise." PhD dissertation, UNSW Art and Design, Sydney, 2017.

Brooks, Daphne. *Bodies in Dissent: Spectacular Performances of Race and Freedom, 1850–1910*. Durham, NC: Duke University Press, 2006.

——. *Liner Notes for the Revolution: The Intellectual Life of Black Feminist Sound*. Cambridge, MA: Harvard University Press, 2021.

Brooks, Daphne A., and/for José Muñoz. "Open Channels: Some Thoughts on Blackness, the Body, and Sound(ing) Women in the (Summer) Time of Trayvon." *Performance Research: A Journal of the Performing Arts* 19, no. 3 (2014): 62–68.

Brown, Jayna. *Babylon Girls: Black Women Performers and the Shaping of the Modern*. Durham, NC: Duke University Press, 2008.

——. *Black Utopias: Speculative Life and the Music of Other Worlds*. Durham, NC: Duke University Press, 2021.

Brown, J. Dillon, and Leah Reade Rosenberg. "Introduction: Looking Beyond Windrush." In *Beyond Windrush: Rethinking Postwar Anglophone Caribbean Literature*, ed. J. Dillon Brown and Leah Reade Rosenberg, 3–24. Jackson: University of Mississippi Press, 2015.

Brown, Sterling. "A Century of Negro Portraiture in American Literature." *Massachusetts Review* 17, no. 1 (1966): 73–96.

Brown, Vincent. *The Reaper's Garden: Death and Power in the World of Atlantic Slavery.* Cambridge, MA: Harvard University Press, 2008.

Bruce, La Marr Jurelle. *How to Go Mad Without Losing Your Mind: Madness and Black Radical Creativity.* Durham, NC: Duke University Press, 2021.

Brunson, Takkara. "Eusebia Cosme and Black Womanhood on the Transatlantic Stage." *Meridians* 15, no. 2 (2017): 389–411.

Byrd, Brandon. *The Black Republic: African Americans and the Fate of Haiti.* Philadelphia: University of Pennsylvania Press, 2020.

Byron, Jhon Picard. "Transforming Ethnology: Understanding the Stakes and Challenges of Price-Mars in the Development of Anthropology in Haiti." In *The Haiti Experiment: Anthropology and the Predicaments of Narrative*, ed. Alessandra Benedicty-Kokken, Kaiama L. Glover, Mark Schuller, and Jhon Picard Byron, 33–51. Liverpool: Liverpool University Press, 2016.

Caignet, Félix B. "Letter to Eusebia Cosme." February 12, 1936. Eusebia Cosme Papers, Reel 1, Schomburg Center for Research in Black Culture, New York.

Carby, Hazel. "The Politics of Fiction, Anthropology, and the Folk: Zora Neale Hurston." In *Zora Neale Hurston's Their Eyes Were Watching God: A Casebook*, ed. Cheryl A. Wall, 117–136. New York: Oxford University Press, 2000.

Carruthers, Benjamin F. "Eusebia Cosme and Nicolás Guillén." *Theatre Arts* 29, no. 11 (1945): 662–664. Eusebia Cosme Papers, Reel 1, Schomburg Center for Research in Black Culture, New York.

——, trans. "Maracas." LHP, JWJ MSS 26, Box 425, Folder 9447, Beinecke Rare Book and Manuscript Library, Yale University, New Haven, CT.

Carruthers, Ben F., and Langston Hughes. *Cuba Libre.* New York: Anderson and Ritchie Press, 1948.

Casid, Jill H. *Scenes of Projection: Recasting the Enlightenment Subject.* Minneapolis: University of Minnesota Press, 2015.

Césaire, Aimé. "Cahier d'un retour au pays natal." In *The Original 1939 Notebook of a Return to the Native Land*, ed. Clayton Eshleman and A. James Arnold, 2–58. Middletown, CT: Wesleyan University Press, 2013.

——. "Poetry and Knowledge." In *Lyric and Dramatic Poetry, 1946–82*, trans. Clayton Eshleman and Annette Smith, xlii–lvi. Charlottesville: University of Virginia Press, 1990.

Chambers, Glenn A. "The Rise of *Son* and the Legitimization of African-Derived Culture in Cuba, 1908–1940." *Callaloo* 30, no. 2 (2007): 497–507.

Chapman, Dasha A., Erin L. Durban-Albrecht, and Mario LaMothe. "*Nou Mache Ansanm* (We Walk Together): Queer Haitian Performance and Affiliation." *Women & Performance: A Journal of Feminist Theory* 27, no. 2 (2017): 143–159.

Chang, Victor L. "Sylvia Wynter." In *Fifty Caribbean Writers: A Bio-Bibliographical Critical Sourcebook*, ed. Daryl Cumber Dance, 498–508. New York: Greenwood Press, 1986.

Chesnutt, Charles W. "The Future American: What the Race Is Likely to Become in the Process of Time." In *Essays and Speeches*, ed. Joseph R. McElrath Jr., Robert C. Leitz III, and Jesse S. Crisler, 121–125. Stanford, CA: Stanford University Press, 1999.

Chignell, Hugh. "British Radio Drama and the Avant-Garde in the 1950s." *Historical Journal of Film, Radio, and Television* 37, no. 4 (October 2017): 649–664.

Christian, Barbara. "The Race for Theory." *Cultural Critique*, no. 6 (1987): 51–63.

Chude-Sokei, Louis. "Foreign Negro Flash Agents: Eric Walrond and the Discrepancies of Diaspora." In *Eric Walrond: The Critical Heritage*, ed. Louis J. Parascandola and Carl A. Wade, 72–99. Kingston, Jamaica: University Press of the West Indies, 2012.

Chuh, Kandice. *The Difference Aesthetics Makes: On the Humanities After Man*. Durham, NC: Duke University Press, 2019.

Clark, VèVè. "Performing the Memory of Difference in Afro-Caribbean Dance: Katherine Dunham's Choreography, 1938–1987." In *Kaiso! Writings by and about Katherine Dunham*, ed. VèVè Clark and Sarah E. Johnson, 320–340. Madison: University of Wisconsin Press, 2005.

Clark, VèVè, and Sarah E. Johnson. *Kaiso! Writings by and about Katherine Dunham*. Madison: University of Wisconsin Press, 2005.

Clifford, James. "On Ethnographic Authority." *Representations*, no. 2 (1983): 118–146.

Cloutier, Jean-Christophe. *Shadow Archives: The Lifecycles of African American Literature*. New York: Columbia University Press, 2019.

Colby, Jason M. *The Business of Empire: United Fruit, Race, and U.S. Expansion in Central America*. Ithaca, NY: Cornell University Press, 2011.

Condé, Maryse. "What Is a Caribbean Writer?" In *The Journey of a Caribbean Writer*, trans. Richard Philcox, 1–9. London: Seagull, 2014.

Corinealdi, Kaysha. *Panama in Black: Afro-Caribbean World Making in the Twentieth Century*. Durham, NC: Duke University Press, 2022.

Cosme, Eusebia. "Cuban Evening Program." Eusebia Cosme Papers, Schomburg Center for Research in Black Culture, New York.

——. "Eusebia Cosme Radio Show." August 25, 1944, Columbia Broadcasting System. Eusebia Cosme Papers, Scripts, Box 3, Folder 8, Page I, Schomburg Center for Research in Black Culture, New York.

Cowley, John. "Obituary: Boscoe Holder." *The Guardian*, May 1, 2007.

Crawford, Margo Natalie. *Black Post-Blackness: The Black Arts Movement and Twenty-First-Century Aesthetics*. Champaign: University of Illinois Press, 2017.

Crawley, Ashon. *Blackpentacostal Breath: The Aesthetics of Possibility*. New York: Fordham University Press, 2017.

"Cuban Artist Gives Recital: Program in Spanish." *New York Amsterdam News*, June 10, 1939, 4.

Das, Joanna Dee. "Choreographing a New World: Katherine Dunham and the Politics of Dance." Ann Arbor, Michigan: ProQuest Dissertations Publishing, 2014.

——. *Katherine Dunham: Dance and the African Diaspora*. Oxford: Oxford University Press, 2017.

Dash, J. Michael. "Review of *So Spoke the Uncle* by Jean Price-Mars." Trans. Magdaline W. Shannon. *Social and Economic Studies* 34, no. 3 (June 1985): 315–318.

Davies, Carole Boyce. "The Caribbean Creative/Theoretical." In *The Caribbean Woman Writer as Scholar: Creating, Imagining, Theorizing*, ed. Keisha N. Abraham, ix–xiv. Coconut Grove, FL: Caribbean Studies Press, 2009.

——. "From Masquerade to Maskarade: Caribbean Cultural Resistance and the Rehumanizing Project." In *Sylvia Wynter: On Being Human as Praxis*, ed. Katherine McKittrick, 203–225. Durham, NC: Duke University Press, 2015.

Davis, Francis. *The History of the Blues: The Roots, the Music, the People.* Boston: Da Capo, 2003.

Davis, James C. *Commerce in Color: Race, Consumer Culture, and American Literature, 1893–1933.* Ann Arbor: University of Michigan Press, 2007.

——. *Eric Walrond: A Life in the Harlem Renaissance and the Transatlantic Caribbean.* New York: Columbia University Press, 2015.

Dayan, Colin. *Haiti, History, and the Gods.* Berkeley: University of California Press, 1998.

——. "And Then Came Culture." *Cultural Dynamics* 26, no. 2 (2014): 137–148.

de Burgos, Julia. "Con Eusebia Cosme: Gran recitadora cubana." In *Julia de Burgos: Periodista en Nueva York,* ed. Juan Antonio Rodríguez Pagán, 45–49. San Juan, Puerto Rico: Ateneo Puertorriqueño, 1992.

De Torre, Emilio. "Hablando con Eusebia Cosme." *Ecos de Nueva York: Semanario del Mundo Hispano,* December 12, 1946. Eusebia Cosme Papers, Schomburg Center for Research in Black Culture, New York.

Dillon, Elizabeth Maddock. *New World Drama: The Performative Commons in the Atlantic World, 1649–1849.* Durham, NC: Duke University Press, 2012.

Donnell, Alison. "Introduction." In *Pocomania and London Calling,* vii–xxiii. Kingston, Jamaica: Blue Banyan, 2017.

Du Bois, W. E. B. "Five Books." *Crisis,* January 1927, 152.

Duck, Leigh Anne. *The Nation's Region: Southern Modernism, Segregation, and U.S. Nationalism.* Athens: University of Georgia Press, 2006.

——. "'Rebirth of a Nation': Hurston in Haiti." *Journal of American Folklore* 117, no. 464 (2004): 127–146.

Dunham, Katherine. *Island Possessed.* New York: Doubleday, 1969.

——. "Katherine Dunham School of Arts and Research: Brochure, 1946–1947." In *Kaiso! Writings by and about Katherine Dunham,* ed. VèVè A. Clark and Margaret B. Wilkerson, 472–478. Madison: University of Wisconsin Press, 2005.

——. "Letter to Langston Hughes." February 2, 1946. Langston Hughes Papers. JWJ MSS 26, Box 57, Folder 1085. Beinecke Rare Book and Manuscript Library, Yale University, New Haven, CT.

——. "Letter to Nicolás Guillén." June 18, 1946. Katherine Dunham Papers. Box 8, Folder 6. Southern Illinois University Library, Carbondale, IL.

Edwards, Brent Hayes. *Epistrophies: Jazz and the Literary Imagination.* Cambridge, MA: Harvard University Press, 2017.

——. *The Practice of Diaspora: Literature, Translation, and the Rise of Black Internationalism.* Cambridge, MA: Harvard University Press, 2003.

——. "The Seemingly Eclipsed Window of Form: James Weldon Johnson's Prefaces." In *The Jazz Cadence of American Culture,* ed. Robert G. O'Meally, 580–601. New York: Columbia University Press, 1998.

——. "The Shadow of Shadows." *Positions: East Asia Cultures Critique* 11, no. 1 (2003): 11–49.

——. "The Taste of the Archive." *Callaloo* 35, no. 4 (2012): 944–972.

Edwards, Erica R. *Charisma and the Fictions of Black Leadership.* Minneapolis: University of Minnesota Press, 2012.

——. *The Other Side of Terror: Black Women and the Culture of U.S. Empire.* New York: New York University Press, 2021.

Edwards, Norval. "'Talking about a Little Culture': Sylvia Wynter's Early Essays." *Journal of West Indian Literature* 10, nos. 1/2 (2001): 12–38.

Ellis, Keith. "Nicolás Guillén and Langston Hughes: Convergences and Divergences." In *Between Race and Empire: African Americans and Cubans before the Cuban Revolution*, ed. Lisa Brock and Digna Castaneda Fuertes, 159–167. Philadelphia: Temple University Press, 1998.

Ellison, Ralph. *Invisible Man*. New York: Random House, 1952.

Emery, Amy Fass. "The Zombie in/as the Text: Zora Neale Hurston's *Tell My Horse*." *African American Review* 39, no. 3 (2005): 327–336.

Erasmus, Zimitri. "Sylvia Wynter's Theory of the Human: Counter-, Not Post-Humanist." *Theory, Culture, and Society* 37, no. 6 (2020): 47–65.

Farebrother, Rachel. *The Collage Aesthetic in the Harlem Renaissance*. New York: Routledge, 2009.

Fauset, Jesse. "Fauset to Jean Toomer." February 17, 1922. Box 1, Folder 37. Jean Toomer Papers, James Weldon Johnson. Beinecke Rare Book and Manuscript Library, Yale University, New Haven, CT.

Fernando, Mayanthi L. "Ethnography and the Politics of Silence." *Cultural Dynamics* 26, no. 2 (July 2014): 235–244.

Figueroa-Vásquez, Yomaira C. *Decolonizing Diasporas: Radical Mappings of Afro-Atlantic Literature*. Evanston, IL: Northwestern University Press, 2020.

Filene, Benjamin. *Romancing the Folk: Public Memory and American Roots Music*. Chapel Hill: University of North Carolina Press, 2000.

Fiol-Matta, Licia. *The Great Woman Singer: Gender and Voice in Puerto Rican Music*. Durham, NC: Duke University Press, 2017.

"First Novel Wins Acclaim." *Kingston Gleaner*, August 11, 1962, 24.

Fishel, Parker. "Alan Lomax's Southern Journey and the Sound of Authenticity." *Sounding Out!* (blog), April 16, 2015. https://soundstudiesblog.com/2015/04/16/alan-lomaxs-southern-journey-and-the-sound-of-authenticity/.

Fluehr-Lobban, Carolyn. "Anténor Firmin and Haiti's Contribution to Anthropology." *Gradhiva* (2005): 95–108.

Foley, Barbara. "Foreword." In *The Letters of Jean Toomer, 1919–1924*, ed. Mark Whalan, xi–xiii. Knoxville: University of Tennessee Press, 2006.

——. *Jean Toomer: Race, Repression, and Revolution*. Champaign: University of Illinois Press, 2014.

——. "'In the Land of Cotton': Economics and Violence in Jean Toomer's *Cane*." *African American Review* 50, no. 4 (2017): 987–1004.

Ford, Karen Jackson. *Split Gut Song: Jean Toomer and the Poetics of Modernity*. Tuscaloosa: University of Alabama Press, 2005.

Frank, Waldo. "Our American Language: Review of *Tropic Death* by Eric Walrond." *Opportunity* 4 (1926): 352.

Frederick, Rhonda. *Colón Man a Come: Mythographies of Panamá Canal Migration*. New York: Lexington Books, 2005.

Gaines, Kevin. "Black Americans' Uplift Ideology as Civilizing Mission: Pauline E. Hopkins." In *Cultures of United States Imperialism*, ed. Amy Kaplan and Donald E. Pease, 433–455. Durham, NC: Duke University Press, 1993.

Gates, Henry Louis, Jr., and Gene Andrew Jarrett, eds. *The New Negro: Readings on Race, Representation, and African American Culture, 1892–1938*. Princeton, NJ: Princeton University Press, 2007.

Gelado, Viviana. "*What, No Rhumba?* Los recitals de Eusebia Cosme y las tensiones entra 'raza' y 'culutra' en torno a la definicion de la 'poesia negra' hispanoamericana en los anos treinta y cuarenta." *Orbia Tertius* 16 (2011): 1–15.

Gilroy, Paul. *The Black Atlantic: Modernity and Double-Consciousness.* London: Verso, 1993.

Glissant, Édouard. *Caribbean Discourse.* Trans. J. Michael Dash. Charlottesville: University Press of Virginia, 1989.

——. *Poetics of Relation.* Ann Arbor: University of Michigan Press, 1997.

Goldsby, Jacqueline. *A Spectacular Secret: Lynching in American Life and Literature.* Chicago: University of Chicago Press, 2006.

Graham, T. Austin. *The Great American Songbooks: Musical Texts, Modernism, and the Value of Popular Culture.* New York: Oxford University Press, 2012.

Griffin, Farah Jasmine. *Who Set You Flowin'? The African-American Migration Narrative.* New York: Oxford University Press, 1995.

Griffith, Glyne. *The BBC and the Development of Anglophone Caribbean Literature, 1943-1958.* New York: Palgrave Macmillan, 2016.

——. "Deconstructing Nationalisms: Henry Swanzy, *Caribbean Voices*, and the Development of West Indian Literature." *Small Axe* 10 (September 2001): 1–20.

Guillén, Nicolás. "Balada de los dos abuelos." In *Sóngoro cosongo, Motivos de son, West Indies, Ltd., España,* 54–56. Buenos Aires: Editorial Losada, S.A., 1952.

——. "Canción del bongó." In *Sóngoro cosongo, Motivos de son, West Indies, Ltd., España,* 12–14. Buenos Aires: Editorial Losada, S.A., 1952.

——. "Conversación con Langston Hughes." In *Langston Hughes in the Hispanic World and Haiti,* ed. Edward J. Mullen, 172–175. Hamden, CT: Archon, 1977.

——. *Epistolario de Nicolás Guillén.* Ed. Alexander Pérez Heredia. Havana, Cuba: Letras Cubanas, 2002.

——. "Letter to Langston Hughes." April 21, 1930. LHP, Box 70, Folder 1366. Beinecke Rare Book and Manuscript Library, Yale University, New Haven, CT.

——. "Maracas." In *Sóngoro cosongo, Motivos de son, West Indies, Ltd., España* (Cuarta Edición). Buenos Aires: Editorial Losada, 1952. Translation by Ben Frederic Carruthers, LHP, JWJ MSS 26, Box 425, Folder 9447, Beinecke Rare Book and Manuscript Library, Yale University, New Haven, CT.

——. *Obra poética, 1920-1972,* vol. 1, ed. Angel Augier. Havana, Cuba: Editorial de Arte y Literature, 1974.

——. "Pequeña oda a un negro boxeador." Translation by Langston Hughes, "Little Ode to a Cuban Boxer." LHP, Box 425, Folder 9447, Beinecke Rare Book and Manuscript Library, Yale University, New Haven, CT.

——. "Prólogo." In *Obra poética, 1922-1958,* ed. Angel Augier, 101–102. Havana, Cuba: Editorial Letras Cubanas, 1980.

——. "Regreso de Eusebia Cosme." In *Eusebia Cosme: La rosa canela,* ed. Nydia Sarabia, 72–76. Santiago de Cuba: Ediciones Caserón, 2013.

——. "Small Ode to a Black Cuban Boxer." In *Man-Making Words: Selected Poems of Nicolás Guillén,* ed. Roberto Márquez and David Arthur McMurray, 53–54. Amherst: University of Massachusetts Press, 1972.

——. "West Indies, Ltd." In *Sóngoro cosongo, Motivos de son, West Indies, Ltd., España* (Cuarta Edición). Biblioteca clásica y contemporánea. Buenos Aires: Editorial Losada, 1952.

Gumbs, Alexis Pauline. *Dub: Finding Ceremony.* Durham, NC: Duke University Press, 2020.

——. "Keynote: Creative Dialogue with Crystal Wilkinson and Alexis Pauline Gumbs." Then You Don't Want Me: Canonizing Gayl Jones, May 14, 2022. Virtual Symposium.

Guridy, Frank. *Forging Diaspora: Afro-Cubans and African Americans in a World of Empire and Jim Crow*. Chapel Hill: University of North Carolina Press, 2010.

Hall, Stuart. "Lamming, Selvon and Some Trends in the West Indian Novel." *BIM* (December 1955): 172–188.

"Harlem's Spanish Section Raves about Cuba's Premier Dramatic Artist, Eusebia Cosme." *Pittsburgh Courier*, September 10, 1938, 13.

Harney, Stefano, and Fred Moten. *The Undercommons: Fugitive Planning and Black Study*. New York: Minor Compositions, 2013.

Harold, Ellen, ed. "Introduction." In *Haitian Diary: Papers and Correspondence from Alan Lomax's Haitian Journey*. San Francisco: Harte Recordings, 2009.

Hartman, Saidiya. "Preface: The Hold of Slavery." In *Scenes of Subjection: Terror, Slavery and Self-Making in Nineteenth-Century America* (revised and updated), xxix–xxxviii. New York: Norton, 2022.

Hayot, Eric, and Rebecca L. Walkowitz, eds. *A New Vocabulary for Global Modernism*. New York: Columbia University Press, 2016.

Heath, Roy A. K. *The Ministry of Hope*. London: Marion Boyars, 2000.

Heinl, Robert Debs, Jr., and Nancy Gordon. *Written in Blood: The Story of the Haitian People, 1492–1971*. Boston: Houghton Mifflin, 1978.

Hemenway, Robert E. *Zora Neale Hurston: A Literary Biography*. Urbana: University of Illinois Press, 1977.

Holder, Boscoe. "Boscoe Holder Interview." Directed by Bruce Paddington. Banyan Archive, Alexander Street, 2000. https://video-alexanderstreet-com.proxy.libraries .rutgers.edu/watch/boscoe-holder-interview.

——. "Drum Dance." Boscoe Holder's troupe perform Caribbean dancing and drumming at the Cote d'Azure Club in London. British Pathé, 1956. https://www.britishpathe .com/video/drum-dance.

Holder, Christian. "Boscoe Holder." http://www.christianholder.com/boscoe-holder.

Hong, Grace Kyungwon. *Death beyond Disavowal: The Impossible Politics of Difference*. Minneapolis: University of Minnesota Press, 2015.

Hubert, Harrison. "Cabaret School of Negro Literature and Art." In *Hubert Harrison Reader*, ed. Jeffrey B. Perry, 355–356. Middletown, CT: Wesleyan University Press, 2001.

Hughes, Langston. *Ask Your Mama: 12 Moods for Jazz*. New York: Knopf, 1961. Reprinted in *The Collected Poems of Langston Hughes*, ed. Arnold Rampersad and David Roessel, 472–531. New York: Vintage, 1995.

——. *The Big Sea*. Originally published in 1940. New York: Hill and Wang, 2015.

——. "Cuba Libre, Selection of Poems Used for Katherine Dunham 'Cuban Evening Performance.'" 1946, LHP, JWJ MSS 26, Box 425, Folder 9447. Beinecke Rare Book and Manuscript Library, Yale University, New Haven, CT.

——. "I, Too." In *The Collected Poems of Langston Hughes*, ed. Arnold Rampersad and David Roessel, 46. New York: Vintage, 1995.

——. *I Wonder as I Wander*. Originally published in 1956. Ed. Joseph McLaren. Columbia: University of Missouri Press, 2003.

——. "Letter to Carl Van Vechten." November 8, 1941. In *Remember Me to Harlem: Letters of Langston Hughes and Carl Van Vechten, 1923–1964*, ed. Emily Bernard, 198–199. New York: Knopf, 2001.

——. "Marl Dust and West Indian Sun." *New York Herald Tribune*, December 5, 1926, 9.

——. "My Adventures as a Social Poet." In *The Collected Works of Langston Hughes*, ed. Christopher C. De Santis, 269–277. Columbia: University of Missouri Press, 2002.

——. "The Negro Artist and the Racial Mountain." In *The Collected Works of Langston Hughes*, ed. Christopher C. De Santis, 31–36. Columbia: University of Missouri Press, 2002.

——. "1927 Trip South: Memphis, New Orleans, Havana, Mobile, Tuskegee, Zora, New York." Memo Pad, LHP, Box 492, Folder 12433. Beinecke Rare Book and Manuscript Library, Yale University, New Haven, CT.

Hurston, Zora Neale. "Characteristics of Negro Expression." In *The Jazz Cadence of American Culture*, ed. Robert G. O'Meally, 298–310. New York: Columbia University Press, 1998.

——. "Folklore and Music." In *Zora Neale Hurston: Folklore, Memoirs, and Other Writings*, ed. Cheryl A. Wall, 875–894. New York: Library of America, 1995.

——. "Letter to Alan Lomax." November 25, 1936. In *Haitian Diary: Papers and Correspondence from Alan Lomax's Haitian Journey*, ed. Ellen Harold, 19–20. San Francisco: Harte Recordings, 2009.

——. "Letter to Henry Allen Moe." January 3, 1937. In *Zora Neale Hurston: A Life in Letters*, ed. Carla Kaplan, 392. New York: Knopf, 2007.

——. *Mules and Men*. Originally published in 1935. In *Zora Neale Hurston: Folklore, Memoirs, and Other Writings*, ed. Cheryl A. Wall, 1–267. New York: Library of America, 1995.

——. "The Sanctified Church." In *Zora Neale Hurston: Folklore, Memoirs, and Other Writings*, ed. Cheryl A. Wall, 902–904. New York: Library of America, 1995.

——. "Shouting." In *Zora Neale Hurston: Folklore, Memoirs, and Other Writings*, ed. Cheryl A. Wall, 851–854. New York: Library of America, 1995.

——. "Spirituals and Neo-Spirituals." In *Zora Neale Hurston: Folklore, Memoirs, and Other Writings*, ed. Cheryl A. Wall, 869–874. New York: Library of America, 1995.

——. *Tell My Horse: Voodoo and Life in Haiti and Jamaica*. Originally published in 1938. New York: Harper Perennial, 2009.

——. *Their Eyes Were Watching God*. Originally published in 1937. New York: Perennial Classics, 1998.

Hutchinson, George. *The Harlem Renaissance in Black and White*. Cambridge, MA: Harvard University Press, 1995.

Huyssen, Andreas. "High/Low in an Expanded Field." *Modernism/Modernity* 9, no. 3 (2002): 363–374.

Ife, Fahima. *Maroon Choreography*. Durham, NC: Duke University Press, 2021.

Ituarte, Andrés. "Eusebia Cosme." *Revista Hispánica Moderna: Boletin del Instituto de las Españas* 5 (1939): 85–86.

Jackson, Zakiyyah Iman. *Becoming Human: Matter and Meaning in an Antiblack World*. New York: New York University Press, 2020.

Jacobs, Karen. *The Eye's Mind: Literary Modernism and Visual Culture*. Ithaca, NY: Cornell University Press, 2001.

John, Errol. *Small Island Moon* on *Third Programme*. May 27, 1958. BBC Sound Archive, The British Library, London, UK.

Johnson, James Weldon. *Along This Way*. In *James Weldon Johnson: Writings*, ed. William L. Andrews, 125–604. New York: Library of America, 2004.

——. "Letter to Arthur Holly." December 22, 1920. JWJ MS 49, Box 8, Folder 180. Beinecke Rare Book and Manuscript Library, Yale University, New Haven, CT.

——. "Self-Determining Haiti." In *James Weldon Johnson: Writings*, ed. William L. Andrews, 660–687. New York: Library of America, 2004.

Johnson, Paul Christopher. "Secretism and the Apotheosis of Duvalier." *Journal of the American Academy of Religion* 74, no. 2 (June 2006): 420–445.

Jones, Meta DuEwa. *The Muse Is Music: Jazz Poetry from the Harlem Renaissance to Spoken Word*. Urbana: University of Illinois Press, 2011.

Kalliney, Peter J. *Commonwealth of Letters: British Literary Culture and the Emergence of Postcolonial Aesthetics*. Oxford: Oxford University Press, 2013.

Kamugisha, Aaron. *Beyond Coloniality: Citizenship and Freedom in the Caribbean Intellectual Tradition*. Bloomington: Indiana University Press, 2019.

Kaup, Monica. " 'Our America' That Is Not One: Transnational Black Atlantic Disclosures in Nicolás Guillén and Langston Hughes." *Discourse* 22, no. 3 (2000): 87–114.

Kernan, Ryan. *New World Maker: Radical Poetics, Black Internationalism, and the Translations of Langston Hughes*. Evanston, IL: Northwestern University Press, 2022.

Kincaid, Jamaica. *A Small Place*. Originally published in 1988. New York: Farrar, Straus, and Giroux, 2000.

King, Tiffany Lethabo. *The Black Shoals: Offshore Formations of Black and Native Studies*. Durham, NC: Duke University Press, 2019.

——. "Humans Involved: Lurking in the Lines of Posthumanist Flight." *Critical Ethnic Studies* 3, no. 1 (Spring 2017): 162–185.

Komunyakaa, Yusef. *Condition Red: Essays, Interviews, and Commentaries*. Ed. Radiclani Clytus. Ann Arbor: University of Michigan Press, 2017.

Kraut, Anthea. *Choreographing the Folk: The Dance Stagings of Zora Neale Hurston*. Minneapolis: University of Minnesota Press, 2008.

Kuhnheim, Jill. *Beyond the Page: Poetry and Performance in Spanish America*. Tucson: University of Arizona Press, 2014.

Kutzinski, Vera. "Fearful Asymmetries: Langston Hughes, Nicolás Guillén, and *Cuba Libre*." *Diacritics* 34, no. 3 (2004): 112–142.

——. *Sugar's Secrets: Race and the Erotics of Cuban Nationalism*. Charlottesville: University Press of Virginia, 1993.

——. "Unseasonal Flowers: Nature and History in Placido and Jean Toomer." *Yale Journal of Criticism* 3, no. 2 (Spring 1990): 153–179.

——. *The Worlds of Langston Hughes: Modernism and Translation in the Americas*. Ithaca, NY: Cornell University Press, 2012.

——. " 'Yo también soy América': Langston Hughes Translated." *American Literary History* 18, no. 3 (2006): 550–578.

Laferrière, Dany. "Jean Price-Mars: Un intellectual en otage." In *Jean Price-Mars Ainsi Parla l'Oncle suivi de Revister l'Oncle*, 263–270. Montreal, Canada: Mémoire D'Encrier, 2009.

Lamothe, Daphne. *Inventing the New Negro: Narrative, Culture, and Ethnography*. Philadelphia: University of Pennsylvania Press, 2008.

Largey, Michael. *Vodou Nation: Haitian Art Music and Cultural Nationalism*. Chicago: University of Chicago Press, 2006.

Leaf, Earl. *Isles of Rhythm*. New York: A. S. Barnes, 1948.

Leary, John Patrick. "Havana Reads the Harlem Renaissance: Langston Hughes, Nicolás Guillén, and the Dialectics of Transnational American Literature." *Comparative Literature Studies* 47, no. 2 (2010): 133–158.

Lewis, David Levering. *When Harlem Was in Vogue*. New York: Penguin, 1979.

Lima, Robert. "Toward the Dionysiac: Pagan Elements and Rites in *Yerma*." *Journal of Dramatic Theory and Criticism* 4, no. 2 (Spring 1990): 63–82.

Locke, Alain. "The New Negro." In *The New Negro: Readings on Race, Representation, and African American Culture, 1892–1938*, ed. Henry Louis Gates Jr. and Gene Andrew Jarrett, 112–118. Princeton, NJ: Princeton University Press, 2007.

López, Antonio. *Unbecoming Blackness: The Diaspora Cultures of Afro-Cuban America*. New York: New York University Press, 2012.

Mackey, Nathaniel. *Discrepant Engagement: Dissonance, Cross-Culturality, and Experimental Writing*. Cambridge: Cambridge University Press, 1993.

Magloire, Gérarde, and Kevin A. Yelvington. "Haiti and the Anthropological Imagination." *Gradhiva* 1 (2005): 1–37.

Maguire, Emily A. "The Eusebia Cosme Show: Translating an Afro-Antillian Identity." In *Writing the Afro-Hispanic: Essays on Africa and Africans in the Spanish Caribbean*, ed. C. James, 77–96. Birmingham, UK: Centre for West African Studies, 2012.

——. *Racial Experiments in Cuban Literature and Ethnography*. Gainesville: University Press of Florida, 2011.

Marson, Una. *Pocomania and London Calling*. Kingston, Jamaica: Blue Banyan, 2017.

Matz, Jesse. *Literary Impressionism and Modernist Aesthetics*. Cambridge: Cambridge University Press, 2001.

McCarthy Brown, Karen. "Afro-Caribbean Spirituality: A Haitian Case Study." In *Vodou in Haitian Life and Culture: Invisible Powers*, ed. Claudine Michel and Patrick Bellegarde-Smith, 1–26. New York: Palgrave Macmillan, 2006.

McEnaney, Tom. *Acoustic Properties: Radio, Narrative, and the New Neighborhood of the Americas*. Evanston, IL: Northwestern University Press, 2017.

McKay, Nellie Y. *Jean Toomer, Artist: A Study of His Literary Life and Work, 1894–1936*. Chapel Hill: University of North Carolina Press, 1984.

McKittrick, Katherine. *Demonic Grounds: Black Women and the Cartographies of Struggle*. Minneapolis: University of Minnesota Press, 2006.

——. "Plantation Futures." *Small Axe* 17, no. 3 (2013): 1–15.

——. "Rebellion/Invention/Groove." *Small Axe* 20, no. 49 (2016): 79–91.

Meehan, Kevin, and Marie Léticée. "A Folio of Writing from 'La Revue Indigène' (1927–28): Translation and Commentary." *Callaloo* 23, no. 4 (2006): 1377–1380.

Melas, Natalie. *All the Difference in the World: Postcoloniality and the Ends of Comparison*. Redwood City, CA: Stanford University Press, 2006.

Méndez, Xhercis, and Yomaira C. Figueroa-Vásquez. "Not Your Papa's Wynter: Women of Color Contributions Toward Decolonial Futures." In *Beyond the Doctrine of Man: Decolonial Visions of the Human*, ed. Joseph Drexler-Dreis and Kristien Justaert, 60–88. New York: Fordham University Press, 2020.

Michel, Claudine, and Patrick Bellegarde-Smith. "Invisible Powers: An Introduction." In *Vodou in Haitian Life and Culture: Invisible Powers*, ed. Claudine Michel and Patrick Bellegarde-Smith, xi–xiv. New York: Palgrave Macmillan, 2006.

Midgely, Robin. "Memo." September 19, 1958. BBC Written Archives Center, Caversham, UK.

Mitchell, Koritha. *Living with Lynching: African American Lynching Plays, Performance, and Citizenship, 1890–1930*. Champaign: University of Illinois Press, 2011.

Moglen, Seth. *Mourning Modernity: Literary Modernism and the Injuries of American Capitalism*. Redwood City, CA: Stanford University Press, 2007.

Moore, Robin L. *Nationalizing Blackness: Afrocubanismo and Artistic Revolution in Havana, 1920–1940*. Pittsburgh: University of Pittsburgh Press, 1997.

Morejón, Nancy, and Juanamaría Cordones-Cook. "Tertuliando con Nancy Morejón." *Afro-Hispanic Review* 31, no. 2 (2012): 193–220.

Moten, Fred. *Black and Blur*. Durham, NC: Duke University Press, 2017.

Musser, Judith. "African American Women's Short Stories in the Harlem Renaissance: Bridging a Tradition." *MELUS* 23, no. 2 (June 1998): 27–47.

Nicholls, David. *Conjuring the Folk: Forms of Modernity in African America*. Ann Arbor: University of Michigan Press, 2000.

Nunn, Erich. "Folk." In *Keywords for Southern Studies*, ed. Scott Romine and Jennifer Rae Greeson, 189–199. Athens: University of Georgia Press, 2016.

Nwankwo, Ifeoma Kiddoe. "Insider and Outsider, Black and American: Rethinking Zora Neale Hurston's Caribbean Ethnography." *Radical History Review* 87 (2003): 49–77.

——. "Living the West Indian Dream: Archipelagic Cosmopolitanism and Triangulated Economies of Desire in Jamaican Popular Culture." In *Archipelagic American Studies*, ed. Brian Russell Roberts and Michelle Ann Stephens, 390–410. Durham, NC: Duke University Press, 2017.

Nyong'o, Tavia. "The Scene of Occupation." *TDR: The Drama Review* 56, no. 4 (2012): 136–149.

Ortiz, Fernando. "La poesía mulata: Presentación de Eusebia Cosme, la recitadora." In *Eusebia Cosme: La rosa canela*, ed. Nydia Sarabia, 41–50. Santiago de Cuba: Ediciones Caserón, 2013.

Ovington, Mary White. "Book Chat: 'Tropic Death.'" *Amsterdam News*, November 24, 1926.

Owens, Imani D. "'Hard Reading': US Empire and Black Modernist Aesthetics in Eric Walrond's *Tropic Death*." *MELUS* 41, no. 4 (December 2016): 96–115.

——. "Toward a 'Truly Indigenous Theatre': Sylvia Wynter Adapts Federico García Lorca." *Cambridge Journal of Postcolonial Literary Inquiry* 4, no. 1 (2017): 49–67. doi:10.1017/pli.2016.34.

Parascandola, Louis J., ed. *"Winds Can Wake Up the Dead": An Eric Walrond Reader*. Detroit: Wayne State University Press, 1998.

Parascandola, Louis J. "Introduction." In *"Winds Can Wake Up the Dead": An Eric Walrond Reader*, ed. Louis J. Parascandola, 11–42. Detroit: Wayne State University Press, 1998.

Parascandola, Louis J., and Carl A. Wade, eds. *In Search of Asylum: The Later Writings of Eric Walrond*. Gainesville: University Press of Florida, 2011.

Pelayo, Joaquín. "Cubans, Our Neighbors." *Chicago Defender*, February 3, 1940.

Peters, Albert. Entry in "Competition for the Best True Stories of Life and Work on the Isthmus during Construction Days for Non-United States Citizens who Worked on the Isthmus Prior to 1915." Isthmian Historical Society, Canal Zone Library, 1963, 2–3.

Pfeiffer, Kathleen, ed. *Brother Mine: The Correspondence of Jean Toomer and Waldo Frank*. Champaign: University of Illinois Press, 2010.

Pinto, Samantha. *Difficult Diasporas: The Transnational Feminist Aesthetic of the Black Atlantic*. New York: New York University Press, 2013.

Posmentier, Sonya. *Cultivation and Catastrophe: The Lyric Ecology of Modern Black Literature*. Baltimore, MD: Johns Hopkins University Press, 2017.

Pratt, John. "Letter to Langston Hughes." February 2, 1946. LHP, JWJ MSS 26, Box 57, Folder 1085. Beinecke Rare Book and Manuscript Library, Yale University, New Haven, CT.

Price, Hannibal. *De la rehabilitation de la race noire par la République d'Haïti*. Port-au-Prince, Haiti: Imprimerie J. Verrollot, 1900.

Price-Mars, Jean. *Ainsi parla l'Oncle suivi de Revister l'Oncle*. Montreal, Canada: Mémoire D'Encrier, 2009.

———. "Calling Card to Herbert Seligmann." April 1920. JWJ MSS 49, Box 8, Folder 183.

———. *Le bilan des études ethnologiques en Haïti et le cycle du Nègre*. Port-au-Prince, Haiti: Imprimerie de l'État, 1954.

———. "Lemba Pétro: Un culte secret." *Revue de la société d'histoire et de géographie d'Haiti* 9, no. 28 (1938): 12–31.

———. "Letter to James Weldon Johnson." April 17, 1920. JWJ MSS 49, Box 8, Folder 183.

———. "A propos de la Renaissance nègre aux États-Unis." *La Relève* 1, nos. 1–3 (1932): 14–20; 9–15; 8–14.

———. *So Spoke the Uncle*. Trans. Magdaline W. Shannon. Washington, DC: Three Continents, 1983.

———. *La vocation de l'Élite*. Originally published in 1919. Port-au-Prince, Haiti: Editions des presses nationales d'Haiti, 2001.

Procter, James. "The Empire Scripts Back." *BBC History Research Blog*, October 26, 2018. https://www.bbc.co.uk/blogs/bbchistoryresearch/entries/75ecb85c-7c40-4eca-b9bb-8e5f5195ce70.

———. "Una Marson at the BBC." *Small Axe* 19, no. 3 (November 2015): 1–28.

Puri, Shalini, and Lara Putnam, eds. *Caribbean Military Encounters*. New York: Palgrave Macmillan, 2017.

Putnam, Lara. "Provincializing Harlem: The 'Negro Metropolis' as Northern Frontier of a Connected Caribbean." *Modernism/Modernity* 20, no. 3 (2013): 469–484.

Quashie, Kevin. *Black Aliveness, or a Poetics of Being*. Durham, NC: Duke University Press, 2021.

Ramchand, Kenneth. "The Writer Who Ran Away: Eric Walrond and *Tropic Death*." *Savacou* 2 (1970): 67–75.

Rampersad, Arnold. "Introduction." In *Tropic Death*, ed. Eric Walrond, 1–18. Originally published in 1926. New York: Liveright, 2013.

———. *The Life of Langston Hughes, Volume I: 1902–1941*. New York: Oxford University Press, 1986.

———. *The Life of Langston Hughes, Volume II: 1941–1967*. New York: Oxford University Press, 1988.

Ramsey, Kate. *The Spirits and the Law: Vodou and Power in Haiti*. Chicago: University of Chicago Press, 2011.

Reckson, Lindsay V. *Realist Ecstasy: Religion, Race, and Performance in American Literature*. New York: New York University Press, 2020.

Renda, Mary. *Taking Haiti: Military Occupation and the Culture of U.S. Imperialism, 1915–1940*. Chapel Hill: University of North Carolina Press, 2001.

Retman, Sonnet. *Real Folks: Race and Genre in the Great Depression*. Durham, NC: Duke University Press, 2011.

Ring, Natalie J. "Tropics." In *Keywords for Southern Studies*, ed. Scott Romine and Jennifer Rae Greeson, 88–97. Athens: University of Georgia Press, 2016.

Ritter, Luis Pulido. "Notas sobre Eric Walrond: La inmigración caribeña y la transnacionalidad literaria en Panamá: Una excursión por las calles de la memoria, la reflexión y los espacios en movimiento." *Intercambio* 5, no. 6 (2008): 175–180.

Rivera, Mayra. "Embodied Counterpoetics: Sylvia Wynter on Religion and Race." In *Beyond Man: Race, Coloniality, and Philosophy of Religion*, ed. An Yountae and Eleanor Craig, 56–85. Durham, NC: Duke University Press, 2021.

Roberts, Neil. *Freedom as Marronage*. Chicago: University of Chicago Press, 2015.

Robinson, Cedric. *Black Marxism: The Making of the Black Radical Tradition*. Chapel Hill: University of North Carolina Press, 1983.

Roy-Féquière, Magali. *Women, Creole Identity, and Intellectual Life in Early-Twentieth-Century Puerto Rico*. Philadelphia: Temple University Press, 2004.

Rusch, Frederik L. "Form, Function, and Creative Tension in *Cane*: Jean Toomer and the Need for the Avant-Garde." *MELUS* 17, no. 4 (1991): 15–28.

Sanders-Johnson, Grace. "Occupied Thoroughfares: Haitian Women, Public Space, and the United States Occupation." In *Caribbean Military Encounters*, ed. Shalini Puri and Lara Putnam, 71–83. New York: Palgrave McMillan, 2017.

Sarabia, Nydia, ed. *Eusebia Cosme: La rosa canela*. Santiago de Cuba: Ediciones Caserón, 2013.

Scott, William. "Motivos of Translation." *New Centennial Review* 5, no. 2 (2005): 35–71.

Scruggs, Charles, and Lee VanDemarr. *Jean Toomer and the Terrors of American History*. Philadelphia: University of Pennsylvania Press, 1998.

Seabrook, W. B. *The Magic Island*. New York: Harcourt Brace, 1920.

Senghor, Léopold. "Hommage à l'Oncle." In *Témoignages sur la vie et l'ouevre du Jean Price Mars, 1876–1956*, ed. Emmanuel C. Paul and Jean Fouchard, 3. Port-au-Prince, Haiti: Imprimerie du l'État, 1956.

Shannon, Magdaline. *Jean Price-Mars and the American Occupation, 1915–35*. London: Macmillan, 1996.

Sharpe, Jenny. *Immaterial Archives: An African Diaspora Poetics of Loss*. Evanston, IL: Northwestern University Press, 2020.

Sharpley-Whiting, T. Denean. *Negritude Women*. Minneapolis: University of Minnesota Press, 2002.

Sheller, Mimi. *Citizenship from Below: Erotic Agency and Caribbean Freedom*. Durham, NC: Duke University Press, 2012.

Simpson, Hyacinth M. "The BBC's Caribbean Voices and the Making of an Oral Aesthetic in the West Indian Short Story." *Journal of the Short Story in English* 57 (Autumn 2011): 81–96.

Smart, Ian. *Nicolás Guillén: Popular Poet of the Caribbean*. Columbia: University of Missouri Press, 1990.

Smith, Matthew K. *Red and Black in Haiti: Radicalism, Conflict, and Political Change, 1934–1957*. Chapel Hill: University of North Carolina Press, 2009.

Sorenson, Jennifer. *Modernist Experiments in Genre, Media, and Transatlantic Print Culture*. New York: Routledge, 2017.

Soto, Michael. "Jean Toomer and Horace Liveright; or, A New Negro Gets 'Into the Swing of It.'" In *Jean Toomer and the Harlem Renaissance*, ed. Geneviève Fabre and Michel Feith, 162–187. New Brunswick, NJ: Rutgers University Press, 2001.

Stephens, Michelle Ann. *Black Empire: The Masculine Global Imaginary of Caribbean Intellectuals in the United States, 1914–1962*. Durham, NC: Duke University Press, 2005.

———. "Eric Walrond's *Tropic Death* and the Discontents of American Modernity." In *Prospero's Isles: The Presence of the Caribbean in the American Imaginary*, ed. Diane Accaria-Zavala and Rodolfo Popelnik, 167–178. Oxford, UK: Macmillan Caribbean, 2004.

Stewart, Jeffrey C. *The New Negro: The Life of Alain Locke*. New York: Oxford University Press, 2018.

Stulburg, Jacob. "How (Not) to Write Broadcast Plays: Pinter and the BBC." *Modern Drama* 58, no. 4 (Winter 2015): 502–523.

Sublette, Ned. *Cuba and Its Music: From the First Drums to the Mambo*. Chicago: Chicago Review, 2004.

Taylor, Diana. *The Archive and the Repertoire: Performing Cultural Memory in the Americas*. Durham, NC: Duke University Press, 2003.

Thomas, Deborah A. "Haiti, Politics, and Sovereign (Mis)recognitions." In *The Haiti Exception: Anthropology and the Predicament of Narrative*, ed. Alessandra Benedicty-Kokken, Kaiama L. Glover, Mark Schuller, and Jhon Picard Byron, 137–155. Liverpool: Liverpool University Press, 2016.

———. *Modern Blackness: Nationalism, Globalization, and the Politics of Culture in Jamaica*. Durham, NC: Duke University Press, 2004.

———. "Public Secrets, Militarization, and the Cultivation of Doubt: Kingston 2010." In *Caribbean Military Encounters*, ed. Shalini Puri and Laura Putnam, 289–309. New York: Palgrave Macmillan, 2017.

Thomas, Greg. "*Marronnons* Let's Maroon: Sylvia Wynter's 'Black Metamorphosis' as a Species of Maroonage." *Small Axe* 20, no. 1 (March 2016): 62–78.

Tinsley, Omise'eke Natasha. *Ezili's Mirrors: Imagining Queer Black Genders*. Durham, NC: Duke University Press, 2018.

Toland-Dix, Shirley. "The Hills of Hebron: Sylvia Wynter's Disruption of the Narrative of the Nation." *Small Axe* 12, no. 1 (2008): 57–76.

Toomer, Jean. *Cane*. Originally published by Boni and Liveright in 1923. New York: Norton, 1988.

———. *Cane*, dust jacket. JWJ 26, Box 611, Digital Collections. Beinecke Rare Book and Manuscript Library, Yale University, New Haven, CT.

———. *A Jean Toomer Reader: Selected Unpublished Writings*. Ed. Frederick Rusch. New York: Oxford University Press, 1993.

———. "Letter to Gorham Munson." October 31, 1922. In *The Letters of Jean Toomer, 1919–1924*, ed. Mark Whalan, 90–92. Knoxville: University of Tennessee Press, 2006.

———. "Letter to Lola Ridge." January 1923. In *The Letters of Jean Toomer, 1919–1924*, ed. Mark Whalan, 123. Knoxville: University of Tennessee Press, 2006.

Trefzer, Annette. "Possessing the Self: Caribbean Identities in Zora Neale Hurston's *Tell My Horse*." *African American Review* 34, no. 2 (2000): 299–312.

Trouillot, Michel-Rolph. "Anthropology and the Savage Slot: The Poetics and Politics of Otherness." In *Global Transformations: Anthropology and the Modern World*, 7–28. New York: Palgrave Macmillan, 2003.

——. "The Caribbean Region: An Open Frontier in Anthropological Theory." In *Trouillot Remixed*, ed. Yarimar Bonilla, Greg Beckett, and Mayanthi L. Fernando, 160–193. Durham, NC: Duke University Press, 2021.

——. *Global Transformations: Anthropology and the Modern World*. New York: Palgrave Macmillan, 2003.

——. "The Otherwise Modern: Caribbean Lessons from the Savage Slot." In *Trouillot Remixed*, ed. Yarimar Bonilla, Greg Beckett, and Mayanthi L. Fernando, 142–159. Durham, NC: Duke University Press, 2021.

——. "Review of *So Spoke the Uncle* by Jean Price-Mars." Trans. Magdaline W. Shannon. *Research in African Literatures* 17, no. 4 (1986): 596–597.

——. *Silencing the Past*. Boston: Beacon Press, 1995.

Turner, Darwin T. "Contrasts and Limitations in *Cane*." In *Cane: A Norton Critical Edition*, ed. Darwin T. Turner, 207–215. New York: Norton, 1988.

——. "Introduction to the 1975 Edition of *Cane*." In *Cane: A Norton Critical Edition*, ed. Darwin T. Turner, 122. New York: Norton, 1988.

——. *The Wayward and the Seeking: A Collection of Writings by Jean Toomer*. Washington, DC: Howard University Press, 1980.

Ulysse, Gina Athena. "Why Rasanblaj, Why Now? New Salutations to the Four Cardinal Points in Haitian Studies." *Journal of Haitian Studies* 23, no. 2 (2017): 58–80.

Urrutia, Gustavo E. "Letter to Langston Hughes." April 20, 1930. LHP, Box 158, Folder 2926. Beinecke Rare Book and Manuscript Library, Yale University, New Haven, CT.

Vazquez, Alexandra T. *Listening in Detail: Performances of Cuban Music*. Durham, NC: Duke University Press, 2013.

Vilsaint, Féquière, and Jean-Evens Berret. *English Haitian Creole Dictionary*. Coconut Creek, FL: Education Vision, 2005.

Vogel, Shane. "*Jamaica* on Broadway: The Popular Caribbean and Mock Transnational Performance." *Theatre Journal* 62, no. 1 (2010): 1–21.

——. *The Scene of Harlem Cabaret: Race, Sexuality, Performance*. Chicago: University of Chicago Press, 2009.

——. *Stolen Time: Black Fad Performance and the Calypso Craze*. Chicago: University of Chicago Press, 2018.

Walcott, Rinaldo. *The Long Emancipation: Toward Black Freedom*. Durham, NC: Duke University Press, 2021.

Waligora-Davis, Nicole. *Sanctuary: African Americans and Empire*. Oxford: Oxford University Press, 2011.

Wall, Cheryl A. *Women of the Harlem Renaissance*. Bloomington: Indiana University Press, 1995.

Walrond, Eric. "From Cotton, Cane, and Rice Fields." In *"Winds Can Wake Up the Dead": An Eric Walrond Reader*, ed. Louis J. Parascandola, 138–141. Detroit: Wayne State University Press, 1998.

——. "The Godless City." In *"Winds Can Wake Up the Dead": An Eric Walrond Reader*, ed. Louis J. Parascandola, 161–172. Detroit: Wayne State University Press, 1998.

——. "The Negro before the World." In *"Winds Can Wake Up the Dead": An Eric Walrond Reader*, ed. Louis J. Parascandola, 286–288. Detroit: Wayne State University Press, 1998.

——. "The Negro Literati." From *Brentano's Book Chat*, March/April 1925. In *"Winds Can Wake Up the Dead": An Eric Walrond Reader*, ed. Louis J. Parascandola, 130–131. Detroit: Wayne State University Press, 1998.

——. *Tropic Death*. Originally published in 1926. New York: Liveright, 2013.

Washington, Booker T. "The Atlanta Exposition Address." In *Three Negro Classics*, 145–150. New York: Avon, 1965.

——. "Dr. Booker T. Washington on American Occupation of Haiti: Tuskegee Educator Sounds Note of Warning Urging U.S. to Be Patient with Black Republic." *New York Age*, October 21, 1915.

Watkins-Owens, Irma. *Blood Relations: Caribbean Immigrants and the Harlem Community, 1900–1930*. Bloomington: Indiana University Press, 1996.

Weheliye, Alexander G. *Habeas Viscus: Racializing Assemblages, Biopolitics, and Black Feminist Theories of the Human*. Durham, NC: Duke University Press, 2014.

West, M. Genevieve. *Zora Neale Hurston and American Literary Culture*. Gainesville: University Press of Florida, 2005.

Whalan, Mark. "Jean Toomer and the Avant-Garde." In *Cambridge Companion to the Harlem Renaissance*, ed. George Hutchinson, 71–81. Cambridge: Cambridge University Press, 2007.

——. *The Letters of Jean Toomer: 1919–1924*. Knoxville: University of Tennessee Press, 2006.

White, Derrick. "Black Metamorphosis: A Prelude to Sylvia Wynter's Theory of the Human." *CLR James Journal* 16, no. 1 (2010): 127–148.

Womack, Autumn. *The Matter of Black Living: The Aesthetic Experiment of Racial Data, 1880–1930*. Chicago: University of Chicago Press, 2021.

Wynter, Sylvia. *The Barren One* on BBC Third Programme, January 7, 1959. Radio Script. BBC Written Archives Centre, Caversham, UK.

——. "Bat and Ball." *Caribbean Voices*, August 11, 1957. Radio Script. BBC Written Archives Centre, Caversham, UK.

——. "Beyond Miranda's Meanings: Un/Silencing the Demonic Ground of Caliban's Woman." In *Out of the Kumbla: Caribbean Woman and Literature*, ed. Carole Boyce Davies and Elaine Savory Fido, 355–372. Trenton, NJ: Africa World Press, 1990.

——. *Black Metamorphosis: New Natives in a New World*. Unpublished manuscript. Institute of the Black World Papers, Schomburg Center for Research in Black Culture, New York.

——. "The Ceremony Found: Towards the Autopoetic Turn/Overturn, Its Autonomy of Human Agency, and Extraterritoriality of (Self-)Cognition." In *Black Knowledges/ Black Struggles: Essays in Critical Epistemology*, ed. Jason R. Ambroise and Sabine Broeck, 184–245. Liverpool: Liverpool University Press, 2015.

——. "The Ceremony Must Be Found: After Humanism." *Boundary 2* 12/13, no. 3/1 (1984): 19–70. Accessed June 16, 2021, www.jstor.org/stable/302808.

——. "Cleo Laine and Errol John in *The Barren One* [Publicity Statement]." *Radio Times*, Issue 1834, London, January 2, 1959, 55.

——. "Commentary." *Caribbean Voices*, June 8, 1958. Program Scripts, BBC Written Archives Centre, Caversham, UK.

——. "Essay and Play Extract: The House and Land of Mrs. Alba." *Jamaica Journal* 2, no. 3 (September 1968): 48–56.

——. "Jonkonnu in Jamaica: Towards the Interpretation of Folk Dance as a Cultural Process." *Jamaica Journal* 4, no. 2 (June 1970): 34–48.

——. "Lady Nugent's Journal." *Jamaica Journal* 1, no. 1 (1969): 23–34.

——. "Letter to Laurence Gilliam." November 12, 1958. BBC Written Archives Center, Caversham, UK.

——. *Maskarade*. Originally published in 1970. In *Mixed Company: Three Early Jamaican Plays*, ed. Yvonne Brewster, 23–132. London: Oberon, 2012.

——. "Novel and History: Plot and Plantation." *Savacou* 5 (1971): 95–102.

——. "Paramour." *Caribbean Voices*, November 25, 1956. Radio Script. BBC Written Archives Centre, Caversham, UK.

——. "The Pope Must Have Been Drunk, the King of Castile a Madman: Culture as Actuality, and the Caribbean Rethinking Modernity." In *Reordering of Culture: Latin America, the Caribbean, and Canada in the 'Hood*, ed. Alvina Ruprecht and Cecila Taiana, 17–41. Ottawa, Canada: Carleton University Press, 1995.

——. "Preface." In *We Must Learn to Sit Down Together and Talk about a Little Culture: Decolonising Essays, 1967–1984*, ed. Demetrius L. Eudell, 7–21. Leeds, UK: Peepal Tree, 2022.

——. "ProudFlesh Inter/Views Sylvia Wynter." Interview by Greg Thomas. *ProudFlesh: New Afrikan Journal of Culture, Politics, and Consciousness* 4 (2006): 1–35.

——. "The Re-Enchantment of Humanism: An Interview with Sylvia Wynter." Interview by David Scott. *Small Axe* 8 (September 2000): 119–207.

——. "Review of *One Love—Rhetoric or Reality? Aspects of Afro-Jamaicanism*, by Audvil King, Althea Helps, Pam Wint, and Frank Hasfal." *Caribbean Studies* 12, no. 3 (1972): 64–97.

——. "Sylvia Wynter: An Oral History." Interview by Natalie Marine-Street, November 22, 2017. Stanford Historical Society, Stanford, CA.

——. "Unparalleled Catastrophe for Our Species? Or, to Give Humanness a Different Future: Conversations." Interview by Katherine McKittrick. In *Sylvia Wynter: On Being Human as Praxis*, ed. Katherine McKittrick, 9–89. Durham, NC: Duke University Press, 2016.

——. "Unsettling the Coloniality of Being/Power/Truth/Freedom: Towards the Human, After Man, Its Overrepresentation—An Argument." *CR: The New Centennial Review* 3, no. 3 (2003): 257–337.

——. "We Know Where We're From: The Politics of Black Culture from Myal to Marley." In *We Must Learn to Sit Down Together and Talk about a Little Culture: Decolonising Essays, 1967–1984*, ed. Demetrius L. Eudell, 456–499. Leeds, UK: Peepal Tree, 2022.

——. "We Must Learn to Sit Down Together and Talk about a Little Culture." *Jamaica Journal* 2, no. 4 (1968): 23–32.

INDEX

Mars, Louis, 97

Marson, Una, 154, 168, 184

Martinique, 161

Marzedo, Don, 131–132

Maskarade (Wynter), 171, 187

Mason, Charlotte Osgood, 147

massacre, of political prisoners, 91

masses: Papa Guedé and, 103;
 zombification and, 104–105

Matz, Jesse, 53

Maubé drink, 59

McBurnie, Beryl, 161, 184

McEnaney, Tom, 136

McKittrick, Katherine, 4, 157, 164–165

McMurray, David Arthur, 150

Melas, Natalie, 22

Mendez, Julio, 126

Méndez, Xhercis, 178

Messenger (newspaper), 30–31

mestizaje (mixture), 137–139

mestizo history, of Cuba, 138–139

Michel, Claudine, 86

Midgely, Robin, 180

migratory patterns, as portrayed in
 Tropic Death, 47

military intervention, 71–72

Miracle in Lime Lane (Wynter), 167

Miranda (fictional character, *The
 Tempest*), 178

Miss Edna (fictional character,
 "Paramour"), 174–177

Mississippi Delta, 21

Mitchell, Koritha, 166

Mittelholzer (announcer), 174

mixed heritage, in "Paramour," 177

modern Black art, premodern and, 39

modernist expression, in *Cane*, 38

modernity, 10, 12, 14–15, 21, 25, 27, 29,
 45, 49, 51, 55, 58, 68, 82, 165, 171, 189;
 Black hemispheric, 8, 22, 24, 49,
 158; death and, 6; of Haiti, 82, 86;
 Southern, 45; Western, 157, 196n16

modernism: American, 24; global, 14;
 literary, 151

Moe, Henry Allen, 89

Moglen, Seth, 24–25

morals, in "Paramour," 177

Morejón, Nancy, 115

Moses, Man of the Mountain
 (Hurston), 96

Moten, Fred, 42, 163

Motivos de son (Guillén), 114–115, 116,
 147–148

mountain peasants (*paysans
 montagnards*), 73, 79

mulatto spirit, Cosme and, 142

Mules and Men (Hurston), 89, 93

Munson, Gorham, 34

music: in "Cuban Evening," 116–120;
 in *The Barren One*, 183–184; in
 "Paramour," 176; of Vodou
 ceremony, 84

Myers, Emmanuel, 184

NAACP. *See* National Association for the
 Advancement of Colored People

Nardal, Jeanne, 161

Nardal, Paulette, 161

narration, role of women in, 129–130

narrative authority, of Hurston in *Tell My
 Horse*, 98–100

narrator: in "Bat and Ball," 172–173; in
 "Fern," 38

National Association for the
 Advancement of Colored People
 (NAACP), 26–27, 72

national unity, Vodou as model for, 83,
 85–86

native informant, dismissal of Hurston
 of, 98–99

naval ship, in "The Godless City," 60

negro composer, search of Hughes for,
 147

negro de verdad phrase, of Hughes,
 148–149

"Negro Literati, The" (Walrond), 25

Negro Novel in America, The (Bone), 31

negro pobre. See poor negro